RJ, Farrah and Me

A Young Man's Gay Odyssey from the Inside Out

by Jack Hilovsky

NFB Publishing
Buffalo, New York

Cover design by Dick Tahsin
Author photo by John Ulman

NFB
NFB Publishing/Amelia Press
119 Dorchester Road
Buffalo, New York 14213

For my mother Ruth who taught me how to fly,
and my father Frank who grounded me...
and Dick who gave me my wings.

Poco a poco, se va lejos... Little by little, you go far...

Contents

A Whole New World — 1

Balls and Crushes — 8

Standing Tall — 13

Happiness is… — 20

Reality and Fantasy — 23

Obsessions — 28

Summer Revelations 1977 — 42

Behind Closed Doors — 51

You're the One That I Want — 57

The Vacation — 65

Guilt and Pleasure — 84

First Date, First Kiss — 92

The Lifeguard and Hero — 102

Mary Kathleen — 114

Breaking Away — 131

Do You Know Where You're Going — 139

The Audition — 147

High School Musical — 156

The Prom/Playing the Part — 162

Lost Summer — 168

John Carroll, Ready or Not — 172

Something Good — 181

The Pledge and the Fraternity — 190

RJ Graduates and Heads to NYC — 208

Ch-Ch-Ch-Changes   220

Melissa   232

Awakening   250

Revelations   280

Move On   291

The Final Inning   303

Afterward: Coming Out   327

POSTSCRIPT   330

Author's Note:

This is a work of creative nonfiction. The events are portrayed to the best of Jack Hilovsky's memory. While all the stories in this book are true, it may not be entirely factual; some names and identifying details have been changed to protect the privacy of the people involved. In some cases I have compressed events; in others I have made two people into one.

CHAPTER 1

A Whole New World

My parents welcomed me into the world on June 6, 1963, the exact date of their tenth wedding anniversary. Dad turned 50 two months before my 43-year-old Mom gave birth. They kept their ages a secret, but I eventually found my birth certificate and discovered the truth. Not that they were hiding; I think they wanted me to assume they were youthful like all the other parents. There were no other kids, although following Mom's earlier miscarriage, my parents filed for adoption before they struck gold with me, the miracle child!

Despite growing up in the tumultuous 1960's and 70's, my early childhood remained calm, even predictable. There was a stay-at-home Mom, a working Dad, and me living under the same roof in suburban Fairview Park, no divorce here. We were good Catholics. We ate supper together as a family reciting *Bless us O Lord, for these Thy gifts*. We attended weekly Mass at St. Angela Merici. Our vacations often involved visiting family and close friends.

At the dinner table, Dad liked to talk politics. Shaped by the Great Depression, he'd grown up with FDR as the patron saint of the average guy, followed by the no-nonsense, "The Buck Stops Here" Harry Truman, one of his favorite Presidents. We all loved the Kennedys because they were Catholic, young, and charming. We were an anti-abortion family, but Mom and Dad still voted Democratic because "the D's cared about our day-to-day interests," said Dad.

My father often quoted Shakespeare at the table, reciting soliloquys he memorized during his school days, which with his silvering hair, I thought must have occurred over 100 years ago. The verse he quoted most often came from *Hamlet*:

This above all else: to thine own self be true,
And it must follow, as the night the day,
Thou canst not then be false to any man.

The cocoon of my upbringing failed to protect me from a growing awareness I feared sharing with anyone. The truth of the matter was I liked other boys. It's not that I didn't like girls. I had kindergarten crushes and cozied up to several of them in grade school. But I had fantasies about boys; they powered my daydreams in a way girls didn't. Part of me became attached; drew close to them, and I couldn't ignore it. I wanted to be near them, share close physical space, touch their bodies, and run my fingers through their hair. When I allowed these feelings to emerge, my heart soared.

One of my earliest memories happened when I was seven. Mom and Dad took me to a family swim night at the YMCA. Kids squealed and splashed each other under bright fluorescent lights and a cathedral, tiled ceiling. I hopped into the shallow end and swam into Mom and Dad's arms several times, enjoying the feel of the water on my skin. Nature called, and I hoisted myself out and tiptoed to the washroom. In the shower, I passed a hairy-chested man with muscular arms lathering his back. In the locker area, I met the eyes of a teenage boy changing out of his jeans. His buttocks firm, a set of strong abdominal muscles propped above a languid penis. He smiled. My heart thrummed like a drum, and I looked away rushing to a stall to pee. On the way back, both the boy and man were gone.

My fascination progressed. As a pre-pubescent I built forts under the ping-pong table in our rec room and hosted sleep overs with my friends from Cub Scouts and CYO softball. Like typical boys navigating the unknown we played make-believe pirates or space travelers under the blankets. Sometimes we'd strip down to our undershorts and explore each other, my playmate's fascination meeting my own as we'd rub up against each other's quivering boners. Our bodies overwhelmed with all the curiosities and nervousness of approaching adolescence.

"Come and get it," Mom or Dad would call downstairs, announcing lunch was on the table. We'd throw on our clothes like nothing happened, and bound upstairs for tomato soup and Velveeta cheese sandwiches. But the feelings of affection and desire lingered in me.

While the boys with whom I ventured into the unknown never pushed me away, I continued to feel unusual and a bit self-conscious about my preoccupation with exploring their bodies. Shy and gentle, I appreciated when they responded to my cautious advances, but I still worried about my parents finding out. I knew I couldn't share this secret with them because boys were supposed to be with girls, not other boys, when it came to love and gushy feelings. I knew from watching my family that women married men and men married women. There wasn't any variance, and I saw no other examples of romantic differentness. Where did I fit in?

When my Cub Scout friends one summer unearthed the plastic wrapped *Playboy* magazine they hid in the neighbor lady's bushes, they ogled the naked women while my eyes wandered to the disrobed men fondling the ladies in the layouts. We shared the thrill of the experience, despite our very different objects of desire.

Further reinforcing my sense of "otherness," popular television didn't broadcast boys experiencing attachments to other boys. David Cassidy, the heartthrob on my favorite show, *The Partridge Family*, serenaded a mob of screaming girls while singing "I Think I Love You." I later watched the short-lived series *James at 15*, enthralled by the idea of a sensitive boy like me trying to find his place in the world, and when James lost his virginity, imagining how that might feel for me considering my tortured feelings.

My parent's friends included married couples with and without children. Several women in our family were widowed. My mother's first cousin Renata, whom I regarded as an aunt and called Re-Re, remained unwed. I'd never witnessed a male couple together, out in the open, although I'd heard about Otto, an acquaintance of my mother's Canadian friend Edna. Otto worked in interior design and wore a toupee. "Oh, he's just a riot," my mother would giggle over the kitchen phone to Edna while I'd listen my ear to the door in the other room. "And those vests he wears with a stylish scarf knotted around his neck. He's like Tom Jones." She'd adjust her perch on the swivel seat and throw back her head in laughter. Then there'd be a noticeable pause before she'd whisper, "But doesn't he have a girlfriend?" Stinging disapproval tinged her voice. Unmarried, Otto lived a different lifestyle.

"Oh, he's one of those." A series of "tsk, tsks" came next from Mom, as I continued eavesdropping. "But he's so harmless," she'd continue, "I adore how creative he is, all his wonderful ideas about how to spruce up a room. And he's the life of the party!"

More pauses as Edna responded. "Well, our church wouldn't approve," Mom clucked. "I guess the Lutherans are more lenient on those matters." Edna, a Lutheran, didn't seem to subscribe to the same moral high ground as my mom. I wondered how Edna would react to my being different, maybe like Otto. What would Mom think if I were to live with a man?

One Sunday afternoon my parents arranged to meet with potential tenants interested in renting my grandmother's homey duplex, which Mom inherited after Nana's death. We arrived after church to interview the first candidate. Two men climbed the porch steps. "Come on in," Mom said with a tentative smile, "this is my childhood home so I'm sentimental about whom I welcome to live here."

"It's beautiful, Mrs. Hilovsky," said the mustachioed sandy blonde. "I love the hardwood floors and the built-in China display cabinets." His friend agreed, "It's just what we're looking for." They filled out an application before leaving. Out of earshot, Mom turned to Dad and whispered: "They're not our kind of people. I won't rent to them."

I noticed the blonde said his esses funny and the other guy wore tight Calvin Klein jeans. My twelve-year-old mind suspected these men fell into Otto's category.

For these reasons, I hid my attraction to other boys afraid of what I had in common with the male couple. Why would I want to suffer the derision and the prejudice it would surely bring my way? Besides, I believed I would eventually grow out of it, and that the boys with whom I experimented would grow out of it too. Yet underneath my makeshift fort constructed with musty Indian blankets I'd snuggle up against the soft, freckled skin of eleven-year-old Michael McDougal, whose mother Gwenn volunteered with Mom at St. Angela's bake sales, or my little league teammate, Benjamin Waring, who rode bikes with me and lived around the corner from the school playfield adjoining our backyard.

The closeness I experienced with them comforted me and provided a haven from the loneliness I felt as an only child. The sleepovers and forts in the basement I equated with innocent fun.

Not until the summer of 1974, four years after YMCA swim nights began, and following my eleventh birthday, did I ever equate same-sex love, attraction, and desire with a graver condition, a reality I would have to reckon with.

That August in our orange VW Beetle, Mom, Dad, and I took a road trip to Boston and Cape Cod. Our love of all things Kennedy resulted in a stop at Hyannis Port where America's most famous Catholic clan summered. I remembered the sad looks on Mom and Dad's faces when Robert Kennedy was killed on June 6, 1968, on the early morning of my fifth birthday—everything seemed gloomy that afternoon at my celebration, where all the neighborhood kids wore goofy pointed party hats. While we missed encountering the Kennedys, I fell in love with the Cape's glorious white beaches, the salt-spewing Atlantic Ocean, the hot orange-red sunsets, and the sense we'd discovered something new and different from our own Lake Erie, Midwestern habitat.

One day we took a side trip to the artist colony of Provincetown. The streets gleamed with colorful striped flags in red, pink, yellow, green, blue, and orange, all flapping in the light wind. Art galleries abounded. Cottages, thatched and whitewashed, dotted the red brick paved streets. The Atlantic breeze whistled through our hair. I could taste salt as we strolled through the town center, every open door a portal to paintings of sandy beaches, sailboats, and portraiture. People poured through the streets with popsicles and ice-cream cones.

That afternoon a group of towering ladies in high heels and short skirts, and wearing outlandish wigs and heavy makeup, approached us. My mother grabbed my one free hand, the one without an ice cream cone, and pulled me into a hidden alcove. Pointing in the direction of the oncoming Amazons she whispered, "Look, look at those queers." My heart froze.

"Who, Mom?" I responded like I was blind, in the dark.

Her abrupt pronouncement served as my first introduction to the meaning of queer. Doors slammed and latches locked inside my mind, obscuring feelings and desires that had risen in me. Denial. My palms grew sweaty. My stomach catapulted into a free fall. The ice cream cone in my hand began melting, and a bitter taste materialized inside my mouth, suggesting that somehow, I was one of them, while not wanting to be.

At eleven years old I knew my math tables backwards and forwards, but I couldn't figure out this frightening reality. Above all else, I craved approval—from my classmates, my parents, my Church. Though I loved the colorful flags and artistic nature of P-Town; the look and feel of the place, I could now see that up close these women were men dressed as women. I was not one of them, but somehow, we barked up the same odd family tree. They winked and nodded at us, and Mom scowled at them.

From that moment on, I chose to conceal my secret awareness that I was odd. Up until Otto and Provincetown, I had never recalled my parents, or society, mentioning queers or homosexuality, much less equating it with a malady. Even the Catholic priests at our parish never spoke about the subject; it was taboo.

Being gay almost didn't exist as an option in Cleveland. I'm not sure what was worse: being ignored or invisible. All I knew was that my desires felt very different and would be an unwelcome topic of discussion at the dinner table, or anywhere else.

CHAPTER 2

Balls and Crushes

I DUG MY cleats into the batter's box and reset my grip on the bat. *One strike, Jack. No biggie!* I sank into my stance as the lanky pitcher kicked into his wind-up. His foot arced gracefully down, throwing hand appearing from behind his glove. Two of his long, smooth fingers hooked loose across the top of the ball, thumb and ring finger braced around the bottom.

The pitch sailed at me belt level. I swung, but a fraction too late. The ball caught the tip of my bat and skittered away toward the dugout. *Two strikes. No biggie!*

"Hey batta, batta. Hey batta, batta!" A scrawny boy in a royal blue jersey taunted as I crouched, knees bent over the plate, waiting for a decent pitch. I clenched my jaw. *What does he know? He's probably still just eleven. One good pitch, that's all I need to bring the boys on second and third home. And maybe even get there myself.*

"Keep your eye on the ball, #12. That's the way to go, wait for a good one," Mom shouted from the stands.

The pitcher adjusted the cap atop his sandy blond hair. I couldn't take my eyes off his face, still boyishly soft, but with a hint of downy fuzz sprouting along his jaw line. I tried to quell the small flutter in my heart. His blue eyes burned with concentration as he nodded sharply at the catcher.

He wound up and threw a sizzling curve. I blinked, breaking his spell, and swung. The ball smacked into the catcher's mitt.

"You're out," the umpire roared, thrusting his thumb in the air.

"Shit," I muttered as I tossed the Louisville Slugger to Deanie Butkus, a short little tumbleweed of a boy. Deanie gave me the stink eye, while from the dugout I heard cheers of "You can do it!" and "Bring 'em home, Dean!"

Little did my sports-loving mother know when she had registered her only child for Catholic Youth Organization (CYO) athletics she had only added to my brewing infatuation with boys. My first crush, 14-year-old Hank Ferris, played catcher and left field on our softball team, the Reds. A head taller than I, stocky, and a bit of a klutz, the boisterous red head with unruly curls made Mom's ears blush when he'd broadcast his opinions. And he had opinions: on everything from premarital sex (it was okay for the Episcopalians, why not the Catholics?) to how to ensure the batting order on our team delivered the most runs. He loved taking long, hot baths.

On Saturday afternoons when I rang the doorbell to visit Hank, his mother, a visual artist with a patched lazy eye, answered and directed me upstairs. There I'd find Hank soaking proudly in the tub under the bright bathroom lights. I plunked myself down on the toilet seat cover for a chat, awestruck my teammate sprouted hair in places I didn't. Several times he hoisted his oversize pink penis out of the water to show it off. I couldn't take my eyes off the purple veins and bright orange fuzz surrounding it. Like a mysterious sea monster, Hank's penis floated to the surface, then dove under the water. I was fascinated by his wiener since I'd only recently begun growing hair down there, and compared with his showboat, I felt like I'd inherited a dinghy.

Other infatuations overshadowed Hank. Chip Schneider, the dreamboat pitcher with the perfect, sandy blonde, feathered hair, conjured daydreams of *Tiger Beat* idol Leif Garrett. Chip's plump rose-colored lips presided over a mouthful of silver braces, but that didn't lessen my crush on him. Snagging line drives and scoring double plays came second nature to him. Every move Chip made looked effortless and heroic, even popping bubbles with the wad of Bazooka gum he kept tucked in his mouth.

I idolized from afar easygoing, confident Dan Beld, our lanky first baseman. His brown intelligent eyes, offset by dewy eyelashes, kept track of the ball wherever it landed on the diamond. With perfect precision, he scooped it up and sent the opposing players packing.

An earlier season his father Dr. Beld coached the Reds to the playoffs. Whenever the ball sailed to me in right field Dr. Beld cheered me on shouting "You've got it, son. Run it out, run it out!" He molded me into a team player with his encouraging words. Despite my fear of dropping the ball, my game began to improve thanks to his patient mentoring.

Surrounded by competitive, rough and tumble boys who lived and breathed sports, and a mom who studied and critiqued my performance, I recognized I was far from an elite athlete. I had a strong desire to be part of something, to fit in somewhere.

One hot, sunny evening during a championship game, Dr. Beld assigned me shortstop. The humidity hung in the air and sweat gathered on the back of my head where my ball cap sat. "All right, show us what you got, son," he said as he patted me on the shoulder and ushered me onto the diamond. A hush enveloped the stands. Man on first, man on second. The pitcher wound up and sailed a sizzler through the air. The steely-eyed batter thrust the aluminum Slugger behind his head. *Crack,* the bat collided with the ball. My opponent raced toward first base as I scooped the ball off the ground and pulled a Chip Schneider in pursuit of a double play. I tossed the ball over the second baseman's head and watched helplessly as it bounced onto the field. The spectators groaned. Humiliated, I hung my head in shame.

We lost the game, but Mom was undeterred. "Practice, practice, practice," she repeated as we ambled toward the car from the dugout. "You'll improve, my darling."

She attended all my games. Dad often missed them because in addition to his job inspecting buildings for the city of Cleveland, in my early years he spent evenings and weekends at Stelman Realty where he worked as an agent. It seemed like Dad was always away at work. As time passed Mom had asked him to get out of real estate so we all had more family time together. When time allowed, she sent us to the backyard to play catch together.

"If you throw the ball out of your father's reach, run and get it for him," she whispered in my ear. I darted right and left to pick up the runaway balls I threw to my poor, tired Dad. I wondered at times whether he even enjoyed playing catch, or just felt obligated because Mom wanted him to.

"Aim for my mitt, son," he'd instruct me tapping the oiled leather pocket with his weathered hand. He'd catch the ones I pitched directly to him and shook his head in disbelief as more frequent ones sailed every which way.

Forever banished to right field because of my weak, inaccurate arm, I imagined the day I would prove my worth and win over the boys who doubted me on the Reds softball team. Then a fly ball would rip through the air, and like Charlie Brown failing to catch it, I'd land in the doghouse with my teammates all over again. I wanted to be a sports hero, but my daydreaming doomed me.

"Hilovsky," said an exasperated Hank one day, shoving his freckled face within an inch of mine. "Focus. When the ball's coming, focus." Then he plopped his red ball cap on his fiery red curls and trailed me into the outfield.

"I'm trying, I'm trying. I get all nervous when I hear the bat crack and the ball's whizzing toward me and everyone's screaming."

"Tune 'em out," Mom insisted, as we left the game. Back home, she grabbed a mitt and practiced playing catch with me. After a few tosses, I fell into a rhythmic back-and-forth. "There you go, keep it up," she said. She lobbed me a studied pitch, and I returned it, right in her glove. "Much better!"

I had mixed feelings about my mother's drive to mold me into a better athlete. I yearned to please her, even though sometimes I got angry being the primary focus of her attention. Why didn't Dad take more initiative, instead of yielding the field to Mom?

During the summer of 1975, on and off the playfield, visions of Chip Schneider filled my daydreams: Chip with his Bazooka gum, stomping his Puma cleats on the pitching mound, tagging our opponents out if they dared to steal a base. I envied his calm deliberateness while making a play. His confidence beamed far and wide.

After the final championship game of the season, the one we lost, I approached Chip at the card table where moms had set up a cupcake display. It was the end of August. The sun blazed overhead; a chilly breeze blew the sand across the field. "So, ready to go back to school?" I stammered, wiping the sweaty dust from my brow. I stole a glance sideways in search of a chocolate cupcake.

He shrugged, "Yeah, I guess so." Silence.

Oh, my God, I don't know what else to say. "Well, guess I'll see you next year, unless...well, see you." I glanced one last time in his direction, but his eyes averted mine, staring into the distance. The wind danced through his perfectly feathered hair, not disturbing a tendril. I disappeared into the crowd.

CHAPTER 3

Standing Tall

T HE YEAR OF America's Bicentennial, my life changed. That summer of '76 I celebrated my 13th birthday. All the traumas of approaching adolescence descended in one fell swoop: acne, unexplained wet dreams, and unrequited crushes. Not to mention my overwhelming self-consciousness concerning the acne, unexplained wet dreams, and unrequited crushes. In September I entered the eighth grade at St. Angela Merici Catholic School in suburban Cleveland.

Cleveland, "the mistake on the lake." That's what *Tonight* show host Johnny Carson called my hometown following the Cuyahoga River catching on fire. Clevelanders didn't take kindly to Johnny making fun of our city. At one time the metropolis claimed the seventh largest population in the U.S.A. We took great pride in our sports teams and well-respected orchestra. A city of builders—the auto, steel, and tool and die industry prospered here—we were more than a punch line to a joke.

Everything seemed clumsy and awkward during these years, not just my adolescence. When it came to talking to girls, I could barely put one word in front of another. My seventh-grade classmates teased me about the puka shells around my neck and the sporty, yellow denim leisure suit I wore for class pictures—items I had acquired the previous summer on a trip out West with Mom and Dad. No one seemed to care that I had scaled the Rocky Mountains, explored the Grand Canyon, and at a Denny's in Vegas, crammed a coin in a slot machine only to get apprehended by security for underage gambling.

At St. Angela Merici I loved history, English, and art, earning respectable grades in all my subjects—a result of my parents' high expectations and the threat of the nuns' dreaded ruler. The Irish sister, Leona, clad in a black habit and wielding a yardstick alongside her rosary beads, would shriek "you, bold brazen thing, you!" and put the fear of God into any misbehaving twerp. The equally terrifying, diva-like Mrs. Capone wore burgundy-tinted glasses, ponytails, and five-inch platform shoes. She'd arrive to school behind the wheel of her burnt orange Camaro. A petite 5'4", she'd shove troublemakers against the chalkboard while poking them with a rubber-tipped pointing stick.

To avoid Sister Leona's and Mrs. Capone's wrath I completed homework assignments on time, raised my hand to answer questions, and refrained from spitball fights and classroom pranks. These compliant behaviors failed to ingratiate me with the volatile Mrs. Capone, who pinpointed the cracks in my veneer.

On the first day of class, a chubby, little girl with curly blonde hair and a paisley book bag snuck into Mrs. Capone's classroom. Her family moved to Fairview Park from the eastern suburbs of Cleveland. "My name's Philippa Hayward," she announced, as if I should applaud her arrival. Her eyes darted back as she squeezed into the seat in front of me. She wore a forest green poncho. Shiny, black cat-eye glasses sat propped on her nose.

"This place is a zoo," I whispered. "Capone's the lion tamer. Watch out, or we'll both get 50 lashes." Philippa made a cracking sound with her voice, like leather hitting a hard surface. "She'll whip us into shape in no time," my new friend giggled.

She laughed at my jokes, no matter how dark they were, and flung her own quick wit right back at me. And despite the pimples constantly speckling my cheeks and temples— which I popped the minute they arose— somehow, I didn't feel at all tongue-tied around her.

We began passing notes back and forth in class. "S.O.S... latest news bulletin. Joe DeLuca is a space alien. Earth to Joe, Earth to Joe." In small sketches we'd draw stick figures of faculty, staff, and the student body. Our cryptic little messages and etchings mocked the school newspaper S.A.M. and turned the tables on our detractors.

The mean kids teased us about being boyfriend and girlfriend, which wasn't true. Even Mrs. Capone chirped about us being lovebirds. Whenever she did, my face turned red. I knew I'd found a like-minded buddy, and I didn't care if she happened to be a girl.

One day Mrs. Capone sauntered into the classroom. "All right, Hayward and Hilovsky, enough is enough, I'm separating you two." She confiscated our notes and shoved our desks to opposite sides of the classroom. The following semester we were assigned different homerooms. No longer able to pass notes and whisper when we felt like it, we arranged to meet after school. I learned that Philippa and her family had moved into a cul-de-sac around the corner from my house.

On rainy Saturday afternoons in my bedroom with the door shut we'd sit Indian-style and spin 45's on my small record player. Sprawled on the floor we'd listen to the wholesome, cheeky music of The Carpenters, The Captain and Tennille, and John Denver.

One afternoon I turned to Philippa and said, "Ok, tell me everything you like about me."

Her cheeks turned a rosy pink. She grew quiet. "Well, I love your haircut. And your smile makes me happy whenever I see it," she stammered. "And your clothing style is the best. You stand out from the other boys."

A wide grin broke out across my face. "Thanks," I said. I sat up straight and gave Philippa my assessment of her, no holds barred. "You're a pretty girl. You've got beautiful hair and a great smile, especially when your braces come off. But you need to lose weight and get rid of those nerdy glasses." She looked down averting any eye contact, just as "Don't Go Breaking My Heart" began playing on the turntable. "And, the poncho needs to go," I said tugging on the fringe.

She remained silent as Elton John and Kiki Dee wailed about the perils of love and making it. I added," You've got a great singing voice too." She looked up on the heels of my last compliment. "Thanks," she smiled. Despite her polite reply, I could see my brashness hurt.

At a loss for how to proceed I pulled back as I sat across from her. My cheeks turned red. No words came. *Oh God, how could I have said those mean things? Maybe I needed to protect myself, not confuse her?* I felt pulled between wanting to get closer to a new friend and confide in her, while also not leading her to believe romance was inevitable. And yet that's what I wanted, closeness. Alone and misunderstood, I yearned for connection. And here was this girl who liked me for being me and was willing to connect. *Why couldn't I accept this gift and let her love me; love her back?* I didn't have the answer.

Despite the awkward interlude we shared, Philippa and I continued to spend time together at school. I made the mistake of confiding in a squirrely classmate that I'd hung the new Farrah Fawcett poster on the back of my bedroom door. Before long, he and others referred to Philippa and me as Farrah and Lee. And the verbal teasing escalated from that innocent admission.

One day in the schoolyard a forceful hand shoved me from behind. "Fag," a spiteful voice screamed. I looked up to see Mac McBride, a tow-headed bully standing there, his fists clenched. "Shut up," I said, oblivious to the meaning of the word but suspecting it meant I was weak and a sissy. My adrenaline surged, my heart pounding, I yelled "You're a fag." He sneered at me, turned his head, and spat a big hocker on the playground cement before strutting away.

Tears poured down my burning cheeks, tears I tried to hide from other kids, some of whom were pointing and laughing. The recess monitor followed McBride to the outskirts of the playground but didn't report him. I wiped my soggy face with my sleeve and cursed under my breath. *Dammit.* Revenge bled into my mind. I was tall for thirteen but lacked the muscle mass to throw my weight around.

I didn't want to fight. But the relentless taunts didn't stop.

"Oh, Jackie, Jackie," my adopted cousin Jimmy Farrell hooted the following day. Rail-thin and limp-wristed, he embodied the girlie-boy stereotype more than I did and took the hatemongering a step further. "You're so gay," he'd holler while I paced with Philippa in the schoolyard perimeter. Then he'd erupt in a high-pitched cackle. He'd up the ante, catcalling. "Look, there she is, his *so-called* 'girlfriend.' When're you getting married?" Philippa's peaches and cream complexion turned scarlet. My insides felt like they might explode. To make matters worse the acne continued its march across my face, aggravated by the angry confrontations I began to encounter.

I'd come home and hurl myself on my bed, punching the mattress, and screaming, "They hate me. Everyone hates me." I'd burst into tears.

"Who hates you, honey?" my mother asked trying to calm me down to talk. "I'll phone the school principal and report them."

"The kids calling me names and pushing me around on the playground," I'd sniff as the fits subsided. "And don't call the principal. They'll think I'm a narc."

Exasperated she said, "I'm signing you up for self-defense classes. You're going to learn how to put them in their place." And right then and there she picked up the phone and enrolled me in boxing lessons.

"Sweetheart, don't take any guff from anyone, especially that darn old Jimmy," she counseled as she drove me down to the inner-city community center, where we'd attended family swim night. "Give 'em the one-two punch!"

"I don't know," I sniffed, tears filling my eyes. "I just want this to be over." We arrived at the community center and entered a dingy room with punching bags hanging from the low ceiling. A man with a crewcut and big arms waited for us on a bench.

"Here, champ, try these on for size," he said chomping on a wad of tobacco. The oversized gloves made my hands look like red dodgeballs. I slid them on allowing the fabric to cushion my long, thin fingers.

"Okay, buckaroo, watch my jabs." He began hopping up and down and circling around me. "Put up your dukes."

I held up the gloves and began mirroring him, imitating his every move. Punching the air with my leather-bound fists. Gravitating into the personal space of my nemesis.

"Okay, good, straighter shot, there you go," he egged me on. I jabbed him in the gut, and he returned the favor. "Protect your delicates," he growled. "Fists up."

I came after him again, bouncing around like a kangaroo. "Watch out, creepo," I snarled. I went for his nose.

"Here's a counterpunch," he blocked my move and hit me in the sternum. I wobbled and recovered. "And here's a fake out," the coach blurted before punching air and then coming in for a kill. I ducked and made a counterpunch that knocked him on the chin.

"All right, enough," he said after another half-hour round of sparring. "That's a good foundation, champ."

Driving home with mom, I could still feel the adrenaline coursing through my system and a worrisome thought crept into my mind. What if I'd turn into some bully? But I needed to do something to reclaim my self-respect. Humiliation wasn't an option. I needed to stand up for myself. I wouldn't let any sucker terrorize me in front of a crowd.

The next afternoon Jimmy cornered me in the playground. "Oh, come on Momma's boy, whatcha' gonna' cry about today?" he whistled. When he looked away to see if anyone else wanted to join his charade, I grabbed his shoulder and popped him straight in the nose.

Blood spurted all over the place, including his white dress shirt. The nuns gave me a detention. But Jimmy buttoned his lip from that day forward, and I got a temporary boost in popularity from the other kids, who knew he had it coming.

Then in September I met RJ, and everything changed.

CHAPTER 4

Happiness is...

W HEN I FIRST saw RJ, with his jet-black hair, coffee-color eyes, and white smile, I felt an instant pang in my stomach. It wasn't like the intense butterflies with Chip on my softball team, or when I visited Hank soaking in the tub while his mom with the lazy eye painted landscapes on canvas. I felt jealousy, pure and simple, seeing him surrounded by a bevy of cute girls, all of them giving him their undivided attention. I wanted some of that attention, some of that popularity, bestowed on me.

The fall of 1976, at age 13, I returned to Lakewood Little Theatre, or LLT, for a second quarter of study with the children's acting program, which I'd begun earlier that spring landing a small role in *The Emperor Has No Clothes*. The spacious lobby and common areas, recently renovated thanks to a generous donor, were awash in autumn light and brimming with people that Saturday morning.

There he stood surrounded by two blondes, a brunette, and a redhead. The girls resembled the female detectives on the popular new show *Charlie's Angels*. I guess he was Charlie. Despite my same-sex crushes, I still liked associating with pretty girls. These were the "cream of the crop," as Dad liked to say.

Animated in his conversation with all four "Angels," every once in a while, RJ cocked his head and laughed with abandon. His perfectly feathered hair, parted down the middle, framed a narrow almond-shaped face. His olive complexion resembled my own. We could be brothers, I thought.

Although we'd never crossed paths, I drew some immediate conclusions about him. First, he was likely a snob; second, he was arrogant; and third, he was bossy. Little did I know, a few weeks later we'd become best friends.

I watched the girls flirting with him. First, I noticed Janice, the pretty blond with playful blue eyes whose sun-streaked hair and golden tan called to mind a California sunset. Then came dark-haired Marlis, glamorous with high cheekbones and a Southern drawl. The third girl, loud and bubbly Gayle, sported a T-shirt that proclaimed: "To Know Me Is to Love Me." Her boisterous laugh echoed through the hallways.

Finally, my eyes landed on Shelley Lundgren. Shelley wore a pink button-down shirt and fitted Calvin Klein jeans; her red hair pulled back in barrettes. She flashed a shy smile.

In my light blue crew neck sweater, bone colored Levi cords, and white Stan Smith tennis shoes, I strode past this magnetic circle, met their approving eyes, nodded, looked away and then glanced back again.

"Hey," he called out, "what are you looking for?"

My face relaxed. "I'm headed toward Studio B, Jan Brueggemann's speech and enunciation class," I said.

"I'm in that class too," he replied. He stuck out his hand and said, "I'm RJ."

"Jack," I replied, cracking a small smile.

He introduced the girls, who were all registered for Jan's class too. "Hey, Jack," the willowy brunette Marlis chirped. "Come sit with us."

"Yeah, we're all in this together," Janice seconded.

My heart aflutter, I nodded in agreement. "It's nice to meet you," said Shelley rising from her chair to say hello.

A rush of adrenaline coursed through my body. *God, up close these girls are even prettier than at a distance. And they're nice. And RJ's smile, it's blinding, like a Pepsodent commercial. And his twinkling, warm eyes. What a relief. These are my people!* Maybe the awkward feeling of thirteen and not fitting in was soon going to disappear.

My self-defenses no longer on high alert, I allowed the morning light and calming camaraderie to sweep me into an alternative universe. Here I wouldn't worry about getting shoved around by Cousin Jimmy or an avenging nun. Plus, the warmth of newfound friendship erased my anxieties around the daily blitz of pimples peppering my cheeks.

I let go, released my shoulders, and allowed my face to beam. "It's great to meet you all," I said. "Maybe we can sit together in class."

Happiness would be right around the corner. I was sure.

CHAPTER 5

Reality and Fantasy

LAKEWOOD LITTLE THEATRE soon became the antidote to the awkwardness I experienced playing team sports that demanded a prowess and confidence I didn't possess.

"Keep your eye on the ball. Follow through. Give it your all, Jack!" Mom would shout encouraging me from the stands or in the backyard while playing catch. She believed in me and wanted to coach me to excel in the sports she loved as a girl, whether that was softball, basketball, or tennis.

My mother, the natural jock, continued her campaign to involve Dad in my athletic development. "Frank, why don't you two go out back and throw the ball around," she'd say. "Ruth, I've been on my feet all day," he'd reply. I could tell by his less-than-eager response that playing with me felt more like an exhausting chore to him. Mom's investment in time and energy in me, her devotion, created a thickening tension between them that I didn't really understand.

When not involved in hitting, throwing, kicking, or catching balls, I enjoyed countless hours away from the playfield in my own company.

Thanks to a vivid imagination as a young child, I fell in love with story-telling and proudly recited by memory *Snow White and the Seven Dwarfs* to visiting relatives and family friends. Hollywood, with all its fantasy and drama, offered an exciting escape. A favorite cousin shared with me her treasure trove of *Tiger Beat* magazines, featuring teen idols David Cassidy, Leif Garrett, and Bobby Sherman. I dove into their pages soaking up the details and drama. Later *People* and *Rona Barrett's Hollywood* would corral my youthful attention. Celebrity profiles, star-studded movie premieres, impending marriages, and legendary tributes all drew me into an alternative universe. I dreamed I'd one day find myself in this theatrical merry-go-round, the world of television and movies and non-stop adventure. In fact, prior to Lakewood Little Theatre, television offered me an unending refuge. The tube became an entertaining, reassuring friend.

***

THE two-story house with white siding and olive-green shutters sat on a small patch of grass on Belle Avenue. I climbed the steps and rang the doorbell. High-pitched squeals echoed from inside. A little boy with wispy blonde hair threw open the door. "It's for you, RJ," he screamed. Engelbert Humperdinck crooning "After the Lovin'" played on the stereo.

Dressed in a purple V-neck sweater, RJ pushed open the screen door. "That's Keith. He's the baby of the family. I've got three other stepbrothers besides him, all younger than me. It's a madhouse sometimes," he sighed. "Where do you want to go?"

"How about the park? It's quiet there." His musky cologne tickled my nostrils, and I inhaled the woodsy fragrance. We headed north toward the lake, walking under tall oak trees aflame in orange, red and yellow.

"Was it okay that I called your house last week?" he asked. "I figured since you gave me your number, it was fair game."

"Oh, it's fine. My mom wondered who you were since she didn't recognize your voice." I watched his brown leather earth shoes adapt to the tempo of my white Stan Smith's.

"How do you say your last name again?"

"Hilovsky. Hi-love-ski. Just like it sounds."

"Hil—LOVE—ski. Is that right?" he asked.

"Yep, just put the love in front of the ski, like my Irish grandmother used to say." I took a deep breath, and glanced at the clouds above, which looked like galloping horses racing for the horizon. "She was an amateur tap dancer."

"Really?" said RJ.

"Yeah, all her brothers and sisters performed in vaudeville, like 80 years ago."

"That's so cool. I love to dance. Who are your favorite entertainers?"

The colorful trees towered over us. Lake Erie loomed in the distance. I stuffed my hands in my painter's pants and shrugged. "Well, on Saturday nights I love watching Carol Burnett and Mary Tyler Moore. They make me laugh. And then there's this new show on Wednesday nights that's become my obsession."

RJ turned to me. "Wait a minute, it's not the same show I watch, is it?"

Our eyes met, and we broke into laughter. "*Charlie's Angels*?"

"Yeah, oh my God, I worship Farrah Fawcett-Majors."

"Me too! I can't get enough of her. I just bought her poster this summer. It's taped to the back of my bedroom door."

As leaves crunched underfoot, we explored our mutual fixation. "I love her smile and those pearly, white teeth," I confided. "And she plays tennis, my favorite sport."

"Yeah, and I love her hair. That blown-back, tousled style. I've never seen a mane like hers before. And she's glamorous, not like Kate Jackson, who looks like a man," RJ harrumphed rolling his eyes.

"Well, all I know is she's a knockout in that red bathing suit. Hair, smile, the whole package. Not to mention she rules on a skateboard!" I added.

The sun glimmered on the breaking waves as we arrived at Lakewood Park. Our shoulders brushed against each other, and we squinted across the water towards Canada. A widening smile crept across my face while a warm, tingling sensation spread across my entire body. I wondered if this was how the great explorers felt, surveying an endless landscape and all the possibilities that lay ahead.

***

My thrilling infatuation with Farrah allowed me – for once – to feel like one of the guys. And RJ's reaction fed my enthusiasm. Her smile, her hair, her athleticism, and charismatic personality—all were attributes I appreciated about myself, or soon would. Plus, she was a woman unafraid to compete—on a tennis court or television soundstage. Devoid of real-life male role models who mirrored the sensitivity I identified with (well, there was Phil Donahue and Alan Alda), I embraced the women of the 1970s. Mary, Carol, and now Farrah. Comfortable in my own skin, I had no interest in becoming a woman; I just felt at home with the joie de vivre and independent streak the women of that decade embraced, especially the youthful Farrah.

And so, I joined the media frenzy, devouring every news clip or cover story I could find. And RJ grew into my partner in crime, as we formalized our devotion.

"Scrapbooks, that's what we need," he said one afternoon in Burrow's, the arts and crafts store in Westgate Mall.

"What do you mean?" I asked.

"So, we can organize all our clippings and cover stories in one place. What do you say we start a Farrah scrapbook?" he said, like it was written in the sky.

We rummaged in the back of the store and found a spiral sketchpad with a red cover for $9.99. "We'll take two," he told the cashier.

"Let the clipping begin," he said as we headed toward my house shopping bag in hand.

CHAPTER 6

Obsessions

THE MIRROR REVEALED the ugly truth. Staring into its reflection after school one afternoon I spotted an outbreak of acne across my face. Attempting to ignore my racing heart, I turned away hoping it was a mirage. When I looked back, the pimples remained, looming like a bad neighbor. And I began to cry.

"Darling, you're a handsome young man," Mom said when I told her one day after school I felt like Frankenstein. "You don't understand," I whined, tears dripping down my cheeks. "I don't feel handsome. Everybody's looking at me, and all they'll see are zits popping across my face." She threw her arms around me, and I began to sob again. "Why me? Why me?" I repeated over and over.

She cradled my chin in her hands and peered into my bleary eyes. "You are special. When your dad and I saw your little face the day you were born, we knew you were a miracle. This is one small cross you must bear but it will subside. I promise you, my sweetheart." She pulled me close and rocked me back and forth in her arms until my unrelenting sobs receded.

The outbreak I suffered that fall overshadowed the one from a year earlier. What had I done to deserve this? Poor hygiene? A chocolate bar habit? Overactive glands? There were countless theories.

My parents didn't know where to go, how to address my condition. And so, I endured it, hiding behind the bathroom door, obsessed with my face. Wondering when it would go away, how long would it take to be rid of this endless torture?

***

WHEN I first realized my same sex desires, I had no interest in hugging or kissing boys – yet. That felt "gay" to me, and I wanted to grow up and get married to a girl and have a family. But my dark, deep secret, my fascination with men's bodies, would not go away. I wondered whether this secret I couldn't share with anyone else was to blame for the ugliness on my face. Maybe acne was my punishment.

The Catholic Church taught homosexuality was wrong so maybe this was a warning not to have these thoughts, these feelings? Like Nathaniel Hawthorne's scarlet letter, maybe this war zone on my face was my indictment, a hot iron brand, announcing to the world my impurity. But I didn't want to believe my desires were wrong, they were just me. Not all of me, but an important part of me. I didn't know what to do, or whom to tell, beyond Mom. So, I kept it to myself, locked away in a tiny cell, determined to not allow it to ruin my life.

***

"I think you should part your hair on the side," RJ advised as we peered in the mirror. I ran his black comb through my hair channeling the dark waves.

"We could be brothers," I said.

He stood next to me and stared. "Yeah, the dark hair, the almond shaped eyes, the bright white teeth. We could be." I gazed at our reflections. Brothers. Yeah, except he was an inch taller. We both sported that feathered-hair look.

***

THAT fall we prepared for a holiday showcase that Lakewood Little Theatre presented at semester's end for the friends and family of students.

"Do you want to be in my skit?" RJ asked after class one morning. I'm calling it "Angels in Snow." Here's the plot: Santa's kidnapped. And Charlie's Angels are hired to investigate his whereabouts. You'd play a suspicious elf."

"What? An elf?" I groaned. "What about Charlie?"

"Okay, okay, if you insist," he said.

His face lit up, his brown eyes radiating a playful glow. I looked back at him and melted. Even though I was 6 months older, I followed his lead.

***

"Do you like fashion?" he asked one afternoon.

"Yeah, why do you ask?"

He pulled out a copy of *Gentleman's Quarterly*. "I thought you'd want to see some of the clothes." We paged through pausing at photo spreads of male models wearing tweedy sport jackets and elegant tuxedos, dark blue jeans, and bulky woolen sweaters.

"Purple's in this season. I like to wear it with black," he said.

"Well, I like something a little sportier." I pointed to a model wearing a hooded sweater and canvas sneakers. A navy blue and red striped rugby shirt was flung around his shoulders. RJ moved closer to inspect the layout.

"God, we're not exactly in the fashion capitol of the world, are we?" he laughed. "Probably better we have separate tastes, otherwise we'd get in a fight about borrowing each other's clothes."

"We'd probably fit into each other's clothes," I said. A small grin broke into a smile across my face. The sun beamed through the window. I forgot all about the acne.

After theatre class, we walked down Detroit Avenue to RJ's house on Belle. As we approached the porch Barbara Streisand's voice trilled from inside, her latest hit "Evergreen" playing on the stereo. Taking the porch steps two by two. RJ swung open the screen door, which rattled. Inside three little boys were on the floor playing the board game Battleship. In the adjoining dining area behind them, a tall brunette woman with a lavender cowl neck sweater was shining the dining room table with a can of Pledge in her hand.

"Hi honey, come on in. Who's your friend?" She put down the rag and came closer. "I'm Jen Fallon."

"Jack, meet my mother," RJ said.

I extended my hand. "Nice to meet you, Mrs. Fallon."

"RJ told me all about you. Glad you could come by. There's ham and cheese in the refrigerator in case you want to make sandwiches. I'm getting back to my housework." Her sparkling blue eyes looked one last time at me.

Squealing with delight, the three little boys ran over and grabbed me around the legs. "You remember Keith, and this is Danny and Matt."

Hi, you guys," I said brushing their hair back with my hand. "You're the one who threw open the door last time, right Keith?"

He giggled and hid behind RJ "He's the shy three-year-old," RJ said.

We wandered into the kitchen, and the boys scrambled away. "I always wanted a brother," I mused.

"You can have them," he said as he opened the refrigerator door. "And my stepfather too."

"What's wrong with him?" I asked.

"We're just different. He lifts weights and fixes cars. He works at Republic Steel. I'm artsy-fartsy, he laments."

I nodded. "My Dad and I are different too. He thinks work comes first. My mom thinks fun comes first. I'm not into fixing leaky faucets."

Screaming like a banshee Keith bulldozed through the living room with one of the missing pieces of the Battleship game. "Give it back," shrieked one of the boys.

"It's mine," Keith whined.

The shrill arguments continued until Mrs. Fallon shouted, "Stop it, or you're all going to your rooms."

***

WHILE the *Charlie's Angels* holiday showcase was cheesy, like an over-the-top *Saturday Night Live* parody, it set the stage for RJ and me. We worshipped at the altar of Farrah, rivaling most boys' obsession with baseball legend Pete Rose.

"I love the way she stays active, playing tennis, and running outdoors," I repeated to RJ as we scoured the latest issue of *People* comparing notes on the ways we adored her.

RJ continued, "It's all about her hair. And look at her in this evening gown. She exudes glamour. She's no frumpy Diane Keaton."

I laughed thinking about the movie *Annie Hall*, although it was a grownup's film I hadn't seen.

We amassed nonstop articles on our golden girl, a signpost of our devotion. After the show debuted in September, and landed in the Nielson Top Ten, the Angels graced the cover of every magazine in America: *T.V. Guide, Time, People*, and gossip rags galore. Farrah's popular red swimsuit poster broke all sales records for pinups and fueled the country's obsession with her.

The poster, still on my bedroom door, confirmed my adolescent fervor. In seventh grade my parents gave me permission to redecorate my room. We replaced the worn brown carpeting and stale green wallpaper with a fresh décor: cherry red carpet, nautical blue wall-paper, and bright white floorboards. My own homespun decorating version of *The Bicentennial Minute*.

With magic markers, glue sticks, and scissors in hand, RJ and I sat for hours filling fresh pages in our new scrapbooks. We showcased Farrah holding hands with her husband Lee, skateboarding on the set of *Charlie's Angels*, and accepting a People's Choice Award in 1977. On and on the photographic spree continued. Each iconic shot we clipped found a place in the hallowed pages of our scrapbooks.

After assembling our Farrah montage we'd page through and quiz each other on the minutia of her life and career as if we'd met the blonde beauty from Corpus Christi in person. Her friendly, breezy personality only enhanced her girl-next-door persona.

"Did you know she made a movie called *Myra Breckenridge* with Mae West and Raquel Welch?" he asked. "She and Raquel even kiss!"

"Never heard of it," I said, "let's watch it."

Then I'd jump in. "Did you know Farrah grew up a practicing Catholic?"

"No way," he laughed.

Like expert game show hosts, we accumulated a running encyclopedia of every little detail of her life, often outsmarting each other in our thirst for Farrah trivia.

Outside my bedroom window the day's end cast a golden wash on the playfield, site of my childhood softball games. We heard my parents in the other room laughing over an episode of *All in the Family*, while the neighbor's lawn mower buzzed in the distance.

Stretched out on my bedspread we observed the sun sink into the distant trees. Elbow to elbow, our scrapbooks nearby, I'd feel the warmth and weight of his body near mine and inhale the scent of Coast soap on his skin. Red highlights in his hair reflected the evening glow. I smiled thinking how long I had waited for a best friend who liked the same things I liked. My hand almost touched his shoulder before hesitating.

"How does it look?" I'd ask after I finished a section of the scrapbook. He rifled through the pages then grabbed a florescent green marker and Zorro-like drew a splashy headline to tie together a photo collage. "There, perfect," he said, admiring his neon proclamations: "Farrah Ponders the Future" followed by "Farrah Dazzles Cannes."

That's how it all started. Whenever the week's new onslaught of magazines arrived at Rexall Drug, we dove into the racks scanning for cover stories and photos of beatific Farrah and sometimes her co-stars, Kate and Jaclyn. And every month or two, there we were in his bedroom or mine, scissors and glue in hand, incorporating the next chapter of her celebrity saga into our scrapbooks, adding layer upon layer to the memorabilia of Mrs. Fawcett-Majors, one of *People* Magazine's Most Intriguing Personalities of 1976 and our mutual muse.

***

RJ and I shared common interests beyond Farrah. Our love of theatre, inspired by our involvement in the children's acting program, brought us closer together while also fueling competition. In 1977 Lakewood Little Theatre cast us in alternate ensembles of *The Wizard of Oz*. RJ played the Scarecrow in the "A" cast, while I played the Tin Man in the "B" cast. The following year we portrayed dueling princes in the same ensemble of an updated *Snow White*, with me, Prince Charming, at the top of the bill while RJ played the supporting role of the mercurial Mirrored Prince.

Strutting across the stage during one rehearsal I whispered to RJ in his cardboard cutout booth, "Hah-ha. I beat you out for the lead."

"I wouldn't hold your breath," RJ countered, " I plan to break out of the confines of this mirror. Don't plan to rest on your laurels."

When I forgot a line, he'd whisper, "Cat got your tongue?" Then he'd wink and continue, "Cough up a quarter, and I'll give you the first word, or maybe two."

RJ's quick wit failed to rival a greater gift: his ability to move to music. The first time I saw him dance in a talent show, my eyes were glued on him. On Teen Dance Night at the Lakewood YMCA, he entered the Friday night dance off, a monthly competition with $50 prize money. The men's contest began with a solo. Four guys dressed in hip-hugging pants and silky, chest revealing shirts lined up to dominate the spotlight.

"Here I go, kiddo," he whispered as he strutted over in his trademark purple shirt and black pants to take his place, hand on his hip. Donna Summer's "I Feel Love" throbbed from a murmur into a fevered pitch as synthesizers intensified into a cavern of sound. RJ started with a foot-ball-change, foot-ball-change, his arms parallel to the floor, forming a kinetic capital T. Bit by bit, he disappeared in the undulating rhythm, his arms, legs, hips, and head drawn into a pulsating vortex of the repetitious beat.

Teens and parents orbited around him. Watching his body capture the music and energy of the crowd and funnel it through space, like a furnace blasting heat, left me in awe. My heart thumped in rhythm to the music but also in reaction to RJ's sensual, sexy hip gyrations. Sweat poured from every pore—from his brow, from the opening of his shirt, from his armpits as he twisted and twirled, a purple cyclone. Sailing through the air, he came to a stop, soaked in water from head to toe, awash in disco fever. He won the contest and prize money.

During fifth grade Mom sent me to formal dancing classes. There I learned the old-time foxtrot, waltz, and jitterbug. Disco was different: the rhythm, the emotion, the feeling of unbound joy and freedom. RJ's music became my music, the songbook of my teenage life. While I loved witnessing him strut his stuff, I soon realized I wanted some of that attention.

In his basement he'd fire up the jukebox with "I Love the Nightlife" and begin to teach me his moves.

"Remember, the head follows the direction of the body. Avoid looking at your feet," he instructed.

"1-2, 1-2-3, 1-2, 1-2-3," RJ counted as he demonstrated each dance step, grinding his hips and swinging his head in the direction he moved.

Exasperated, I'd complain, "Slow down. Jeez, I can't flex my hips like you!" Then, immediately after picking up a move, I'd demand, "Ok, next."

Sweat rained down all over us as we danced hip-to-hip, arm-to-arm, on the floor. His warm breath tickled my neck when he spun me 360-degrees. Adrenaline coursed through my body, and starry-eyed, I pirouetted across the room.

The disco craze swept Cleveland and the entire nation by storm with its glamor and seductive rhythms. Downtown nightclubs to neighborhood taverns retrofitted their interiors with pulsing disco lights and illuminated dance floors.

One Sunday afternoon our group of friends attended a teen dance at The Electric Mining Company, a local club. I slipped into a brand-new powder blue shirt, with a plunging "v" neckline. RJ wore his signature purple top, while Shelley Lundgren from LLT and her high school pal Beth donned faux-silk dresses that sailed through the air when we spun them.

Music boomed through the cavernous space filled with dancing teens not old enough to drink. Shag carpeting covered the walls overhead. Shelley grabbed RJ's hand as they neared the dance floor. I gestured to Beth, whose pearly white smile accentuated her dimples. Her glasses slipped to the tip of her nose.

"Wanna' dance?" I asked, as the Bee Gees broke into a high-pitched siren call from loudspeakers above the deejay booth.

We began to sway our shoulders and hips in unison while "Staying Alive" repeated its incessant beat. I reached for Beth's hand and began spinning her around the room, like RJ had taught me.

"You're good," Beth shouted over the din of the music.

"I learned from old Twinkle Toes," gesturing toward RJ. I looked over my shoulder to catch a glimpse of him twirling Shelley in several directions before dropping her into a dramatic dip. "Sometimes I can't keep up with his moves," I sighed. "He'll always be #1."

I sailed Beth across the rainbow-colored blinking dance floor. Her honey-brown pageboy flew in every direction.

"Okay, how about we try the bird of paradise move?" I trumpeted with a big fat smile.

"Are you sure you can lift me?" she asked.

"No problem, you'll be a feather. On the count of 1-2-3."

I leaned over and hoisted her petite frame over my shoulders as she squealed with glee. Her arms outstretched like Supergirl, Beth reached for the stars while I pirouetted in place. Then I delivered her back to the floor in a graceful pivot.

"You were, well, great," Beth swooned as she leaned into me for an embrace. My heart thumped in my chest, but it wasn't beating for Beth; so light and airy she might float into the ether. My confidence overflowing, I'd accomplished moves that most of my peers might never have the knowhow to execute. And I'd stepped up to contest RJ's outsized presence, whether he noticed or not.

"C'mon," I whispered in her ear, "Time for a break. I'm boiling." We found a private corner off the floor and ordered a 7-Up to share. Meanwhile Shelley ran over to Beth, grabbed her hand and they spun around the floor a few times together, looking my way in between their moves.

"Impressive," RJ whispered as he sat down next to me at the small table. "You're learning your lessons."

"Some," I said. "Lessons, I mean. Thanks. I love leading on the dance floor. I kinda get lost."

"Yeah, I know," RJ replied. "It's like nobody can see you because you're a flash of light, and then it's gone, onto the next move or song."

I nodded and looked down. "Of course, I'll never outshine you. But I can try."

That moment, I felt both separate from and connected to RJ. Our passion for showmanship brought us together. And while I loved witnessing his talent, I needed my own laurels.

Girls adored RJ because he knew how to make them look elegant and graceful on the dance floor. And thanks to his tutelage I too became popular with them. Two fourteen-year-old boys riding high like Fred Astaire and Gene Kelly. Dating wasn't the top priority. We enjoyed the fun we found with each other.

I guess that's the beauty of reinvention, creating a new persona, making art, and losing oneself in that creation. You are the medium. You are the message. Lost in the swirl of bright lights and uncompromising rhythm, it was nothing short of intoxicating.

Other shifts, more physical, began happening. My voice started changing, and my body followed suit as I raced toward adolescence. Dark hair under my armpits, light coats on my arms and legs, a smattering on my chest and sprouts above my penis. The growth, the change, felt so alien and yet intriguing. I stood on the cusp of something exciting.

All I knew is the more time RJ and I spent together, laughing at life's silly triumphs and pitfalls, co-creating our Farrah scrapbooks, and dancing with wild abandon, the more I felt close to him in a way that was superior and far removed from the days of my Cub Scout sleepovers and makeshift forts.

***

"Do you want to be an actor?" I asked RJ one Saturday afternoon while strolling along Madison Avenue. It was springtime, the cold air blew north from Lake Erie, but the sun emerged from behind the gray clouds offering a momentary glaze of warmth.

He laughed, "Why not a dancer? I don't think I have the discipline to be an actor. Besides, I like to draw." We'd recently taken a charcoal drawing class, and RJ had completed several portraits of Farrah from movie magazines. They were lifelike and captured her free-spiritedness. In one she stood draped in a floor length gown, in another she sat curled up in a striped boat neck sweater. In both, her leonine mane tumbled down her sexy shoulders.

During lunch at the burger joint Leonard's, we'd trade gossip about the girls from Lakewood Little Theatre, whom we referred to as our Angels. Girl-next-door Janice, the blonde, pert-nosed lifeguard. Willowy Marlis, the brown-eyed brunette with a subtle drawl from New Orleans. And strong-willed Gayle, the brassy, fun-loving dishwater blonde who spoke her mind and wore her thoughts on her sleeve. And of course, red-headed Shelley and her Calvin's.

"Would you date Janice?" I asked. The master of the hypothetical, I framed questions out of the blue in hopes to learn a new or exciting tidbit about my friend. Or provoke controversy. I liked playing the instigator at times.

"I think she has a boyfriend," he said with a mouth full of fries. "But if she didn't, I would date her in a heartbeat."

I remembered the black and white dance stills taken with Janice that RJ showed me one afternoon. Arm in arm, dressed in matching satin baseball jackets, they were a striking couple. With her fair, soft features complimenting his dark, good looks, they resembled a 1970's version of Astaire and Rogers.

"She's beautiful," I cooed. "I think I've got a crush on her."

"You, me, and everyone else," RJ sighed.

As summer approached, I became determined to teach RJ how to play tennis, an activity I excelled at. "C'mon, try something new, you can do it." At Linden Park I tossed the ball into the air and demonstrated my serve.

"Ugggh," he'd shout, rolling his eyes as the balls he hit sailed out of the court.

"Patience, you gotta have patience," I repeated. "First, hold the ball above your racquet. Now toss it above your head."

He would follow my directions and then ka-boom!!—the ball would fly over the fence. The second or third time RJ succeeded in serving the ball in the box.

"I'm sizzling now," he'd shout, until the following serve ricocheted into a neighboring court. I smiled and nodded to the court's occupants. "Thanks, we'll take that ball."

"You're improving," I'd say, my hand on his shoulder. "We'll keep on practicing until you're a natural."

"Yeah," he'd nod with a characteristic twitch of his neck. "Until the end of time."

RJ had a mind of his own when it came to sports or activities in which he didn't excel. I always felt behind the learning curve when he taught me a new dance, but I eagerly rolled up my sleeves to learn the routine. Not so much with him and tennis, though he humored me by agreeing to play.

We found greater commonality with our families. He'd join mine on picnics near Lake Erie, where we'd eat a prepared lunch of grilled chicken, potato salad, and fresh watermelon and cantaloupe before playing a game of lawn darts on the grassy cliffs overlooking the water. At his house I met his Aunt Mimi, Uncle Bill, and a steady stream of cousins and friends. His family embraced me, while my family embraced him.

"Okay, bucko, let's go to the movies," he'd say when I tired him out from an assortment of outdoor activities and family picnics. "You are always on the go."

"I'm not on the go," I'd counter. "I'm just wanting to take advantage when an opportunity presents itself." I'd fall onto the leather couch in his basement and listen to the latest 45-record RJ spun on the jukebox. Music helped me relax. And when we disagreed, I didn't mind letting him have his way.

Luckily, we both shared the same love for scary movies and romantic comedies, and while disco was tops, we found room in his parent's jukebox for schmaltzy Barry Manilow songs like "Looks Like We Made It," sentimental guys that we were. And I continued to welcome his tutelage on the dance floor, while he tolerated my coaching on the tennis court.

Days stretched endless, yet summer had only begun. And I was endlessly happy!

CHAPTER 7

Summer Revelations 1977

"OH, MY GOD, did you see what I saw?" RJ whispered in disbelief. We had been sitting in the backyard with handsome Tom, his hunky parochial school classmate, before excusing ourselves to grab popsicles from the kitchen freezer.

"He didn't seem to care; everything was in plain sight," I deadpanned.

Tom Brandon, who ran cross-country with RJ in eighth grade, dropped by to say hello. While sitting on the back lawn Indian style, his large balls peeked from outside his tiny Adidas running shorts. He seemed oblivious to the sideshow. I tried averting my eyes but couldn't help noticing. His knockers, pink and low-slung, kept grazing Tom's muscular thighs, not to mention his adjoining bulge. I wondered if he knew he was hanging out.

We handed him a popsicle. The conversation hit an awkward lull until he looked down to discover he was exposed, blushed, and tucked himself back into his shorts. "Whoops," he said with a light-hearted shrug of his shoulders.

"What are you guys planning to do tonight?" Tom asked, his boyish grin revealing an adorable gap between his two front teeth.

"Probably head to the YMCA," I replied. "Why don't you join us? There's another dance contest, they're playing music from *Saturday Night Fever.*"

"Oh, I don't know if I'm up for the Y tonight." Tom laughed and once again adjusted himself. His twinkling blue eyes, wavy sunlight-streaked brown hair, and broad shoulders reminded me of teen heartthrob Parker Stevenson in the 1970's television series, *The Hardy Boys*. Thirteen-year-old Tom, who lettered in basketball, football, and cross-country, had the physique of a 24-year-old.

"We'll have to teach you how to dance, Tommy Boy," a coy RJ teased.

"I'll need a lot of help; I'm not the dancing kind. And I haven't seen the movie yet. Does it matter?"

"It's all in the hips," RJ reassured him. "You can pick it up quickly, you're an athlete."

Tom shrugged his shoulders again and flashed his mischievous grin. "We'll see, I've got baseball practice tonight. I may run over time."

After Tom left, RJ and I collapsed on our wool Indian blanket. The sun warmed our bare backs, and the light wind muffled our words.

"I can't believe he just let himself hang out of his shorts," RJ repeated

"I think he knew," I said. "Tom's very confident; he probably enjoys showing off. He's teasing us."

"That's for sure. That stud can tease me anytime," RJ purred.

We both began laughing out loud recognizing we'd ventured into unexplored territory for us.

"One time he stayed over after a cross country meet," RJ confided. "He fell asleep in the bottom bunk. From the mattress above, I watched his chest rise and fall, rise and fall," he sighed. "I wondered what it would feel like to plant a kiss on him."

I'd no interest in kissing boys on the mouth but had curiosities about exploring their bodies with my hands and lips, continuing the adventures I'd begun with my Cub Scout friends under the ping-pong table.

In between pining for Tom and the innuendo that entailed, RJ and I enjoyed the silences in each other's company. Free to tread the waters of uncertainty and ambiguity, we cast off any fear of judgment from the other.

"Hey, RJ what do you really want to do with your life?" I asked one moonlit night during a sleepover at his house.

"Probably go to New York and design beautiful clothing for women," he replied from the upper bunk. I lay still on the lower bunk, listening to the light wind rustle the muslin bedroom curtain.

He peered over the edge of the ladder down at me. "What's your dream, bucko?" I smiled, recalling how he'd adopted that endearment when he felt playful with me.

I shrugged and rolled over on my side facing the window. "Well, if I can't be an actor, I think I'd like to write."

"Why not be an actor, if that's what you want?" he said.

"I don't think I'm good enough. It's too competitive. Dad says it's unstable. They're all drunks and addicts. He lived in California for a while before he met Mom."

"Well, why not try?" His voice sounded optimistic.

My heart grew warm as I heard RJ drift off to sleep above me. Fond feelings stirred in my chest, ones I hadn't felt before. How great to be understood, encouraged, challenged to be myself and to consider all the options. In that room, that warm May night, I felt surrounded in a womb of security.

The whoosh of passing cars on Belle Avenue lulled me into a sound sleep.

***

"HEY, what's that--above your mouth?"

"What are you talkin' about?" I said planting my finger on the space between my nose and upper lip. It was Sunday morning. Stuffed after Mrs. Fallon's delicious breakfast of bacon, eggs, and waffles, we were sprawled on the living room carpet watching an old Doris Day and Rock Hudson movie, *Lover Come Back.*

RJ laughed. "Your mustache. That fuzzy stuff, silly." He looked at me with a gleam in his eye.

"Are you teasing me?" I shot back.

"No, just thought you should know it makes you look like the Frito Bandito. Unless that's the look you're after...."

"Well, not really." I slowly got up from the chair in the living room and climbed the stairs to his family's second floor bathroom. RJ followed.

"Oh my gosh, you're right." I touched the fuzzy down lining my lip, sliding my finger back and forth.

RJ pulled the drawer open in the bathroom vanity and unearthed a Bic razor. "Here's your answer. How about shaving it?"

"But won't it grow back thicker?" I stammered.

"Yeah, but it's never going to grow back lighter. Off with it."

I took the razor from his hand and began scraping the downy fuzz, which cascaded like snowflakes into the sink below.

"Welcome to the club," RJ patted me on the shoulder. "I started shaving two weeks ago. Don't worry, you're not alone."

Underneath the unforgiving light on the bathroom wall, I smiled at my friend while my heart went thump-thump-thump. Initiated, I'd taken one step toward manhood and could never go back. What would Mom say when she learned I'd shaved my face? I imagined she might express disappointment, tell me now that I'd done the irrevocable deed, I'd have no choice but to shave every day. My childhood over, I was no longer a boy and would be forced to daily remove the whiskers from above my lip.

Even though on weekend mornings I'd observed my father with his shaving brush, he'd never explained how I might begin this rite of passage. Kind of like how I'd woken up recent mornings to discover my undershorts all creamed inside. Nobody said a word about why or told me, "*You're having wet dreams.*" I felt embarrassed and a bit panicked. Unprepared for my changing body, I threw the messy underwear down the laundry chute each morning after washing it out in the bathroom sink to get rid of the evidence. Part annoyed, part ashamed, I wondered what was happening.

In eighth grade health class we'd learned the biological names of private parts, but no practical discussion of what they might do in the middle of the night. Not a word about it being a natural occurrence.

And nobody ever said, "*By the way, if you begin growing whiskers, maybe it's time to get a razor.*" I felt alone, in the dark, left to figure it out for myself. I knew my parents meant well and expected health class would fill in the gaps. But there were gaps. Nobody had explained anything about different sexual desires or even the benefits of pleasuring yourself. Until RJ.

I stepped away from the mirror and exhaled. "I think it looks better now, don't you?"

"Trust me," he said. "Much."

***

"Do you wanna' sleep over at my house, or should I sleep over at yours?" became our mantra of the summer of 1977. My newly redecorated Bicentennial bedroom housed my grandmother's hand-me-down double bed. If we stayed at my place, we didn't have to kick RJ's kid brother out of the lower bunk to make room for me.

Whenever RJ spent the night, I felt like we grew closer. I liked how he smelled-- his honey scented hair, skin that whiffed of coconut oil, the light perspiration that clung to his neck.

"Do you think Marlis has had sex before?" I asked him one hot summer night in July as we lay in my bed.

A long pause permeated the quiet, while crickets chirped in the humid night air.

"Well, she certainly is older looking than fourteen," he replied. He rolled toward me and said, "I guess it really doesn't matter."

I strained to see his eyes in the dark of my bedroom, even though the moon cast a yellow sheen on our entire backyard.

"Let's go outside and run naked under the stars," I blurted.

He laughed, "Are you serious? What if we get caught?"

"Everyone's asleep," I reasoned. "Nobody will even know."

Quietly, careful not to raise a stir, we snuck out the back garage door. In the moonlight I slipped off my cotton shirt followed by my boxers.

"Oh, my God, are you crazy? What if your parents see us?" RJ whispered.

"Shh, follow me." My heart raced. My penis stirred, blood rushing in to awaken me to nervous destiny.

I began sprinting around our backyard, the badminton net sprawled in the middle of the lawn, the family garden with fresh tomatoes and lettuce asleep in the dark, humid, summer soil, the neighbor's pool glistening shiny blue and transparent under the moonlight.

A moment later he removed his shirt and underwear and chased after me, our milk white bodies, like apparitions, silhouetted in the moon's glow. We rolled on the dewy grass performing cartwheels and flips. Like circus clowns, off the grid, home on leave, in no need of an audience.

Breathless and with flushed faces, we finished our lap around the yard and plopped on the curb of the cement patio. "It's too warm to go back inside," I panted catching my breath "Let's sleep out here, okay?"

It was 2 AM. Surrounded by the indoor/outdoor carpeting, redwood furniture, and family bikes, RJ and I assembled a makeshift mattress from patio furniture cushions, which we covered with my old Boy Scout sleeping bag and a lightweight blanket.

"This doesn't look very comfortable," he grimaced.

"Oh, come on, it's summer," I countered with a wink and a devilish grin. Goose bumps suddenly ran down my arms, and I hurried to cover us up. My heart pounded.

Underneath the itchy blanket our bodies were lined with a thin layer of sweat. I could feel RJ's silky skin rub against my own and held my breath.

"Have you ever whacked off?" RJ whispered.

"Ummm, no, not really," I said. "Why, have you?"

Quiet stretched for what seemed like forever. "Well, yeah, of course, it's natural when you're horny, or trying to go to sleep but can't relax."

"Hmmm, sounds interesting," I replied. I rolled on my back and sighed, grazing his shoulder.

He reached over and touched me under the covers. "I can show you how."

Conscious, and embarrassed of my already stiffening cock, I took a deep breath and said, "Sure."

As RJ stroked me from north to south and back again, it was as if a locomotive began coursing through my loins. As I screamed out into the dark surrounded by my Schwinn bike and the family lawnmower, thrill and fright enveloped me at the same time. The skin-to skin-contact, the pleasurable force of my friend's hand, the velocity of the release—my first orgasm. Everything seemed new and different, like the world had changed, converted to Technicolor, like Oz once Dorothy set foot. And amidst this newfound wonder, tinges of shame and embarrassment once again circled around me. Knowing I could never discuss this interlude with anyone, including my devout Catholic Mom. That it must remain a secret; that this was the beginning of something many considered sinful.

What happened three years ago in Provincetown with my awareness of the Amazon ladies was now culminating in this very act, this liberating, pulsing, throbbing awareness that yes, I was different, and who might I tell other than the boy who brought me here?

***

Throughout that summer RJ and I stole countless moments to explore each other's bodies. Touching, caressing our necks, nipples, and backs, exchanging provocative groans and whispers, myriad blowjobs and hand jobs. My body shed the mental constraints of sin, relented, and embraced the tactile ecstasy that my best friend bestowed on me. Giving and taking with playful abandon.

We'd sneak down his basement or upstairs into our attic for "love in the afternoon." "Close your eyes," he'd say as he held my wrists and made his way down my treasure trail with tongue tracing each inch of skin. Or we'd wait until the quiet of the evening when our parents, fast asleep, wouldn't hear our explorations in the dark.

"Shh.... did you hear that, I think someone's awake?" I'd whisper. Silence. A shift of my parent's mattress across the hall, or one of RJ's brothers getting up to pee, would force a pause before we'd begin our sensual adventures again.

Secrecy and a prevailing fear of being caught hovered in the air. The friend who'd convinced me to shave my peach-fuzzed mustache and taught me disco dancing had joined me down a path I was too afraid to pursue on my own. All I knew is our togetherness felt safe, reassuring, and unique. We would walk, and sometimes sprint, down this carnal road together. The thumping in my chest, voracious and needy, accelerated whenever he stirred my naked desire.

CHAPTER 8

Behind Closed Doors

An impatient RJ, whom I'd convinced to see the movie, crossed his arms and repeated, "This better be good."

"Oh, come on," I replied. "You saw *Logan's Run*, and you liked it."

"Granted, but Farrah was starring in it. Not a bunch of robots and a Wookie monster!"

As the summer of '77 progressed RJ and I grew inseparable. I continued dragging him to the tennis court, while he continued instructing me on the finer points of disco dancing. I felt like each day held something new and special. I was growing up.

Star Wars blasted into theaters Memorial Day weekend, and although neither of us were sci-fi geeks, we made the pilgrimage to The Fairview to catch moviemaking history. The line stretched down the block of the outdoor plaza while we waited with an army of kids in shorts and baseball caps and their starry-eyed parents.

Once in the theatre, we swooned over Harrison Ford, the sexy hunk playing Han Solo. "God he's *hot*," I sighed.

"Yeah, I'll give you that," RJ said.

"You two boys remind me of Millie, Renata, and me," Mom said after picking us up at the theatre. "I get such a kick out of watching you both, seeing you laugh and giggle and have such a good time. You're like twin brothers. And we were like sisters, went all the same places, did everything together. Renata and I even wore similar outfits."

I liked my mom comparing RJ and me to her childhood buddies. And I also knew that Mom and Re-Re had their share of fights and petty disagreements, which I hoped RJ and I would never experience. For them, closeness bred competitiveness and at times contention. Maybe the closer you grew to somebody, the more they got on your nerves, even if you loved them to death.

Mom coined the nickname "Richie-bird" for RJ, which she used when she wanted to tease him. She loved to suntan and despite his olive complexion would tease him about looking pale. "Oh, Richie-bird," she'd say. "We need to get you all lathered up with Hawaiian Tropic and out in the sun. You're as white as a bar of Dove soap."

RJ would roll his eyes and flash a big flirtatious grin. "I already use Bain de Soleil, Mrs. Hilovsky."

Meanwhile there was no letup in Farrah's pop cultural juggernaut. Men wanted to date her, and women adopted her sporty feathered hairstyle. When she announced she would quit *Charlie's Angels* after one season to pursue a movie career, the uproar landed on the front page of *The Cleveland Plain Dealer* newspaper. The series producers Spelling and Goldberg filed a lawsuit, insisting she'd violated a contract she'd never signed.

I loved the chameleon in Farrah. When she appeared on the cover of *Bazaar* magazine, I asked RJ, "Do you like this new look?" The fashion shoot recast her into a modern-day Veronica Lake, hair pulled behind one ear and cascading over the opposite eye. She threw the camera a seductive sideways glance. The two-piece suit she wore with narrow lapels and pencil thin trousers projected an androgynous flair. Yet her soft femininity persisted.

"She kinda looks like Annie Hall," RJ observed.

"Yeah, but sexier. And they added a beauty mark on her cheek, like Marilyn Monroe," I pointed out. RJ drew a headline in the scrapbook "Farrah Conquers the Fashion World. What's Next?" The pictures punctuated the bright neon words.

While Farrah mania sizzled, our dancing and desire for each other intensified. We loaded his parent's jukebox in the basement full of our favorite 45-records: Taste of Honey's "Boogie Oogie, Oogie," Evelyn "Champagne" King's "Shame," and Gloria Gaynor's anthem "I Will Survive." RJ taught me more dance routines, and we created new moves together. Once the jukebox went silent, we collapsed on the cool-to-the-touch black leather couch bathed in our sweat. Our dance workouts elevated our raging hormones; hungry for more of the physical connection we'd shared, we no longer hesitated to reach out to each other for a sexual release.

The laundry room beckoned underneath the downstairs staircase. With loads of dirty clothes piled high on the floor, he began undoing the metal clasp on my denim overalls while I fiddled with the zipper on his cords, both of us stifling a giggle.

"Shhh," RJ cautioned, "make sure nobody hears us."

"Don't worry, I'll be careful," I promised while trying to avoid tripping on the laundry Mrs. Fallon amassed with all the boys in the house. The last thing we needed was to be found out by one of his little brothers, our ears always attuned to the staircase and floor above us.

Our amorous summer afternoons continued at my house whenever Mom took her afternoon siestas. We'd tiptoe upstairs to the attic and make our home on the cast iron frame bed, surrounded by gift boxes and Christmas decorations. RJ's skin, warm to the touch, burrowed against my body.

My fingers ran through his black wavy hair and reached down to squeeze his balls as my mouth teased his ear lobes. Those afternoons I'd lose inhibition, devouring him in my relentless desire and offering myself in return. Night and day we listened for the changing rhythms of the house on Story Road.

One night in my bedroom, RJ diverged from our usual repertoire and attempted mounting me from behind.

"Oh my God, what're you doing?" I hissed as he rolled me across the cool sheets onto my stomach.

"Shhh. Just relax," he whispered. "Breathe, tell me how it feels." I inhaled his warmth on my back and neck. His rigid cock rubbed against the opening to my anus. I felt tense, uncomfortable, wanted to pull away.

"Owwh, not good! That's not going to happen, get off me!" I nudged him away and slid under the thin blanket. Without so much as a warning, the bedroom door burst open, my father's towering presence filling the frame.

"Are you two asleep yet?" he asked, the harsh hallway light illuminating him from behind.

"Not now," I squinted with a note of sarcasm, my heart pounding. "Dad, knock first, please."

"Get to bed," he said clucking his tongue and pulling the door closed behind him.

I lay there next to RJ quivering with the knowledge that my father may have heard us and came to investigate. Had he opened the door one minute earlier, he would have discovered our secret, and there would have been no turning back. He would have witnessed his son engaging in an act considered immoral, outright repugnant, and sinful in many people's eyes. Especially our Church.

I shuddered to think what he would have done. Thrown us both out? Forbid me from seeing RJ? Send me to a psychologist or psychiatrist? I didn't know, but feared he harbored suspicions. Would he tell Mom? Memories of Provincetown and her reaction to the strange Amazonian women flooded my mind. I knew those women were men, but I didn't want to be a woman. I liked my body, and I liked other guy's bodies too.

I could sense RJ found it difficult to fall asleep. We both sighed and rolled away from one another before I heard his smooth exhalations.

"I feel guilty," I admitted to RJ the next morning behind the closed bedroom door. Earlier I'd sat across from him at the kitchen table finishing the pancake breakfast Mom prepared for us. In his eyes I saw my own reflection, a mirror, and a reminder of our encounter the night before. I felt disturbed, dirty, and bothered peering back at him. "Maybe we should stop," I said. RJ rolled his eyes and gave me a confounded look.

I began a pattern of distancing from RJ following Dad's late night "raid." The burst of reality, the door flying open, scared me. I still wanted to have sex, and enjoyed the thrill of keeping it secret, but after each encounter there was a temporary pulling away. We cleaned up in a hurry, allowing no time for languishing or permitting the feelings of euphoria, of closeness to linger.

Two weeks passed before he confronted me. "What's up with you? How come I feel like you give me the evil eye at breakfast every morning when I sleep over?"

I shrugged. "I don't mean to, but I'm confused. I like the sex we have, but afterward I feel tormented, like I'm doing something wrong. Like I'm hurting my family, or being dirty, or something. I'm sorry, I just feel bad."

"All right, if you don't want to have sex, we can stop. But I know we like it. And it's only part of who we are. Maybe all that Catholic school stuff is getting you down. We can still date girls."

The thought of whether we were dating didn't even cross my mind. All I knew is RJ meant the world to me, like the brother I never had, and we enjoyed giving and getting pleasure from each other. I didn't really want to stop. I didn't know anybody else like us, at least out in the open. There was no public display of our affection, or discussion of attending a school dance together. It wasn't a possibility. I knew I didn't feel comfortable kissing him; we weren't boyfriends; and we weren't gay.

How could we be? Nobody would accept us; we'd be ridiculed. We could never get married, a tradition I was raised to revere. There was no place to go with this relationship. RJ and I were best friends, and confidants, and we enjoyed sex together, and while I'd like that to continue, I worried about how I'd cope with being found out, how I'd ever meet a girlfriend, and whether at this point, there was no turning back.

CHAPTER 9

You're the One That I Want

"STUDYING LATIN WILL make you stand out from the crowd, men," Mr. Dowd informed us. "You will always be distinct from those who study French, or Spanish, or German."

In 1977 I started freshman year at St. Ignatius, a Jesuit preparatory high school for young men. My homeroom included many intelligent boys from across Cleveland, all grouped together based on our shared interest in studying Latin, a "dead" language no longer spoken outside the church, but highly valued according to our Latin teacher, Mr. Dowd. I already felt quite different in this new all-male environment, regardless of the foreign language denominator. Testosterone, and macho intimidation, filled the air.

During gym class, the buff, mustachioed Mr. Wilson, his feathered hair parted down the middle, assigned all of us regulation sweatshirts and gym shorts in gold and navy blue, the school colors. In the locker room I changed into and out of my one-size-fits-all uniform, while surrounding me stood boys in various stages of undress: in jock straps, shirtless, some marching in or out of the shower room, others snapping their towels at each other. Rank body odor reigned, intermingled with the smell of soap and deodorant.

After flag football and basketball games, Mr. Wilson distributed white towels, and we hit the showers. Self-conscious and painfully self-aware, I dreaded showering with my classmates for fear I'd notice an attractive boy and pop a boner, the ultimate embarrassment. So, I shut down my feelings with the hope I wouldn't be caught ogling my classmates despite my curiosity about their bodies. I forced myself during the usual locker room banter to not allow my eyes to wander below the neck as we changed, but occasionally, copped a peek when nobody was looking. A muscled arm, tight buttocks, or amply filled jockstrap didn't need a face attached for me to feel rapt desire.

While my fourteen-year-old classmates gabbed about the Cleveland Browns or sports teams they liked, I tried to adapt to the all-male camaraderie. Once safely clothed I was in the clear, only later could I allow the flash of naked images to flood my imagination.

There were no feminine influences at St. Ignatius, other than Sr. Capilano, the freshman biology teacher, and Mrs. Small, who taught theology, and at 4'10", well, befit her name. There were no longer any girls to talk with either —no Janice, Marlis, Gayle or Shelley to assure me "you're one of us." No chatty friends like Philippa, now attending a parochial all-girls school, to make me smile and laugh while passing notes back and forth.

The same-sex environment of St. Ignatius, rather than putting me at ease, stirred more awkwardness and tension. On the other hand, I loved the academic challenge of studying demanding subjects like algebra with the eccentric Mr. "Be-deep, Ba-dop" Peronelli, or AP World History with the wild-eyed and crazed-about-his-subject Mr. Haskin.

My lingering attraction toward some classmates distracted me, making it difficult to concentrate. I felt like I stood out, at the same time I felt invisible, afraid to reveal my true personality for fear of judgment or rejection. And watching how other kids judged anyone who they deemed too different, I had plenty of reason to worry.

Two episodes left a permanent imprint. Our freshman speech teacher Mr. Rush arrived the first day of school with a guitar and at the top of the class began singing "He Ain't Heavy, He's My Brother." Suddenly, several boys in the back row catcalled "Hoot, hoot, get off the stage," and began laughing and hurling paper airplanes. Flabbergasted, Mr. Rush stood there without disciplining them. He was ridiculed behind his back the rest of the school year.

Then later that September several upper classmen pushed a tall, effeminate sophomore to the ground. "Faggot," they screamed as they kicked him and yanked the leather handbag (they called it his "purse") draped across his shoulder.

Witnessing his torment, I shuddered, so grateful it wasn't me. A boy couldn't afford to look weak, or reveal his soft side, or else dickheads would take advantage of that weakness and subject him to mockery and assault.

I began to befriend other brainy boys in my classroom who, like myself, enjoyed learning and helped me adjust to the academic demands of St. Ignatius. Math and science whiz Don Hiller and I studied Latin in the library, breaking into fits of laughter while memorizing our verb declensions. Yearbook editor and hyperactive goofball Denny Gustavus shared a love of history and film with me. And salty, opinionated Mitch Toscavich from Marching Band worked with me on algebra and chemistry problems. I felt no physical attraction towards these boys; our connection sprang from the life of the mind. Thanks to our combined brainpower, we inspired each other to greater academic achievement, and along the way friendships bloomed.

Off campus, RJ remained my best friend and a refuge from the narrow confines of St. Ignatius High School. The pleasure of each other's company fed our creativity, humor, and sexual desire.

"How are classes?" I asked over the phone.

"I don't know why I need to take science and math if I'm going to study art and design."

"Well, you need to measure material and determine how much fabric you'll need."

"Hmm, I like you in as little material as possible," he said with a slow, flirtatious drawl.

I laughed. "You're trying to get some, aren't you?"

"No, just letting you know the truth." My face turned several shades rosier, but he couldn't see it. I wanted to reach across the line, pinch him, and pinch me.

Several weeks later we both pinched ourselves when we learned Farrah would make a surprise last-minute stop in Cleveland to accept a check for one million dollars from Revco Drugstores, which planned to carry her Farrah Fawcett Shampoo and Conditioner on their shelves.

She landed at Burke Lakefront Airport on the afternoon of Wednesday, May 3, 1978. I wasn't aware of her impending visit until I heard about it on the radio en route to St. Ignatius. Mayor Dennis Kucinich's wife Sandy gave her a key to the city while the mayor planted a big fat smooch on Farrah's cheek. A gaggle of fans crowded in the terminal but other than a friendly wave, she avoided signing autographs. They hurriedly whisked her away in a big black limousine to the Bond Court Hotel for a press conference. We snipped the front-page headline and pictures out of *The Plain Dealer* and glued them into our scrapbooks.

"How could we have missed her?" RJ whined over the phone.

"If only I knew she was coming," I sighed. "I could have played hooky." Even though I was too much of a goodie-two-shoes to even try.

***

FOLLOWING his smash film debut in *Saturday Night Fever*, John Travolta delivered another blockbuster movie in 1978 when *Grease* hit the screen pairing him with lovely Olivia Newton-John. Cleveland's local radio station WGAR sponsored a ticket giveaway for the first ten call-ins to attend a sneak preview at Loewe's Theatre East, and RJ and I won a pair. Because neither of us were old enough to drive we hopped a bus across town for the special opening. A surprise guest star from the movie would be there to sign autographs, and I couldn't wait to see who it was.

"Do you think we'll meet him?" R.J asked as the #75 roared down Euclid Avenue past the Higbee and May Co. department stores.

"Travolta? I'm hoping for Olivia." We leaned our heads against the window, fifteen-year-olds watching the world fly by on a hot August day. Full of dreams of movie stars and autographs, our heads spun. My imagination ran wild fantasizing stealing a glimpse of John Travolta or shaking the hand of Olivia Newton-John and hearing her Aussie accent.

Once the bus dropped us off, we trudged across a deserted parking lot to the theatre entrance. Standing next to the film's framed poster was a tall brunette woman wearing a red pantsuit. Little did I realize she was a celebrated Broadway actress who played bad girl Rizzo in the film. When we approached her with our movie pass, she courteously said hello and cheerfully scribbled *All the Best, Stockard Channing*.

Hiding disappointment that we didn't meet a "real" movie star, RJ and I took our autographed passes and found our seats in the theatre. From the first still of Danny on the gravel playground and Sandy registering for classes, Travolta and Newton-John wowed us with their romantic chemistry. We reveled in the flashy dance numbers of "Greased Lightning," "Summer Nights," and "You're the One That I Want" and left the theatre with starry-eyes, dancing feet, and song-filled hearts. A week later, RJ played the movie soundtrack. Nimble with choreography and eager to add a new dimension to the disco dance craze, RJ reimagined dance routines for the major tunes, which Beth, Shelley, and I learned and performed with him. Even while at St. Ignatius I continued staying in touch with my Lakewood Little Theatre friends.

"How does this move look?" he'd ask as he whirled a make-believe lasso in the air for "You're the One That I Want." I marveled at his pelvic thrusts and confident grin as he recreated *Grease's* signature numbers.

"Holy mackerel, your choreography's sexier than the film version," I'd laugh while trying to emulate his moves. "Foot, ball change, foot, ball change," I repeated to myself. The record spun repeatedly. Sprawled on his dad's leather chair I watched him piece together one sequence after another. His talent overflowed.

***

"DON'T you ever get tired of playing second fiddle on the dance floor?" Beth asked me one night as we sat on RJ's front porch while he snuck into the kitchen to make root beer floats. Her eyes fell like laser beams on me. Her apple cheeks, like Shelley's, glowed from an early summer tan.

"He's like my big brother, I always learn from him, you know?"

"Okay, but you're capable of dancing as good as he. In a few more months…well, you could rival him," she insisted.

Shrugging my shoulders, I turned a light shade of red. "He's a natural. I need to work at it."

RJ continued racking up accolades. In addition to winning first prize in the local YMCA dance competitions that summer, he and Shelley were invited to join other couples on a local broadcast called *Weekday Fever* filmed at the downtown dance club Rumors. I would rush home to watch the pre-recorded show on weekday afternoons and gaze at them in envy and admiration.

One humid summer evening we sat rocking on his parents' front porch swing. The creaky springs made music with the chirping crickets. "How do you do it?" I asked him. "You make dancing look effortless."

"It's just like Farrah," he said. "We've both got a passion for collecting her. And we're spending our time on that. Dancing's the same way. I never get tired practicing, getting better. What about you?"

I sat silent for a split-second. "I've never had this much fun before, but I'm not sure dancing is my one and only love." For a moment I felt this loneliness descend upon me. I smiled and shrugged my shoulders. I really didn't know what I wanted. For now, I was happy just being RJ's sidekick, basking in the glow of his talent and inspiration, as he shared his dancing spotlight with me and encouraged me to find my own happy medium. When we danced, I felt united in spirit with him, part of something bigger, more than just me but a part of a whole, a universe that was throbbing and full of life. The same feeling arose whenever we strolled to Rexall Drug and discovered Farrah splashed across another magazine cover, the world her forever oyster. I had my oyster, and it was the exciting, splashy world of disco dancing, free-spirited and happy, one in one with my best friend and our adventures in exploring our bodies, our beliefs, and our future dreams.

To figure out what else excited me, I began exploring activities separate from RJ's interests. Freshmen year, when I returned home from school, I'd run three miles around the block. I loved the movement, the sound of each foot hitting the pavement, my breath escalating and evening out. Afterward, my brow drenched in sweat, I'd do several sets of push-ups and sit-ups in the backyard. I could feel my body strengthening, observe the muscles building in my arms and legs, my core growing firm and stable. Like Farrah, healthy living made me high, gave me a glow.

I continued playing tennis too, at times inviting RJ, more often heading to the court without him. On Thursday mornings after delivering my paper route I'd join Mom and her girlfriends at Lakewood Park. One of the women brought her teenage daughter Jenny, and we'd play on a separate court, sometimes rallying at the baseline, other times waging a hard-fought game, like Farrah when she competed in tennis on the celebrity-laden *Battle of the Network Stars*. From my perch on the tennis court a wavy, green-gray Lake Erie stretched into the distance and children squealed during swimming lessons at nearby Foster Pool.

In that moment, all I knew was a summer with RJ melting into a collection of memories, sweeter than any summer thus far: the countless YMCA dances, the times on RJ's front porch with our friends, and a much-anticipated vacation in August to see my godparents at their getaway home on Lake Templene.

Everything, every single thing, brought me closer to him. Yet all the while I struggled to find my own path, separate from his large imprint. I wanted to savor these times, but avoid getting overshadowed in the bigness of RJ, who always drew the spotlight thanks to his huge dancing talent. Besides besting him at tennis, what major gift did I have to offer the world? I felt excited, like new experiences and feelings awaited me around the corner, but how would I react to them? How would I know what to be? Who to be?

CHAPTER 10

The Vacation

"Your friend is welcome. We'd love to meet him," Fran said over the phone when I asked if it would be okay for me to bring RJ. My godparents Hugh and Fran invited Re-Re, great aunt Lola, Mom, Dad, and me for a visit to the home they built on Lake Templene, a small lakeside community in southeastern Michigan. I couldn't wait to introduce them to RJ.

We arrived on a hot, sunny August day. Our Chevy Monte Carlo pulled off Route 3 onto a narrow gravel road. Amidst the tall pine trees emerged a two-level wood framed vacation house tucked into the side of a hill with a lake view and water skiers zipping across the quiet surface.

My godmother Fran dressed in a red skirt came to the front door and waved at us. "You made it in good time."

"We knew where we were going this year," Dad smiled as he embraced her. He was referring to last August when we made a wrong turn and got lost on the other side of the lake. "Jack here was my eagle-eye navigator this time round," he chuckled giving me a playful wink and pat on the shoulder.

"Fran, I love the flowers you planted in the front," Mom said as she touched the purple and red geraniums in the wicker planters on the porch step. "Last summer you were still filling in the front lawn."

"Well, hello there," came a buoyant voice from the side of the house. Dressed in a blue Arnold Palmer golf shirt and khaki shorts, my godfather Hugh wrapped his forearms around my head and hugged me close to his chest. "Hi, there Johnny, is this your new friend?"

Hugh loved to ruffle my hair and embarrass me with his clever witticisms that verged on teasing. "What's a matter, cat got your tail?" He butchered clichés and made us laugh. He was one of the few family members who called me "John," my baptismal name, even though I went by Jack.

"Yeah, I told RJ about you."

Hugh put his hand on RJ's shoulder. "Welcome to our humble abode. *Mi casa es tu casa.*"

My godmother assigned us the downstairs study, a makeshift guest room with a fold out bed. She smiled at both of us, and I felt immediately at home. "Are you hungry, or do you want to take a dip in the lake?"

RJ and I looked at each other, excited at the chance to get out in the sun after the four-hour car ride. "We'll take a swim first," I said.

We changed into our swimsuits and trotted down the grassy path to a small dock at the water's edge.

"How deep is it?" RJ asked.

"Oh, waist high, I think."

"Okay, ready when you are," RJ shouted. With a running start, we raced each other and jumped feet first off the dock. Splashing each other in the early afternoon light, the chill water flew in my eyes and mouth as I sent torrents of water skyward.

"Hey, you're getting my hair wet," RJ shouted.

"Oh, c'mon now!" I insisted. "You're supposed to get wet. We're at the lake." I splashed him again and wrestled him down into the water. His skin, now cool to the touch, felt soft like velvet.

We came to the surface coughing and sputtering. "Who knows what's in this water anyway," he said gazing toward the bottom. "It's kind of dark and murky." After some more splashing around we toweled off and with dripping feet snuck through the sliding door and into the bathroom. My godfather lay snoring on the couch with the *USA Today* sports page splayed across his chest. His handlebar mustache twirled on the edges, speckled with blond and grey.

"How do you turn on the water?" RJ whispered behind the shower door, twisting the uncooperative shower knob.

"I think we have to fiddle with the water pump but I'm unsure where it is," I said. "Remember, this is the country."

I slipped off my red Speedo swimsuit and stepped into the shower with him. Suddenly, a burst of water exploded from the showerhead pummeling us both.

"Woo, it's ice COLD---," I shrieked as the chilly water hammered our skin, and goose bumps popped out all over me. We were all elbows and knees and feet and cock in the compact stall. The light hair all over my body stood on end and my nipples turned into knobs. Gradually the temperature warmed.

"All right, time for a scrub down," I whispered grabbing the green bar of Irish Spring. As I lathered him with a washcloth from behind, I could see a faint cocoa tan on his neck and shoulders. I kissed the spot between the broadness of his shoulder blades.

"And I'll work on your hair," he said uncapping a bottle of Johnson and Johnson Baby Shampoo. He applied a juicy, golden dollop on my scalp, massaging it into the dark wet roots.

"Okay, I know it's not the soon-to-be released Farrah shampoo we keep hearing about," RJ continued. "But I gotta say 'gee your hair smells terrific.'" The most precious smile brightened his face, and we broke into uncontrollable laughter. My back now turned to him I could feel his silky skin grazing my neck and shoulders, his hands playing with my sudsy hair and scalp. Our constant Farrah references served as the glue stick that sealed our friendship. We loved dropping her name into every conversation as if she were a close intimate: our mother, our lover, or a girlfriend. A part of us. She united us in a common bond. Her teeth, hair, smile, laughter, trim athletic build. Her vivacious youthful energy fed our teen spirit.

"Shhh, we're making a racket," I whispered, holding my breath before bursting again into fits of laughter. "I don't want them to get any ideas." We both sported raging boners. I grabbed his and squeezed. His hardness made me harder.

"Oh, come on," RJ whispered. "You can just say we're sharing the bathroom, that you're drying off while I'm showering. Even though you'd be lying." He grabbed my erection and knelt to kiss the mushrooming head of my cock.

At this joyful, intoxicating moment, part of me didn't care what my family thought. I still wondered, even feared, whether my parents or godparents sitting 50 feet away on the outdoor patio had any inkling of our carnal involvement. That two 15-year-olds took showers together and rough-housed might seem normal, or not. What did they think? All I knew is my pulse raced, the warm water splattering over me, over us, felt delicious and sinful and I could have begged for more. But too much of a good thing.... well, my Catholic sensibility held me in check.

I couldn't forget Dad barging into my bedroom -- the near miss of him catching us -- flat naked, RJ on top of me. My heart racing from the close call. But now, I was bathing only in happiness, pleasure. The playfulness of our grabbing each other, R.J kissing the head of my cock, propelled me into another world.

And yet, despite the closeness, a nagging undercurrent loomed like a pit in the depth of my stomach. Somehow, I couldn't sustain this joy. Somehow, someday, I'd face a reckoning. Nagging guilt, always the unwelcome visitor the day after. My young mind dreamed that one day I'd find the power to fling this monkey off my back.

The next morning my godfather Hugh drove us all to an inland stream, where he had purchased canoes for a family daytrip. The unbearable humidity made us drowsy, and huge horseflies and gnats swarmed far and wide. Trying to conceal our yawns, RJ and I decided we didn't want to be shooing critters the whole afternoon.

"This is not my idea of a good time," RJ groused.

"These gnats are relentless. They're eating me for lunch." I slapped my neck. My shirt dripping with sweat clung to my skin. "We've had it, Hugh, we want to go home."

An irritated look on his face, he pointed the way, and we began walking back to the house. Thanks to my godfather's vague directions, we promptly got lost.

On a farm in the middle of nowhere, the heat cooking our backs I suddenly got the crazy idea I wanted to run naked through the fields. Self-conscious at first, R.J followed my lead. We first stripped down to our Speedos. Moments later we removed our bathing suits leaving nothing between our skin and the sun's hot rays.

"What if we get caught?" RJ said, shyly placing a hand over his crotch.

"Don't fuss about it," I said. "What's the worst that could happen? They arrest us for streaking?"

Before you could say jackhammer, we were racing through fields, our cock and balls swinging above the rows of alfalfa.

"Are you nuts?" RJ screamed.

"Just inspired," I called back to him. "Doesn't it feel good, no sweaty shorts or tops, just the wind and sun on bare buns?" I felt confident and free as I led the way.

The heat penetrated our skin. Overcome with laughter we squatted in the middle of the field and grabbed our quivering bellies. No longer able to hold his water, RJ peed on top of a shrub.

An hour later, we came to a dirt road. Lost as could be, our asses in full view, we saw a car way in the distance with dust clouds billowing around it. "Holy shit," I shouted, "I think that's Hugh's car." We quickly slipped on our swim trunks, barely in time before my godparents climbed out of the automobile. They'd come to get us. My godfather said, "You know, I was pissed at you for taking off." I was relieved to see that he was chuckling. Sheepish, we got in the car.

"Hugh, how did you ever know where to look for us?" I asked.

"We gave you the roundabout way to get home," he replied. "Your godmother and I spent a lot of time planning that canoe trip, and it burned my arse to see the two of you walk away from it. We played a little trick, knowing we'd find you if you didn't get back by such and such a time."

In the backseat of the car, RJ and I leaned into each other, relieved we were not discovered while sporting our wares in the middle of farmland U.S.A. In our minds we'd managed to keep our secret, but we couldn't resist daring the fates. I closed my eyes, imagining all the ways we could get naked together. Then I heard a small voice in my head chuckle, "Goody two shoes, say goodbye."

***

"It's all yours, Johnny." My godfather gave me the keys to his motorboat along with instructions on how to start, stop, and park at the small wooden dock near the house.

The white boat, brand-new and sleek, sat moored to the dock. The morning sun glistening over the lake beckoned. I untethered the canvas ropes, checked the gauges, and turned the key to hear a bright va-va-vrooom before steering our course toward the opposite shoreline.

RJ sat behind me in the white leather seats at the back of the boat. He rested his hands behind his head and relaxed into our inaugural ride.

"Look at you, Speed Racer," he flirted over the din of the motor as I shifted into a higher gear and gripped the steering wheel, a bit uncertain how the boat would handle at a faster clip.

The light wind caressed our faces, the sun warmed our shirtless backs. The glade of the water spilled onto the surface of the boat and kissed our cheeks. Last summer Mom, Dad and I had spent a week here. I remembered canoeing, diving off the dock, riding my bike down the quiet country road with the abandoned farmhouse off the side of the curved gravel path – I had been by myself, all alone.

This year was different. With RJ in tow, I had a buddy and a partner in crime. Like Butch Cassidy and the Sundance Kid, we could escape the confines of my parent's watchful eye and pursue our own adventures. This vacation was the first time I brought a friend. The excitement and pride of sharing my family with RJ, like he shared his family with me, buoyed my spirit.

RJ and I manned the controls of the speedboat and watched the world whirl by. The herons flew overhead, diving for fish on the water's surface. An unidentifiable bird cawed above us. The cotton candy clouds punctuating the sky made the lake seem small in comparison, like a fishbowl dwarfed by heaven.

The water's surface, calm and glassy, captured our reflections as we put-
tered to a stop and found a quiet resting place in the middle of the lake.

"I love the sound of nothing, just the lap of the waves," RJ sighed.

The blue sky, a perfect blue, smiled on us. I'd turned fifteen that summer
and felt happier, more content, than I'd ever felt my entire life. I fell back
into the comfortable white cushion next to RJ and rested my head on his
shoulder.

"Do you think we'll be friends forever?" I asked.

RJ looked at me with a twinkle in his eye. "Why wouldn't we?"

"Sometimes friends take different paths. You know, move away, or grow
apart."

"Well, I'm not planning a getaway in the near future, not until I head to
New York for college."

I recalled him mentioning that dream at a sleepover at his house and
sighed. "New York City? That's great. That's exciting!" I repeated these
words of support but deep inside I didn't want RJ to go away. I didn't want
him to go anywhere.

"That's my goal if I get a scholarship. Otherwise, it's Virginia Marti."

We both knew option two was no option at all. The Virginia Marti College of Art and Design offered classes in fashion design and merchandising
but was more of a community college for Cleveland kids. If you wanted to
make a mark in fashion, you got out of Cleveland and headed to the Big
Apple. That would be RJ--the escape artist. "I could see you scaling the
Empire State Building, like King Kong, with a flailing Farrah in place of
Fay Wray in your right hand." He laughed but my stomach felt funny even
thinking about losing him.

A cloud drifted over the boat. RJ opened a bottle of Hawaiian Tropic and
poured the oil over my pink shoulders while gently massaging it in around
the contours of my terry cloth tank top. I thought about how the world

changed from black and white to Technicolor the day we met each other at Lakewood Little Theatre. Our eyes collided, he said hello, and it was like instant chemistry, like a switch went off and I could hear a different kind of music than the station I'd been listening to my entire life. The more time we spent together, the more we could read, even predict, each other's minds. And from there, we moved into exploring each other's bodies. God, it was everything I wanted, everything I'd dreamed of. Like a soul mate, someone who understood me, made me feel accepted and safe in the world.

His strong hands spread the oil from my shoulders to my mid and lower back. My entire body relaxed, like air released from a balloon. For a moment I reflected on the last childhood friend I lost when his family moved to Sandusky in fourth grade. I'd never forgotten bright-eyed Mark, but it pained me to think that it could happen again.

I refused to waste another moment worrying about what might happen if RJ and I went our separate ways. He first had to finish Lakewood High School, where he'd begin as a freshman next month. I'd return for my sophomore year at St. Ignatius. Having survived the challenges of freshman year with a class of hormonally challenged Catholic school boys, I wondered what sophomore year held for me in what my Latin teacher referred to as the year of "wise fools." Feelings of wariness and uncertainty mixed in with the reassurance I had one friend who understood me. RJ wasn't going away anytime soon. Many more good times lay ahead, I was sure of that.

As late morning melted into early afternoon, the heat grew more intense. Sweat began pouring down my brow. The back of my tank top and cotton shorts began sticking to the leather cushions. I leaned over the side of the boat and splashed ice-cold water on my forehead and face.

"Getting a little warm, tweedy bird," RJ teased.

I flashed him an all-knowing smirk. "Hot is more like it. In fact, I'm boiling." I peeled my orange tank top over my head and threw it in a ball in the corner of the boat. Slipping off my neon green running shorts, all that remained was my fire engine red Speedo.

"Why don't you take it all off," RJ dared from the other side of the boat.

"What?" I screeched, "What if people see me?" My chest puffed up.

"Oh, c'mon, tweedy, we're in the middle of the lake. Who's going to notice? Besides you don't have to stand up. We're protected here."

"Only if you do, and if another boat comes close, the suit comes back on zip quick." Now I was the shy one.

For the second day in a row, we got naked out in the open, hanging our gonads in the wind. More and more comfortable with our sexuality, we took turns playing the antagonist, egging each other on, challenging each other "to take it off." I liked the playfulness, the gibes, the erotic one-up-manship. We pushed each other to go places that might feel uncomfortable but led to more freedom and vulnerability. I loved seeing RJ naked.

Sunglasses perched on our noses we slathered sunscreen on our pale parts and lounged on the white leather until our bare butts could no longer withstand the mid-afternoon heat radiating from the cushions and the clear blue sky. Together we found a resting place in the bottom of the boat, our heads perched on a shared cushion.

All the muscles in my body relaxed as we baked in proximity. Our pale white feet touched. Our cocoa-colored legs with downy brown hair turning golden blonde became emblems of summer. I reached over and grabbed his hand. "Hmmm, that feels cool to the touch," I whispered. I could see his penis shifting in the heat of the sun, a light mulatto shade like coffee and cream mixed in a dish. A tuft of black fur arose from above the shaft, wiry and dense. The sun continued to warm our bodies and the inside of the boat, our refuge and hiding place. I listened to the rise and fall of his breath, his chest following in due course. Happy.

Suddenly, I heard a motor off in the distance and grabbed my Speedo fumbling to get into the tiny swatch of fabric.

"Hey, that's not fair," RJ chirped. "Keep that off."

"I'm not taking any chances after yesterday. Besides, it's getting close to dinnertime," I said.

He followed my lead, and we looked up to wave at a water skier zooming by. With my Kodak camera I snapped a few photos of us, posing like GQ models, in our skimpy bright suits. Hair blowing in the wind, our smiles forecasting good days ahead. Then I turned the key to start the engine and aimed the boat toward shore.

As we raced home, we bounced along the waves, splashing and spewing the water in all directions. Above the roar RJ shouted, "Don't forget, lower the throttle when we get closer, we don't want to hit the bottom."

Suddenly, I heard a groan and an awful grinding noise.

"Oh, shit, what's going on," I panicked. "Oh, fuck. What the hell." Smoke began rising from the back of the boat, and I could not get the motor to start as we drifted toward the dock.

"I don't think it hit bottom," RJ said. "Maybe some seaweed got stuck in the blade."

We glided alongside the edge of the dock. RJ threw me the rope. I secured the boat. My face crimson I slunk toward the house to confess we'd destroyed the motor thanks to my cruising too close to shore before lifting it away from the bottom, or the seaweed, or whatever the heck it struck; and after blowing off canoeing yesterday I feared my otherwise good-natured godfather would be mercilessly pissed.

I found him in the garage tinkering with his CB radio.

"Hugh, I broke the boat."

Through his bifocal lenses he gave me a disapproving look. I bit my lip trying not to cry. Silent we walked down to the dock. He attempted to re-suscitate the motor, but nothing worked.

He harrumphed and stroked his mustache. "Well, Johnny, I think it's dead."

"Hugh, I'm sorry. I didn't mean to mess it up."

"It's okay, son. I'm just disappointed you didn't follow my instructions."

"I tried, when we neared dock, I thought I had plenty of time. But I didn't." I put my head in my hands. Waves buffeted the shore.

He put his arm around my shoulder, and we walked up to the house, where my cousins and a sheepish RJ awaited. My godfather never asked me to replace the motor. Maybe I should've offered but I had no job other than my weekly newspaper route.

"Johnny, you've got to watch what you're doing," my godfather said. "When I do fix or replace the motor, I'm afraid I won't be able to let you take the boat out unsupervised. I can't take that risk."

While I didn't get punished, I felt embarrassed and ashamed I'd let him down. I admired my godfather, his patience and his forgiveness. We didn't discuss the incident again nor did he mention it to my parents.

That night I crawled onto the sofa bed next to RJ and rested my head against his golden-brown shoulder. "I'm sorry that happened," he said. "We did the best we could."

I shook my head. "Yeah, I thought we were paying attention. All eyes focused on bringing the boat safely to shore, right?"

He ruffled my hair. "You can come over to my aunt's some time and wreck her pool, okay?"

I pushed him away and laughed. "You're a real stinker, you know?"

We even shared the same dark humor, like my grade school friend, the poncho-wearing Philippa and I had shared. She and I hadn't spoken for over a year after graduation from our parochial school took her to St. Joseph Academy and me to St. Ignatius.

RJ and I played a game of gin rummy by ourselves. After we finished, I turned out the light. Our fingers tiptoed across each other's bodies, caressing shoulders, neck, nipples, and chest. My mouth engulfed his penis, he groaned softly before lifting my head away. "Stop, I don't want to cum," he whispered. He then returned the favor, but it was hard for me to relax due to the same fear someone might walk in on us. We fell fast asleep curled next to each other, the adults still chatting in the other room as we drifted into dreamland.

***

The next day the heat continued but RJ and I avoided boats and water. We sat on the back-patio steps and tried to figure out how we wanted to spend the day. I'd bought a copy of *People* Magazine and rifled through the pages of celebrities and advertisements. The curly-haired Willie Aames, the older brother on the television show *Eight is Enough*, was featured in a story. "I want to look like him," I told RJ as we scoured the magazine.

"With that mop of curls, you're gonna need to stick your finger in a socket," he joked.

"Stop it, silly. I've got a better idea. Why don't we convince Mom to give us both a perm? She does it all the time with Re-Re. They take turns fixing each other's hair."

"Are you sure you want to do this?" she said after corralling her. "It's irreversible, at least for the next month, until it grows out a bit." Mom agreed to play beautician and drove us to the K-Mart in town. We found the Toni Home Permanent kit on a forlorn shelf. The guy on the box, a cute redhead, smiled at the camera, loose tendrils of hair falling on his forehead and along his ear lobes.

I turned to RJ. "Have you ever had a perm?"

"Never."

"Let's do it. What's the worst thing that could happen?"

"An awful 'do?" RJ said with his characteristic bluntness.

We made our pact and carried two boxes to the checkout counter. This was our chance to experiment while on vacation.

Back at the lake Mom was barely able to contain her zeal. "You boys are going to love the results," she said as she mixed the fizzing formula, like a bartender whipping up a favorite cocktail.

RJ volunteered to go first. "We'll keep the solution on for a short time, so your curls are more relaxed," she reassured him. We both sat in the bathroom on a kitchen stool while Mom clad in an apron and flip-flops worked her magic on us. The air conditioning hummed in the background keeping the stifling heat and humidity at bay.

My mother, the beauty bartender, expertly completed her task, first wetting his hair, rolling sections into tiny pink hair curlers, and applying the solution. She doused a curler and twisted, doused a curler, and twisted. RJ scowled, his face caught between expressions of pain and embarrassment.

"Oh my God, will my hair fall out?" RJ croaked as he watched her firmly weave his hair into the tight bend of the curler. Mom chuckled saying, "I've had permanents my whole life, RJ dear. Trust me, you've nothing to fear."

Once the job was done, she seated him in the corner of the bathroom, set the timer and turned to me. Stifling a laugh, I tried to contain my amusement. RJ looked like a pink-headed Q-tip.

"Okay, Jack, let's get down to business."

I sat down in front of the bathroom mirror while my mother wet my hair. She yanked and tugged the curlers along my tender scalp, giving me the same treatment RJ received.

"Owww, that hurts!" I screeched after she pulled one strand with more force than I'd expected.

"Sorry dear. I'll try to be gentler."

I looked in the mirror at my wet head, tan face and shoulders, suddenly nervous about the end results; worried about how it would all turn out. Would I have a new, cool look when I arrived back to Ignatius later this month? The guys didn't spend a lot of time primping. I wanted to look "natural" like I woke up one day only to discover my hair turned curly. I would tell people it grew out over the summer. Kinda' like girls who came back to school with golden blonde locks after three months of summer vacation. "The summer sun lightened my hair," they'd explain in matter-of-fact innocence. Except for that secret ingredient, the lemon juice. Ha!

The thought ricocheted in my head: would Toni make me a new man?

When the timer rang for RJ a layer of pink curlers spanned my entire scalp. She sat me down opposite him as if preparing two opponents for a boxing match.

She rinsed RJ, removed the curlers, and voila.

"Wow!" I said when I saw the end results. His hair, a field of relaxed curls, resembled dreamboat Willie Aames. Bullseye!

Forty minutes later Mom removed my rollers. Hesitant I approached the mirror like a car accident survivor seeing the results of his plastic surgery for the first time.

I stood speechless. My hair, twice the height and circumference of RJ's, had turned into an Afro. "Holy mackerel, I'm Michael Jackson," I whimpered. My fingers ran up and down my scalp attempting to stretch out the tight, knotted curls.

RJ laughed and started singing "I'll Be There."

"Not funny," I snapped. Then a wide grin emerged as I looked at myself again in the mirror. I began snickering, laughing at myself. I couldn't stop. What a joke. The hair would eventually return to normal after a few trips to the barber.

My mother smiled and shrugged her shoulders. "You wanted curls, dear. We can probably use a neutralizer to scale them back a bit. You do look a bit bushy."

Mom dug her hands into my white man fro and trimmed some of the excess volume, but my sophomore class photo with curly, big hair still resembled Michael more than Willie. Lucky RJ got to carry the mantle of my *Eight is Enough* heartthrob.

After the Toni debacle we both agreed that from here on out we'd stick with our straight hair. Between the motorboat fiasco and permanents on parade, we'd managed to turn the routine of our Cleveland existence on its head. Our unbridled experiment with freedom led to unintended consequences. We learned a few lessons. There were more to come.

***

THE final night of our vacation in Lake Templene I talked my family into accompanying RJ and me to a local tavern that hosted a disco night. We would teach them how to boogie to our kind of music. The Imperial, a shed-like hole in the wall on Main Street, seemed an unlikely place for a discotheque. Mom, Re-Re, my godmother, and my cousins Liz and Annie followed RJ and me into the bar. The management ignored the fact most of our party was under-age. A kaleidoscopic dance floor and rotating disco ball dominated the space. "Staying Alive" from *Saturday Night Fever* rocked the sound system while strobe lights flashed overhead. Like John Travolta and his dance co-star Karen Gorney, we strutted toward the center of the light, thrusting our hips, twirling our bodies, and raising our hands into the air.

Out on the floor RJ glided from one female member of my family to the next, giving them his undivided attention. While I danced solo alongside my cousins Annie and Liz, I watched him couples dance with Mom, then my godmother Fran, and lastly Re-Re, who reminded me of an infatuated schoolgirl, swooning and shaking her hips and derriere, entertaining us with a comic impression of Spanish-bombshell pop singer Charo.

"Oh, my gosh, Jack," a blushing Re-Re exclaimed. "Your friend trips the light. He reminds me of the jitterbug guys I used to date way back when. They burned up the floor." Now approaching 60, Re-Re had loved the big band music of the 1940's and 50's. The sticker on the rear bumper of her White Pontiac Trans Am proclaimed "I'd Rather Be Dancing."

"That boy is the cat's meow," she purred.

RJ and his smooth moves also delighted my cousins Liz and Annie as he swept them across the neon blinking dance floor. I watched with amusement as he taught them how to couple's dance and then let loose with characteristic flair. He guided their hands to his back and then taught them fancy footwork as the voices of divas Yvonne Elliman, Evelyn "Champagne" King, and Taste of Honey provided musical inspiration.

When Donna Summer's "Last Dance" signaled the end of the night, we coaxed everyone to the floor. RJ grabbed Liz's hand and spun her in circles like a ballerina.

"Slow down," seventeen-year-old Liz laughed as her curls flew through the air. "I'm getting dizzy. You're a lightning rod."

Eleven-year-old Annie got into the action too. Tall and streamlined, she followed his every move, twirling and twisting in half circles.

"Please, please show me how to spin," she insisted while watching RJ lead her big sister Liz across the floor.

"It's easy," RJ called out. "Just pick a focal point to center your attention while I twirl you. Don't hold too tight and stay in place." He arched her hand over her head and began the circular motion.

"I'm doing it," she screamed while Donna's carefree voice soared in the background. "I love it, I'm a disco dancer." Pure joy radiated on her face as she completed the revolutions with RJ leading the charge.

"C'mon, Mom, I'll show you a few steps I learned." My mother placed one hand on my shoulder and the other on my hip as we glided along the floor on a foxtrot step I adapted to disco. Then she added her own cha-cha step. "Honey, one thing I'll say, you've got the rhythm. Those old Grady genes from your tap-dancing aunts and uncles are alive and kicking."

I shrugged. "Well, it's not square dancing or tap, but this music's in my heart and soul."

"Aren't you glad you met RJ?" she smiled. "He's changed your life. You're not the same boy."

She was right. In a way, RJ's friendship gave me permission, liberated me, to find my own path. Like disco created an alternate musical universe compared with rock, my universe with RJ had turned life on its head. The two of us laughed, we teased, we dreamed, we imagined, we loved, we hungered, we challenged, and we competed. Like stars, we lit up the skies, reflecting the light of our own galaxy. Sometimes he stood in my shadow, but more often I stood in his. And many times, our galaxies intersected, and we enjoyed the limelight together.

Here and now this time with my family was one of those shared galaxies, and it was beautiful.

As Donna Summer's anthem to romance rose to a fevered crescendo, I broke away from my mother and joined Annie, Liz, RJ, and Re-Re as they improvised their own steps under the kaleidoscopic light of the disco ball. My godmother watched with glee. We twirled and swirled, flying free, nothing daring to keep us earthbound. Gravity had taken a holiday.

The passion of the music, our music, provided a never-ending soundtrack to our carefree summer. A summer of freedom where the Bee Gees, Donna Summer, and John Travolta ruled. The summer sun kissed our sun-tanned brow. And we imagined the dancing would never end.

CHAPTER 11

Guilt and Pleasure

THAT OCTOBER MY eyes met the bathroom mirror after my morning shower. "Shit." I repeated it under my breath, "Shit." Rippling like a constellation across my face, I discovered a swath of acne in places I'd never seen it. My cheekbones, my temples, now stood like breeding grounds for the return of an alien invader. Horrified I turned away, attempting to ignore the mirror even though I wanted to slap it. Even though I wanted to crack it. Self-conscious that everyone was staring at me, I spent the day at school avoiding eye contact. I could endure a blackhead or pimple here or there, like in eighth grade, but now I couldn't pretend away what I saw, or isolate it. There was no way to hide it.

That afternoon I got off the bus and hurried the six blocks home, each block felt like an endurance race, heart pounding, chest ready to explode. When Mom greeted me at the door my eyes flooded with tears. "Honey, what's wrong? What happened?" she called out as I ran into my bedroom slamming the door. I could barely see where I was going. I threw my book bag on the floor and hurled myself onto the bed.

Mom knocked before entering.

"Don't look at me," I wailed. "I'm ugly, I'm ugly, and I don't want anyone to see me." A pained, panicked expression grew on her face. She rushed over and ran her fingers through my hair. "Honey, that's not true. You're my beautiful boy, and you're not ugly. You're handsome and full of joy."

I met her gaze trying to breathe in between my hysterical gasps and a nose full of snot. "I can't go out there, I don't want people looking at me. Help me." Stuffing my face into my pillow, I fell into another crying fit.

"Stay here," Mom said squeezing my hand. Her hurried footsteps headed toward the kitchen. I heard her dialing the phone. Moments later she'd reached a dermatologist who agreed to see me.

After waiting two agonizing weeks, we met Dr. Zorn who prescribed tetracycline and UV light sunlamp treatments. The combined regimen turned my face a bright cherry red. I felt like an Oompah, Loompa in *Willie Wonka and the Chocolate Factory*. Relief followed that finally we were doing something to alleviate the scourge erupting all over my face.

Battling adolescent acne wracked my self-image. It was as if I'd made it to the top of Chutes and Ladders, surviving my freshman year while collecting an oddball assortment of friends, only to roll the die and tumble all the way down to the bottom rung again. The time I spent in the bathroom popping zits and applying endless hot compresses, nightly facemasks, and emollients left its mark. My critical eye viewed every outbreak as gargantuan, and I wondered when the merciless attacks would cease. Beyond losing it in front of Mom, I suffered in silence and misery. Slowly, thanks to time and Dr. Zorn's double-pronged protocol, the tide of acne subsided. However, the lasting physical and emotional scars colored my sophomore and junior years at St. Ignatius, making me brutally self-conscious.

My biggest saving grace was time spent with RJ who began his freshman year at Lakewood High School that fall. If he noticed, RJ never mentioned my blemished complexion. He'd look in my eyes, and we'd get lost in conversation. Our relationship sustained me. At school, Don, Denny, and Mick also offered a shelter from my inner turmoil, engaging my mind, imagination and funny bone. The constant conversation, kidding, and uproarious laughter freed me from obsessing about my imperfect life and my imperfect looks. Out of school, the closeness RJ and I shared bolstered my outlook on the world.

To our friends and family, RJ and Jack were like the inseparable twins from the famous *Patty Duke Show*. We laughed alike, walked alike, and at times even talked alike. Every Friday night during summer the conversation repeated itself: "Want to come over for dinner and spend the night? We can go to the movies tomorrow afternoon; my mom can give you a ride home if your mom can drop you off here."

Mrs. Fallon gave birth to RJ a few months after her sixteenth birthday. She was much younger than my mom, who'd become a parent at 43. Sitting on the couch in their living room while she smoked cigarettes and monitored the three other boys in the family, Mrs. Fallon drew me into conversation. Effortlessly releasing plumes of smoke into the air, Mrs. F. once asked, "Honey, are you born-again?"

I knew that RJ's mom was a practicing Catholic, but had recently gone through a conversion, where she'd dedicated her life to Christ.

"Well, yes," I said. "I'm baptized and believe in God."

"But you need to accept Christ as your savior to be born-again," Mrs. F. repeated.

I guess I thought by virtue of my Catholicism and the sacraments I received or would receive, I was saved. But the more my physical involvement with RJ progressed, the more I wrestled with shame. Would declaring myself "born-again" save me from damnation, despite my sexual trysts? Would it rescue me from my urges? I didn't dare ask.

I sensed no hostility toward gay people from Mrs. F. the way I did from

Mom. Still, I wrestled with my conscience. I loved having sex with RJ, but at the same time I felt it was very wrong. I didn't know how much longer I could continue to keep this secret. I loved the raw physical contact we shared and yet couldn't imagine how, if ever, a same-sex relationship would work in the real world.

I knew where the Catholic Church in its silent disapproval stood. Sex between men was unacceptable, sinful, and I would go to hell. My youthful awareness expanded so that I became aware of any new developments around anything gay. First came Anita Bryant, the country singer and orange juice lady, who ignited a national furor over her opposition to gay rights, followed by the assassination of openly gay San Francisco City Supervisor Harvey Milk. *The Cleveland Plain Dealer* newspaper and national television broadcasts featured these sensational stories. The controversies stoked a media conversation about the existence of gay people; a frightening conversation that confirmed it was not safe to be gay. The news reinforced the brutal reality that gay people would face oppression and outright death for living their lives out in the open.

Despite the scary outside hostility, I continued to find pleasure and felt bonded to RJ as we shared our bodies. He found me attractive during a period when I felt undesirable. In those tender moments we'd laugh, ruffle each other's hair, and let the world blow by. I allowed my feelings to surface: to desire him, to fully lose myself in his embrace, and give myself the freedom to enjoy it. Yes, we were young, but we understood each other and communicated in a way we didn't with other boys. Talking, listening, and sharing secrets in the dark, our hands would wander, our lips would collide with skin, and we'd bring each other to ecstasy, falling asleep in each other's arms.

But hours later, upon awakening, guilt would plague me. I'd once again sit across the breakfast table from RJ, Mom and Dad serving us pancakes or bacon and eggs. Nagging, confused resentment would spill over me. I couldn't resist his touch and attention; despite the disapproval I'd surely get from society if people ever discovered our secret. More shame arose.

Farrah helped disperse or at least distract from the guilt. We continued our homage to her as her breach of contract lawsuit dragged on with the producers of *Charlie's Angels*. "I wonder if she'll ever return to the set," I said while pasting the black and white photos of her testifying on the stand against Aaron Spelling and the contract she never signed.

"She said they promised her she'd be home by 6 o'clock to cook dinner for Lee, and then claimed they didn't honor that agreement," RJ responded.

"The show won't be the same without her," I lamented.

We celebrated news of her three-picture movie deal with Paramount Studios, resulting in the release of her first major motion picture, *Somebody Killed Her Husband*, in which she shared top billing with Jeff Bridges. While one scathing critic labeled the film "Somebody Killed This Movie," we crossed our fingers for Farrah's success, thrilled to see her name atop a movie marquee.

After we'd turned 16, RJ and I snuck into a showing of our first R-rated film, the controversial and disturbing *American Gigolo* with Richard Gere. As a kid, I recalled seeing *The Towering Inferno* with Dad and shrinking in my seat when Faye Dunaway appeared in an early scene wearing an open kimono, her breasts fully exposed. I averted my eyes from the sight, my stomach tightening. Nudity on the screen…. what did Dad think, should I even pretend to notice? I wasn't turned on, just titillated by the idea someone famous would take that risk. When Richard Gere fully disrobed in *Gigolo* a momentous thrill arose in my chest. A Hollywood movie dared to show a beautiful man naked! The funny part is that his penis, barely visible in the dim shadows of the bedroom scene, seemed so small on the screen you could barely see it. And yet the fact it was a man naked thrilled RJ and me.

"Wow, I didn't expect him to shed everything," RJ remarked as we walked home from Westgate Mall, snow flurries pouring from the dull white sky.

"Would you ever want to be a gigolo?" I asked, knowing full well the answer but wanting to provoke a conversation.

"No, I wouldn't want to get paid to have sex with people I didn't love," he replied.

"That scene where he kisses the man's wife before lashing her with a strap was freaky," I replied. "I don't think he loved her, but he wanted to make her happy. She was so sad though."

A long silence passed between us as we walked the ten blocks back to my house. I was thinking about why people endured pain and unhappiness. Now and then I saw it in Mom and Dad's relationship but then it would lighten, and on another day they'd be happy. Maybe that's how people were, like clouds and sun. You could be partly cloudy or partly sunny depending on how you looked at it.

That night while Dad snoozed through an episode of *The Love Boat* and Mom read a biography of talk show host and fellow Catholic Phil Donahue, RJ and I camped in my room with the door shut. He pulled out his sketchpad and flipped through the charcoal drawings of Farrah and fellow Angel Kate Jackson.

"Hey, why don't you draw me? I can add a little flair with an accessory or two."

"Whaddya mean?" RJ asked sitting down on the bed.

I found a lead pencil set in my desk drawer and handed it to him. Then I rummaged around in my closet. I emerged wearing a cowboy hat with no shirt.

"Why don't you make it more interesting?" he smiled locking the bedroom door. He unhitched the top button of my jeans. I lowered them to reveal my pleasure trail and the waistband of my briefs.

While I posed on the bed, jeans pulled down to my ankles in case someone knocked on the door, RJ sketched me with his pencil. I flashed a broad grin, relishing my first experience playing sketch model. I liked him drawing me this way. I felt vulnerable and desirable at the same time. When he finished an initial draft, I took the pad. He had captured the lanky tone of my slim build, my muscular legs, and trim arms. The cowboy hat cast a shadow on my face, which he drew serious, with accentuated dark eyes and lips. The jock held my package, full and plump and leaning to the right. He adorned my bare feet with tiny wings. The image took my breath away. He'd drawn me idealized, and it was beatific. A smile blazed across my face.

"Sexy, huh?" he said with a satisfied grin and glimmer in his eye.

"You make me look like Mercury, the speedy messenger of the gods. I love it."

I could barely collect myself when Mom called us to come into the kitchen for a piece of her delicious homemade carrot cake and a glass of milk.

That night after the lights were out, and my parents asleep, RJ and I crawled into my small double bed. As we lay there in the dark resting against the maple wood headboard he reached across the bed and touched me. I curled up next to him, and he enfolded me in a warm embrace. I could hear him breathing, but he didn't shift his attention.

"Hey, I just want you to know I'll never hurt you. I wouldn't do that." I could barely hear him whisper it in my ear, tucked away as I was in the crook of his arm. Smiling I nuzzled up against him enfolded in his comfort and warmth. Before I knew it, he'd fallen asleep.

In the past we'd reach over and grapple each other's excited flesh, but that didn't happen this time. I lay awake that night thinking about what he'd said, feeling happy and safe, before finally nodding off. His arms slowly loosening around me, but his presence remained constant, consistent, abiding.

CHAPTER 12

First Date, First Kiss

"C'MON HILOVSKY, LET'S do it," said Mick as we reviewed the audition sheet.

"Do you think I'll get a part?"

"You can sing, can't you?" Denny responded.

The spring of 1979 word spread all over St. Ignatius about tryouts for the school musical *Where's Charley?* The show was based on the play *Charlie's Aunt* about a young man who tries to fool a girl into falling in love with him. Now that I'd gained some experience performing in several children's shows at Lakewood Little Theatre, I wanted to give my Catholic school turf a try. My trio of friends, Don, Denny, and Mick, all decided they'd sign up to audition.

For the last eight months, I'd dreamed of venturing out on my own, separate from RJ. While I didn't mind ceding the attention to him in dancing, I wanted to discover my own limelight. Rumor had it lots of upperclassmen would be auditioning for *Charley* so it would be competitive to land one of the leads. Any speaking part would allow me to get my foot in the door and graduate from the fairytale roles I'd played at the children's theatre.

"Okay, let's do it. I'm ready for a change," I told my bookish friends.

"All right folks," the lanky music director announced. "We're going to learn a song called "Once in Love with Amy." I took a deep breath and began mouthing the words, listening to my deeper voice take root in the lyrics. We learned the song in groups then sang a verse on our own. My stomach tightened into a ball of nerves. *Relax*, I told myself. I took a breath and released the tension. My voice soared. A smile rippled across my face.

"Hilovsky, can you take the role of Jack, please?" the disheveled director Mr. Molina asked. "From the top of the page."

My heart leapt. Jack, Charley's best friend, was a lead role, even if it was the sidekick. *Remember, any role is a good one*, I told myself.

I read the five- or six-line scene with a young woman from a Catholic girls' school who would be cast as Kitty, Jack's girlfriend. Careful not to exaggerate, I played it straight with minimal flourishes.

The next day Don and I scrambled up the stairs to the sixth floor of the Admin Building to check the final cast list on Molina's door. Our eyes traced the long list of names until we found our own. Don and Mick landed roles in the chorus. I was selected to play the cameo role of Reggie, Charley's egotistical rival for Amy's affection in addition to a chorus slot.

"Yes!" I shouted practically pirouetting, in mid-air. I wanted to dash for joy. My first role not playing a storybook character like Oz's Tin Man, Snow White's Prince, or Alice's White Rabbit. I could put Lakewood Little Theatre and the kid parts behind me. I was moving into the high school musical big leagues.

Don adjusted his clunky glasses and slapped me on the shoulder. "See, I said you could do it. Way to go."

Adrenaline raced through my entire body; my imagination full of possibility. No longer would I be pigeonholed as a bink, the pejorative for us

uber-smart, Latin students and other wiz-kids from the freshman class of
1H. Now we were sophomores and breaking out!

I'd finally begun settling into friendships with my high school classmates. Every afternoon when classes let out Don and I met in the school
library to review our Latin homework. Sophomore year we added a Greek
class. We laughed to ourselves translating stories about Odysseus and
Achilles, Grecian heroes with cursed fates, and the beckoning monsters
Scylla and Charybdis.

Where Don exuded gentle humor, shyness and humility, Mick ratcheted
up the conversation with a healthy dose of sarcasm and wit. "Where's your
yacht?" he'd tease me glancing at my Docksider boat shoes.

"Hilovsky," Mick would say every time I mentioned a female friend.
"When are you going to get a girlfriend?" Never mind Mick didn't have
one. He was interested in getting us all coupled.

And then out of nowhere he'd get serious.

"You know," he'd sniff, "I'm just pulling your leg. You don't think I'm
obnoxious, do you?" When I wagged my head no, he'd chuckle and say,
"Good."

With all the testosterone swirling around me, it was a welcome pleasure
getting to know young women who came from neighboring girls' schools
to participate in the plays. Magnificat, Beaumont, Holy Names. These were
the schools, among others, that sent their most talented young women to
audition. I noticed how much more comfortable I felt relating to my male
classmates when females were present. The guys acted nicer, more polite.
They cared what the girls thought of them. Guys didn't want girls to discover they were jerks.

That spring I asked one of them to attend my first Junior-Sophomore
dance with me. Debbie Lannigan from Holy Names Academy. "I thought
you'd never ask," she squawked in that brassy, confident voice of hers. "I've

got the perfect dress." We double dated with my friend Craig and his grade school sweetheart Julie. The night started out great. I felt dressed to the nines in my unconstructed tan jacket, brown knit tie, and khaki low-rise pants, all purchased at the teen fashion outlet Merry-Go-Round.

We grinned as we had our photo taken by the yearbook photographer upon our arrival to the gym. I escorted Debbie to the dance floor, and we danced to Michael Jackson's "Rock with You." All seemed perfect until halfway through the dance Debbie pulled away from me in distress. "You popped a button on the back of my dress!" Her voice got even louder as she bellowed, "What do you think you're doing? You've got some nerve!" She pushed me away. We tussled. People were staring.

I began to sweat. "Look, I swear, I'm not doing anything. Just because we're slow dancing, doesn't mean I'm trying to undress you."

"I don't believe you," Debbie shouted, her arms folded protectively over her chest. "How do you explain the two undone buttons in the back? This is a brand-new dress."

"I don't know," I replied. "Maybe the dress doesn't fit. It's too tight.... you're practically squeezed into it."

I covered my mouth. *Did I say that, or just think it?* I couldn't remember.

"How dare you even suggest?" she said in a hysteric voice, as if she read my mind. Clutching herself she ran away and approached a chaperone on the sidelines.

"He tried to tear my dress off!" she said pointing toward me. "What?" said Mrs. Ghostley, the mother of one of my friends in Latin class. "Mr. Hilovsky, please behave yourself and respect your date here."

I didn't even try to explain and instead cajoled Debbie to come back for a dance. When Debbie returned to my side, I smiled and said, "Why don't we start over? We can still be friends, right?" She nodded and put her hand on my shoulder. While the deejay spun "Dreamweaver," I positioned my hands on her hips to avert any more embarrassing wardrobe calamities that might arise.

I danced with her wide curves and tense demeanor when what I desired was the litheness of a fit male physique, not curves and softness. And while I would have enjoyed the freedom to touch that kind of physique it wasn't on the menu.

"Can you believe Jack tried to unbutton my dress on the dance floor?" a wide-eyed Debbie told Craig and Julie afterward while we were eating at Heck's, the popular local hamburger joint. She twisted the wilted iris corsage on her wrist and barely concealed her giggles, erupting like insistent hiccups. "I give up," I said rolling my eyes heavenward, deciding to stop contesting her story.

When Craig pulled up to the front of her house, she emerged from the backseat, then leaned toward me and whispered, "That was fun. We'll have to do it again sometime." Then she pecked me on the cheek and popped out of the car.

***

"I don't get it," RJ replied with a perplexed look on his face. "She accused you of trying to pop the buttons on her dress in public?"

I nodded in silent agreement and arranged the Polaroid pictures, evidence from the dance, on the table.

"She's a cow, I'm sorry. You shouldn't get in trouble for her bad decision on which dress to wear. Besides, that white knitted shawl has to go. It looks like her grandmother's."

"It probably is," I sighed. "It's okay, RJ. Maybe it's a lesson to avoid taking someone to a dance unless I'm totally crazy about them. Next time I'll be better, more selective." All I knew is that it would be someone who wouldn't be as embarrassing as Debbie. All the guys who heard the story of our disastrous date ribbed me. "Hey, Hilovsky. We hear you've got some loose fingers, hee-hee, ha-ha," they'd say. "Better watch out, before you're in deep girl pudding," they teased.

For God sakes, I wasn't even attracted to the girl! And now I had to endure jokes about pudding.

Where's Charley? opened the following weekend. During tech week Debbie behaved herself, and we agreed we were better off as friends. My cameo role as Reggie required me to wear a white tuxedo, my eyebrows accentuated with a heavy black pencil a la a young Groucho Marx. Happy and excited to be on the Ignatius stage, my self-confidence bloomed. I liked flirting with the female leads while Charley, his sidekick Conrad, and I shared laughs backstage.

RJ attended opening night with his mother and his Aunt Mimi. "Nice job with the slick character, Bucko," he said. "Those acting lessons at LLT came in handy." I beamed. After three years competing for roles at Lakewood Little Theatre, I still valued his approval.

Delivering over-the-top comedy, music, dancing, and a pinch of drama, *Where's Charley?* drew sold-out audiences during its two-weekend run and closed at the end of April. Riding the buoyant response softened the thud of reality when academics reemerged to demand my focus.

Once the papers were done and the exams completed, school let out. The Summer of '79 leapt to a racing start. Farrah continued dominating the headlines: rumors suggested she and Lee had "called it quits," and she'd started dating Lee's best friend, the film actor Ryan O'Neal. "I liked her with Lee," I told RJ as we read the cover story in *People* Magazine. "Ryan O'Neal's a bubblehead."

"But he's cuter," RJ contested.

The saga of her contract dispute with *Charlie's Angels* finally resolved, she agreed to complete several more appearances over the next year before departing from the show that made her a household name. We couldn't wait to see her second movie, *Sunburn*, in which she'd play a beautiful secret agent. "At least she'll be in a bathing suit rather than the cowl neck sweaters and trench coats she wore in the last movie," RJ sniffed. "You're such a fashion snob," I teased.

More important events loomed beyond our Farrah obsession and the circus around her. On June 6th, I was to turn sixteen. RJ insisted on throwing me a party at his Aunt Mimi's in suburban North Olmsted. An above ground swimming pool dominated her spacious backyard surrounded by woods and tall oak trees. We picked a weekend night and invited a small group of friends, many from Lakewood Little Theatre and our disco dancing entourage. I loved celebrating my birthday; as the day grew closer, my excitement grew.

During my involvement with *Where's Charley?* RJ had grown inseparable from his neighbor and new dance partner Tricia, which I didn't mind since rehearsals consumed my time. A junior at Lakewood High School and two years RJ's senior, she began dancing with him when Shelley bowed out due to other after-school commitments. Tricia lived in a two-story bungalow across the street from the Fallons. Her beautiful, pale, creamy white skin made the small, cute freckles on her nose even more obvious. She loved to flirt with RJ and me and tell racy jokes, some of which the punch line was lost on me. "Why does Dr. Pepper come in a bottle?" she asked. "Because his wife died," she giggled slapping my knee. When she learned I was Catholic, she said, "Oh, Jack, you need to loosen up, dear."

At my birthday gathering Saturday evening we played the pool party game Marco Polo, diving under water and toward opposite ends of the pool. The cool night air subdued the heat from earlier in the day. The waves and all the splashing from the games and racing and swimming wore us down. At sunset, a seductive voice followed by a wandering hand emerged from the roughhousing.

"Come here, lover," Tricia mewed in the warm shallow waters. Her purring, like a cat awaiting a little nip, grew insistent. Soft, long fingers glided along the water's surface.

Without warning she grabbed my waist and glued her body to mine. Her tongue, wet and insistent, invaded my mouth. Her lips, like suction cups, locked on mine. Totally unprepared I was unsure how to even greet her aggressive pounce. I felt awkward, clumsy, self-conscious. Underwater I came alive, an awkward boner rising in my swimsuit, my heart pounding, like I had no control over my body. My physical reaction didn't sync with my helpless feeling of being ambushed by a girl who had more experience in the love department than I.

Something sharp nicked the inside of my cheek and—Oww, *geez, I forgot she had braces. What's that stinging--* I unhinged her mouth from mine.

Then RJ's Aunt Mimi flipped the switch; the backyard floodlights illuminated the entire pool. Mimi emerged from the house carrying a birthday cake ablaze with sixteen candles. Unaware she'd caught us in an awkward make-out session she started singing *Happy Birthday* and all my friends joined in.

When I touched my lip a trickle of blood appeared on my hand. I caught Shelley looking at me and turned away in embarrassment. Here was another disastrous girl-encounter on display for all to see, another romantic entanglement gone awry. What was wrong with me?

"Ow, dammit."

"What?" Tricia flashed me an impatient look. "What's wrong now?"

"The braces, I forgot about your braces," I mumbled, my hand over my bruised and bloody lip. I'd stuck my tongue in her mouth and got entangled in the chicken wire.

"Well," she said, "despite the braces, nobody's complained about my kissing before. You just need to get used to working around the metal. We can try again?"

"No, I think I've had enough tonight. Thanks, though."

Embarrassed, I swam over to the deck and hopped out of the water to defuse the flaming birthday cake. Everyone clambered out of the pool and circled around to watch me.

With one deep breath I blew out the candles on the strawberry infused vanilla pound cake with "Happy 16th Birthday, Jack" strewn across the top. My pals hooted and hollered.

But I couldn't stop thinking about Tricia--Girl Number Two--another failed experiment. Another opportunity to test the waters of teenage normalcy had backfired. Kissing a girl, or taking one on a date, didn't guarantee smooth sailing. It bothered me that I didn't respond to female wiles; well, I did with my involuntary boner but not on a feelings level, where it felt, dare I say, unnatural. Most guys relished the chance to dive in, but I felt hesitant, like part of me wasn't there with the girl at the receiving end. It was like a performance at Lakewood Little Theatre, or a romantic scene in the movies, done for the sake of the crowd with part of me separate from my own body.

Yeah, I might get aroused, but I also felt scared. Scared about feeling the need to perform or respond to sexual aggressiveness. Scared about an even greater question: what did I want to do with my life now that college was fast approaching? Did I even have a clue about my calling or the career I might want to pursue?

Aunt Mimi gave me a hug and passed the knife. "I didn't mean to embarrass you there, honey."

I winked. "Oh, no, you did me a favor. I was ready to come up for air."

Then RJ with his warm brown eyes came over and elbowed me. He was

cupying him while getting into physical shape consumed my after-school hours.

"How do I look?" I'd ask him after completing a set of curls and push-ups, then showering, and meeting him at Leonard's.

"Fine, I don't see much of a difference. You've always looked fit and out-doorsy."

"What does that mean?" I asked, crossing my arms.

"You're more rugged and athletic, I'm more artistic and sophisticated," RJ replied.

"Is that a putdown?" I asked.

"No, think of it this way. You're…autumn leaves, earthy, you know what I mean? I'm more like silk, more into luxury and glamour. We're different, alike in some ways, but not all ways. One's no better than the other."

I shrugged, thinking I'd just been given a backhanded compliment, but I loved my friend anyway. We always tried to define how we differed because it amazed us how much we shared in common.

As the days passed, I dove more and more into training for my lifesaving exam. I'd need to pass both a physical endurance and written test. As my day of reckoning approached, I felt prepared yet apprehensive. I knew my drills, now if I could survive the water test, I'd be home free.

***

"How would you rescue someone drowning in a lake without a pole or buoy to throw them?" the instructor asked.

"Swim front crawl with my head above the surface…. maintaining eye contact…. once I'm six to eight feet from them, dive underwater…. Turn them away from you and climb ladder-like up their torso maintaining firm contact while assuring their head remains above water…. Reach across

their chest and restrain them with a crossover arm grip.... Swim to shore."
I smiled.

"Excellent," she replied. "Now, demonstrate."

As I changed into my Speedo, I remembered my first scary lessons as a kid. My breathing turned shallow; perspiration dripped down my armpits. I slammed the locker shut and crossed through the shower room. On the pool deck stood four other lifeguards in training. I counted them. Three girls, another guy, and me.

"Mr. Hilovsky" announced a woman I didn't recognize holding a clipboard. "You'll be the first to go. Is that all right?" She smiled as if she were doing me a favor.

"Oh. Sure," my voice cracked. I cleared my throat.

"But why don't you all get in the water and do a few laps to warm up?" she suggested.

Once we'd finished, I leaned near the edge looking down towards the deep, where I'd execute my rescue. Then I climbed out.

"Oh, Mr. Hilovsky," said the examiner. "I'd like you to meet Chuck Daniels who will evaluate you."

I looked up to see a Cleveland version of the television character Grizzly Adams standing in front of me, all 200 plus pounds of him!

"Pleasure's mine, Jack," Grizzly stuck his paw-like hand out. "Good luck, here, on the water test. Ha-ha. I'll just jump in over there and swim to the deep end and you can rescue me when I give you the thumbs up. Sound good?"

I broke into a sweat. Debbie Lannigan and her faux accusations about her popped buttons on her dress didn't come close to bringing me to this level of anxiety. Now I looked at my faux drowning test case. *Oh, my God, this brute is a mountain man!*

The six foot three Mr. Daniels lumbered over to the deep end and dove in headfirst making a splash bigger than Shamu in the practice pool at Sea World. Water flew into the air and splattered on the deck.

He's a whale, I thought. *How in the hell am I going to rescue him?*

"Mr. Hilovsky, are you ready? Mr. Hilovsky?"

I snapped to attention.

"Uh, yes, thanks, ma'am." I took another deep breath and gulped tossing my fear out the window. "Shall I assume my victim will be active and flailing in the water?"

"Yes, Mr. Daniels may actively resist your attempt to rescue him. You'll approach him from the shallow side of the pool and swim out to execute the underwater approach with the two-handed arm lock, returning him to shore. You must be prepared for any reaction."

"All right then. I'm ready," I announced and nodded at the others who would follow me. They all looked stupefied, deliriously happy I would be the first to go.

"When I blow the whistle," said clipboard lady.

Grizzly nodded, clearing his stringy, wet hair away from his face, and scratching his brown beard, before giving the thumbs up. "Ready," he called out.

The whistle blew. I dove feet first into the pool and laser focused on the victim. My freestyle stroke powered me. Arm over arm I motored, kicking with fervent speed. Grizzly, who had remained eerily composed from a distance, like the Great White in *Jaws*, began flailing in the water once I reached the halfway mark, belting his arms to make big splashing waves. "Help!" he called out. "Help!"

Adrenaline exploded through my body. I approached him 15 feet, 13 feet, 11 feet, 9 feet, 7. I dove under the water after meeting the whites of Grizzly's panicked eyes.

"Haaalppp!!" he screamed from above.

I grabbed his flailing propeller like legs, arching every which way, slammed them together, and twisted him like the wheel on a runaway truck careening down a watery embankment. I climbed up his thick, glutinous trunk, arched his back and lifted myself to the chaotic surface.

"Haalp!!" he screamed. Thrashing from side to side and trying to evade my grip.

I crashed my bony hip into his back and threw my arm crossways over his hairy, barreled chest.

"Relax," I demanded. "I'm taking you to shore."

Each time Grizzly tried to escape I arched my bony hip further into his back. I wanted him horizontal and under my control.

Arriving at the pool's edge, both of us winded and exhausted, we coughed up water.

The clipboard lady rushed over. "Excellent job, Jack. Now please demonstrate how you'd remove him from the water."

I lopped Grizzly's one hand over the side of the pool, while maintaining contact, hoisted myself out, and lifted Grizzly's upper half onto the deck. Gasping for breath I rolled his legs over the pool's edge. Then I collapsed.

"Not too bad, kid," said Grizzly Chuck. "Don't forget to cushion my head on this hard surface. And watch it with that hip action. You really did a job on my back."

I smiled and nodded. "Thanks, Chuck."

I left the pool that evening, floating on a cloud, the first candidate out the door of the aquatic center where my instructor had attempted to "drown" me 11 years earlier to teach me the basics of swimming. The June light blinded me as I threw open the door; it cast a brilliant gleam on everything: the trees, grass, the school building and library, and the track and field course across the street.

Mom pulled into the school parking lot tooting the horn to get my attention. She rolled down the window, her warm eyes twinkling with anticipation. "How did it go, sweetheart? Did you knock 'em dead?"

I started laughing, giddy, like I'd won the million-dollar lottery.

"You're looking at a certified lifeguard," I exclaimed pumping my two middle fingers in the air, a "V" for victory gesture. She reached through the window to kiss my forehead and muss my hair. "I didn't expect anything less from my one and only. Remember, you can do anything you want in life."

Wow, when she said those words, the power of them hit me like a Mack Truck. I could do anything I want in life. I closed my eyes trying to envision how that might look.

As we pulled out of the parking lot, my chest puffed up and I leaned back on the headrest releasing a slow exhale. "You'll never guess—I wrestled a Grizzly out of the water," I chortled while mom kept saying "Oh, my. Oh, my," failing to contain her laughter. My mother--my coach, critic, and cheerleader—all folded into one. We were a team.

From an early age, she'd tell me, "Jack you're special. People will be jealous. Make sure to stay humble." How could I, how could any child, resist such a tempting elixir? How could I not believe that I was called to accomplish great things?

I could do anything I want in life. I couldn't be a lifeguard my entire life, even though that's the only job I wanted right now. I loved people, helping them, inspiring them. And people were drawn to me. How did I make that into a life's work?

***

NAILING the water exam by rescuing "Grizzly" Chuck Daniels signaled a major life turning point. On June 13, 1979, a week after my sixteenth birthday, I became an official Red Cross Certified Lifeguard. I proudly tucked the ID card into my wallet.

I'd arrive at Foster Pool early and swim a few laps before chatting with fellow lifeguards and co-workers. I took seriously my obligation to guard people's lives by strictly enforcing the rules—no running on the deck, no diving in shallow water, and routine breaks every quarter past the hour.

More than anything I loved the initiation and new sense of self I encountered working at Foster Pool. Surrounded by other people drawn to the water and outdoors, I'd found another place, like the children's theatre before, that I now could call home. While I loved the freedom to dance I discovered with RJ over the past three years, maybe now I could be the star of my own life production. Confident, breezy Jack emerging on center stage as Teen Lifeguard.

***

AT Foster Pool all new guards began their careers as lowly "coolies" while awaiting their first assignment. A coolie scrubbed the grimy pool decks, hosed and disinfected the changing areas, and assisted with other tasks, like pool cleaning and monitoring the chemicals in the water. When a lifeguard slot opened, usually on the night shift, we were on our way to full-fledged lifeguard status.

I started working nights. The typical evening shift promised a quieter, less chaotic atmosphere with fewer kids and more adult lap swimmers. All of us lifeguards wore a regulation royal blue nylon swimsuit with a bright yellow side panel ensuring we stood out from the crowd. We sat high above the Olympic size pool like gods and goddesses perched on white lookout chairs. Every fifteen minutes a replacement guard arrived and the seven of us on duty rotated chairs, which entitled the final guard to take a break. From several hundred yards away, Lake Erie stretched north into the distance, all the way to Canada. I loved looking out toward the lake and its endless horizon. Like a perpetual mirage, it signified possibility. Every night I marveled at the brilliant orange, purple, and red sunsets.

After my night shift ended, I walked to RJ's in the summer dusk. By that time, he'd returned from his part-time job bagging groceries at Heinen's. We sat on the front porch swing and exchanged tales of our day.

"Wow, they pay you $7.50 an hour to get a suntan. What if it rains?"

"Well, the pool stays open until the pool manager makes a final call," I explained. "We'll shut down if there's thunder or lightening. Or a prolonged rainstorm. Basically, we're paid until the pool's closed."

A light breeze rustled the large oak trees along RJ's street. Stars twinkled in the night sky. I could hear crickets followed by a train whistle in the distance, the tracks only several blocks north. Summer had begun. My heart raced with anticipation of all the new adventures awaiting us.

RJ sighed. "*Weekday Fever* is on hiatus until school starts again. I guess this summer I'm not going to see you or Shelley much. She's lifeguarding at Marine Towers on the Gold Coast. And you'll be busy too. At least Tricia is willing to dance with me."

"Well, yeah, for now I'm scheduled to cover the night shift. I'm on call during the day, but that doesn't mean we can't get together before or after work."

RJ smiled and leaned closer into me. "That's true, but it won't be the same. Things are changing."

Dad arrived to pick me up and tooted the horn. That spring I'd flunked my driver's exam after failing to make a complete stop before turning right at a red light. I was to take a remedial class in the fall. Driving fell to the bottom of my priority list, and my parents were more than happy to chauffeur around their only child. It allowed them to keep tabs on me, though I wasn't the type to get into trouble.

As we headed home, I asked, "Dad, when did you know Mom was the one for you?"

"The minute I laid eyes on your mother, she had the most beautiful smile, and her laugh. It made me happy to hear her laughter."

"What else?"

"Her blue eyes. Her eyes danced when she looked at me."

I rolled down the car window while Dad zipped along Warren Road and across the Fairview Bridge. The warm night air gently ruffled my hair. I peered into the dark wooded expanse of the Cleveland Metroparks below. Nobody in my sixteen years had touched my heart in this way. Except for RJ. When we were together, laughter and joy, mixed with a healthy dose of tender sarcasm, were our constant companions. Closing my eyes, the night wind caressed my face, and we were home in no time.

***

As summer progressed, a whole new clan of teenagers entered my social circle. The majority of lifeguards came from Lakewood High, the public school RJ attended. A ragtag team, our personalities ranged from shy and sweet to loudmouth and bossy.

Each morning white haired Marion Becks arrived at the pool. Meticulously dressed in walking shorts and a sleeveless white cotton shirt, along with sunglasses and a large brim straw hat, Marion ran the Lakewood Parks Aquatic Program. She ensured all lifeguards were properly certified and that all of us wore the regulation suit. While most of the guards hated the suit, I loved it. Modest but brief, it allowed for maximum sun exposure and tan lines that coincided with my slimmer cut Speedo. In my book any-thing was better than baggy boxer swim trunks.

One day in late June Marion approached me and asked if we were near full registration for the swim classes.

"Uhhmm, I don't know, I'm not an instructor." I shifted in the lifeguard chair to make better eye contact in the glare of the late morning sun.

"Well, you should be," she replied. "You're friendly and the children re-ally like you. Let me see if we have a class where you can assist."

"Thanks, Mrs. Becks," I smiled. "I'd be interested. I've not taught be-fore…"

"Oh, you'll be a natural," she interrupted adjusting her straw hat. "Check in later with me."

The next week I learned I'd be teaching a class of pre-school swimmers called Tadpoles. Scott Meenan would lead the session, and I'd assist. Scott, with sun bleached curly blond hair, a wide, bright smile, and wicked sense of humor, was two years older than I. All the kids loved him.

"All right, Tadpoles, let's practice blowing bubbles," he said on the first day of class clapping his hands to get their attention.

A dozen 4- and 5-year-olds plopped their faces in the water and with varying levels of success, fomented a bubble brigade along the side of the pool.

"This should keep 'em busy for awhile," Scott winked. "Why don't you make sure they don't stray too far from the edge? These little guys always have the itch to wander."

I glided from child to child observing their bubble-blowing prowess, amazed at how each kid seemed to embrace the water.

Alonzo, a small, olive-skinned boy of Italian descent, doggy paddled further and further away from the edge. "Hey, look at me, mister, look at me. I can swim," he shrieked. He splashed his way into my arms.

"Not yet Alonzo. It'll take a little more time. But you're doing good. Let's stay focused on the bubbles, that'll help your breathing." For a moment an image of my childhood swimming instructor, the woman who "tried to drown me," flashed in my memory, and I smiled inside.

I grabbed him by the waist and held him horizontal, while he poked his head in the water and then came up for air, smiling with wide brown eyes and eyelashes flapping with excitement. "Yippee," he squealed in utter delight. "I'm swimming!"

"Good, good, Alonzo, that's a start." I steadied his kick as he powered along, his small legs up and down and all around. With a firm grasp I cradled him in my arms. Then and there, amidst the splash of the water and the chatter of the kids and the sun beaming down and the light breeze dancing all around me, I decided teaching swimming lessons and lifeguarding at Foster had to be the best job I'd ever had.

People told me I glowed at work. Maybe it was the summer light or the golden suntan I'd managed to cultivate. No longer glued to RJ's side, I was making my own way in the world. My afternoon routine consisted of preparing to teach the Tadpoles. I slipped into my blue suit, slathered a layer of Hawaiian Tropic sun tanning lotion on my shoulders, and sunglasses perched on my nose made a beeline for the pool deck. The scent of coconut oil sailed through the air, summer's aphrodisiac.

When my fellow guards Dirk Freska and Henry Brewer arrived, we discussed the rotation for the upcoming shift. Everyone, including me, was drawn to playful, sexy Dirk. With his ripped chest and his curly short brown hair peeking from behind a bandana, he loved playing practical jokes, while his goofy, pale sidekick Henry looked serious and sullen behind big circular frame, Barbara Walters's eyeglasses. Like RJ and I, they too were an inseparable duo. Henry the straight man to Dirk's clown.

The summer peaked in August with temperatures climbing into the 90's.

I devoured the lunches Mom carefully packed for me. In addition to large turkey sandwiches piled with lettuce, tomato and cheese, protein milk shakes were her specialty. Assembled with a host of ingredients to keep me from wilting in the summer heat, she tossed banana, vanilla ice cream, egg yolks, and bran into a blender and voila, poured the concoction into an ice-cold thermos, which I gulped before manning my lifeguard station. Most of the other guards were lucky if they got a power bar to last through the afternoon.

One day, towards the end of the summer of '79, I sat guard at the empty children's wading pool. I felt such a great responsibility for people's lives in my new summer job. The breeze off the lake and warm intensity of the sun for a moment melted away my hyper alertness. My windblown hair and skin baking in the desert-like heat, I grew lost in my own time and space--the outdoors, the sunlight, the high-pitched squeal of kids in the larger pool beyond my control.

Beaming and content, like Tarzan in my lifeguard suit, I needed nothing else. All life sang in concert. No need for a uniform, or a shirt and tie. No need for a costume. No need to please anyone. Lake Erie lapped in the distance, nature's partner in a gentle wind dance. My surroundings coalesced in one glorious life canvas. God was here. There was nothing else I needed.

CHAPTER 14

Mary Kathleen

"OH, FOR CHRIST'S sake," a voice boomed from the middle of the racks. "I'm stuck. Can someone help me out of this?"

I was in the St. Ignatius costume shop one September afternoon trying to find out information about future auditions when I encountered a girl attempting to squeeze herself into a much too tight wedding dress. Wedged in between the racks of clown suits, formal gowns, and tweedy professor jackets, she had somehow got her head caught in the dress' bodice. A red, puffy face emerged from the collar of the ivory dress. Her brown hair, swept like a windstorm across her face, fell to her shoulders.

"Man, that was a bitch," she said smiling after we had freed her. "How does it look?" She buttoned the fitted sleeves and smoothed the wrinkled train.

"Good, with a little ironing. Are you planning on a fall wedding?" I joked.

"You're a wise guy." She paused before a widening smirk spread across her face. "One day, yes, but for now I'm faking it. I'm Milady in *The Three Musketeers.*

I bowed. "Nice to meet you, Milady."

"Oh, my real name's Mary Kathleen." She looked in a nearby mirror and fiddled with the bridal train. "And who are you?"

"I'm Jack. You look familiar."

She brushed her flyaway hair back and gave me a playful wink. "I'm sure I'll see you around," she said grabbing the bustle and sashaying into a dressing room.

I watched her and the trailing ivory gown. Pizzazz, I said to myself. That girl's got pizzazz.

***

I'd always wanted to be a cheerleader. Since its early days Ignatius had organized an all-male cheerleading club called The Spirit Squad. My junior year the school decided to permit women to join this club, a step sure to generate more enthusiasm for the struggling, come from behind St. Ignatius Wildcat's football team.

That fall I tried out, and soon found myself hoisting girls on my shoulders while leading cheers for the home team. "Let's go Wildcats, we want some action!" rumbled across the playfield unleashing a roar from the spectators. I loved the spectacle, the theatre of it. Better yet was the adulation of the all-male student body when they observed me throwing pretty girls in midair and catching them while the crowd yelled its approval. I felt big, important, and popular. Applause, yes applause rang in my ears. My stature in the eyes of classmates rose because access to the opposite sex was everything in an all-boys' school.

The crowd went berserk as the six of us guys hoisted the cheerleaders and created a human pyramid. In the stands my gaze alighted on the girl I'd met the week before in the costume shop, Mary Kathleen. She had traded the snug ivory wedding gown for a bright fuchsia jacket and her hair was now pulled back tight in a bun. Her two male co-stars in *Three Musketeers*, sat on either side of her, engrossed in the game. She waved at me.

When the game resumed, I casually wandered up to posture against the front bleacher. "Hey, small world. What are you doin' here?"

"Homecoming's around the corner. I figure I'll eventually get a date if I just show up enough." She smiled, her baby blue eyes steadily gazing into mine. She leaned in toward me and whispered, "Woody Allen says 80% of life is showing up. Of course, the girls from Mags have the dance all tied up."

"Ohhhh, so you're a Magnificat girl?"

"Unfortunately. It's really a terrible holding cell for debutantes and Stepford Wives in training. Yeeesh. Thankfully I only have one more year. I'm a senior soon to be set free."

I grinned. "You should have no problem getting a date. You've got moxie and look stunning in a wedding dress."

Sure enough Milady's leading man, D'Artagnan in *Musketeers*, turned to Mary Kathleen later that afternoon and asked her to join him at the Homecoming Dance. She happily accepted, only to learn a week later he'd begun seeing another member of the cast who played the virginal handmaiden to the iron-fisted Milady.

While that drama played out, I began running into Mary Kathleen on campus. She'd always call me by my last name, like a football coach addressing a member of the squad.

"Hey, Hilovsky, I think I know how we met. You deliver *The Sun Herald* every Thursday morning to my house. My sister Katherine said she's answered the door when you're collecting. She thinks you're cute."

I turned red. "The Cassidys of West Valley? Now it all makes sense. I've seen your brother and sisters, but never you."

"I'm smart. I don't answer the door."

Every time she volleyed a snappy retort, I rolled my eyes and shook my head. I was at a loss for words around her, but she didn't mind. Like oil (me) and vinegar (she), we found a way to intermingle in the crazy salad bowl of high school. Soon she became the big, sassy-mouthed sister I never had, double daring me to dive into a wider world. I discovered while she liked disco, she also saw a universe far beyond it.

In November after *Musketeers* closed and I finished *Alice in Wonderland* at Lakewood Little Theatre, Mary Kathleen and I began calling each other. "Hilovsky, you gotta get out more. Have you ever been to *The Rocky Horror Picture Show?*

My stomach fluttered with butterflies. "Isn't that about transvestites?"

"Oh, it's more than that—it's about freedom of expression and telling the boring status quo to fuck off!" I paled. She grinned. "Hilovsky, live a little. You gotta come with me."

The next weekend on a cold December night, we drove to The Hilliard, an old, neglected movie house in Lakewood, for a midnight showing of *Rocky Horror*. MK, as I'd taken to calling her, didn't tell me she planned to come dressed as Dr. Frank N Furter, the mad scientist in drag.

"How do I look?" she asked with an unabashed grin when she picked me up on Saturday night.

"Different than I've ever seen you," I said, my eyeballs almost popping out of my head. Her hair coated in Dippity-Do, her blue eyes outlined in heavy black mascara, her ruby red lips accentuated with black pencil. Enveloped in a snug black bustier, and towering over me, she wore knee-high leather boots with gigantic heels.

When we arrived at the theatre, a whole host of characters awaited us, from Brad and Janice in their signature white underwear and oversized black frame glasses to the blond hunk Rocky adorned in metallic paint and stuffed in gold metallic gym shorts. I couldn't take my eyes off his bulging crotch though I tried to conceal my fascination.

Standing in the aisle wearing a beige hooded sweater and blue jeans, I felt like a virgin at an orgy. I'd never participated in such a scene and lacked the costume, but MK equipped me with the requisite flashlight, toast, and rice. Various characters mimicked the story in front of a big screen amidst the rain, lightning, and thunder of the opening scene. Guys in tight fitting spandex charged across the stage, girls wore skimpy dresses. My eyes widened and feasted on the uninhibited sexuality surrounding me.

In a blink the *Rocky Horror* anthem "Let's Do the Time Warp" erupted on the screen and a mass of flailing bodies filled the aisles of the darkened theatre. Big wigs and tiny costumes all competed for floor space.

Mary Kathleen merrily took in my wild-eyed dancing and vocal interpretation of the song and crowed "Hilovsky, not bad, you've got some vocal chops there."

"What do you mean?"

"Dear, you can sing. That's what I meant. I can't string two notes together without hitting B flat."

Then the toast began to fly, followed by a whiteout rice storm, and flashlights flickering everywhere. I looked to my left, and then to my right. MK was nowhere to be found.

Then I saw a tall vision on stage, with black hair and a white face. It was MK spotlighted in all her phantasmagorical wonder: her body wriggling, jumping, writhing in a state of reckless abandon, reciting the lyrics on the screen, and keeping rhythm with the relentless staccato beat of the song.

When the chorus began again, I dove into the sea of sweaty bodies and echoed the refrain: "*Let's do the time warp again.*"

Bumping and grinding with a cast of unknowns, I felt both alien and accepted. I was still the only one without a costume, but nobody cared.

The freaks of *Rocky* both attracted and repelled me. Freedom and rebellion flooded the theatre in the dark post-midnight hours. Multiple versions of Rocky, Brad and Janet haunted the room, titillating me, arousing both my curiosity and disdain. Uniformity was dispelled and replaced by thunderous waves of the queer and unique. I couldn't escape – and I didn't want to. I felt mesmerized, and breathless, as if all the oxygen would be squeezed out of me by the stampede.

"Welcome to a new world," MK chortled with a wide grin, squeezing my shoulder as we strolled arm in arm into the star-filled night.

***

I couldn't wait to introduce Mary Kathleen to RJ. After *Rocky Horror* I invited her to join us at our favorite hotspot in Lakewood. The Lido was a vintage 1970's bar turned discotheque with a lenient policy about checking IDs for underage youth. Since we only danced and drank soda, the owners never bothered to card us. Thanks to our dressy open-necked shirts and form-fitting pants, RJ and I could easily pass for eighteen.

I'd finally nailed my driving exam in October, but Mary Kathleen insisted on manning the wheel since her family had 4 cars to share among 8 members of the Cassidy clan.

"Be home by midnight," Dad called after me, as I dashed out of the house. I nodded knowing I'd never missed a curfew. MK was dressed in her signature quilted fuchsia jacket, a cherished Christmas gift from her father who bought it at Saks Fifth Avenue in New York. She bounced out of the car, removed her coat, and struck a pose. "How do I look?"

Her makeup was perfect, and her hair carefully clasped in a silver barrette with volumes of curls cascading down her shoulders. An aquama-

rine camisole shimmered above a tight charcoal pencil thin skirt. A pair of
black stiletto heels accentuated her chorus girl legs, bringing us eye to eye.

"You look.... magnificent." Completely awed, I stumbled for the words.

"A little tongue-tied?" she chuckled. Her eyes twinkled, and she gave me
a hug. "Oh, come on Hilovsky, don't get too warm and fuzzy on me, this'll
all wear off in no time, and I'll be back to my old self."

"Well, RJ will be impressed."

RJ and Shelley greeted us in the foyer of the Lido. Shelley, her red hair
pulled back in a headband, was dressed in a simple pink – her favorite col-
or – sweater and Calvin Klein jeans. At least for this night, she'd abandoned
the flowing dresses she wore on *Weekday Fever*. RJ in his trademark black
pants and a floral poly-silk green shirt, looked ready to tear up the floor, his
toes tapping to the background beat of "Night Fever."

Shelley ran over to hug me while RJ followed eyeballing Mary Kathleen
from head to toe.

"Glad to see you made it, Bucko. We thought you got lost now that you
finally earned that license." Ever since I'd passed the driver's test, he loved
to tease me about my poor sense of direction. "Who's the pretty girl on
your arm?"

"Meet Mary Kathleen Cassidy. She starred in the fall play at Ignatius and
now is setting her sights on Broadway."

RJ extended his hand. "Jack has told me all about you and your performance last weekend. You sound like quite the sensation."

Mary Kathleen blushed.

"Don't mind him," Shelley whispered. "He's just a flirt especially on the
dance floor."

Once in the main hall, the loud music overwhelmed any conversation.
Disco lights blinked in unison with the percussive beat. A group of platinum blonde and red-haired girls outfitted in the latest punk garb, safety

pins hooked on black leather jackets and denim miniskirts, spun in circles on the dance floor. Blondie's "Heart of Glass" shook the room. Then "I Will Survive" followed with its insistent chorus.

"C'mon, let's boogie," RJ insisted as he grabbed Mary Kathleen by the hand and led her to the middle of the floor. Shelley and I broke away and found a quiet corner to talk.

"How's everything with your music?" I asked.

"I'm playing first flute in our school orchestral concert next weekend. And marching band is a blast. We're done for the season." We chatted for a minute or so before the deejay upped the volume.

"Let's dance, okay?" I grabbed Shelley's hand as the first notes of "Funky-town" blasted from the speakers. She beamed and laughed as I twirled her across the floor, her pink sweater inching up to reveal her pale midriff. RJ and I mercilessly teased her about her pink fetish and her omnipresent hair barrettes, but I loved her sweet, girlish way. I related to her innocence and admired her grit. Despite RJ's desire to mold her into a disco princess, she held true to her own sweet style, while on occasion she ditched it removing the barrettes, letting her hair down and revealing her wild red tresses that magnified her beauty.

Okay, I'll admit. I had a crush on Shelley. Not that I was in love with her, it wasn't that kind of crush at all. More that I felt comfortable in her presence, I liked the person she was. She didn't exude a sexual vibe, like Tricia, that felt threatening, or that expected me to act in a traditional male way. Her sweetness and honesty made me feel safe, at home.

When I'd asked and she'd accepted my invitation to my upper-classmen dance in September, I was elated. That night I told her about my desire to cultivate an identity separate from RJ's influence. She admitted to feeling encumbered by his all-encompassing dance talent and told me their partnership was coming to an end. They'd completed their run on *Weekday*

Fever and now that the show was on hiatus, they hardly danced together. RJ's premonition the previous summer was accurate: Shelley was moving beyond silk-polyester and Lycra Spandex. She'd discovered new social circles in high school, mostly centered on her love of music.

I could see Mary Kathleen filling Shelley's seat, the rumble seat, in between RJ's and my triumvirate. I had no doubt she'd offer the possibility of something exciting, different.

While the disco lights of The Lido flashed like camera bulbs, Shelley told me about Philip, a shy guy she'd begun to date in marching band. I nodded my head, happy for her, knowing we'd remain friends even as she ventured on a new path. In our dancing cocoon we beamed and laughed, while the swirl of light, tempo, and rhythm engulfed us. Lost in the music that colored our lives, unaware what the new decade 1980 would bring.

***

I knew I wasn't attracted to Mary Kathleen in the way most guys are to girls. Yes, she was pretty and clever. I liked her strength, the power of her personality, and how we shared a mutual interest in fashion, theatre, and dancing. These were the same passions that bound me to RJ, but without the sex.

When she asked me to her senior Christmas Ball at the Avon Country Club, I eagerly accepted. I donned the same stylish grey herringbone suit I'd worn to other dances that year.

The night of her formal ball Mary Kathleen glided down the staircase in an emerald green velvet off-the-shoulder gown. Her hair swept up in a French twist, she wore a silver pendant around her neck. Mr. and Mrs. Cassidy snapped several pictures of us seated on a plush loveseat in their formal living room, so rarely used it reminded me of a roped-off gallery in a museum.

"This is great," I said, backing my parent's car out of her driveway. "We can stay out all night. Dance until the sun comes up. I've got a car!"

Upon our arrival at the country club a crowd of Magnificat girls lined up with their tuxedo-clad boyfriends for formal photographs.

"Mary Kathleen, don't you look nice. And who's your date?"

"Umm, Jack, meet Jenny, our reigning Student Council President."

"A pleasure," she squeezed my hand. "I like your suit. All the guys are wearing the same old boring black tux. You've got a little personality."

"Thanks," I said as Mary Kathleen pulled me away.

"That girl's a bitch," she said as we headed toward the dance floor. "She's never given me the time of day, until now that I'm here with you. She's nothing but a lousy, soon-to-be Stepford wife."

"MK, give her a break; she's trying to be friendly. Maybe she's turned a corner."

"Knights in White Satin" blared from the deejay booth. I reached for her hand. Her dress and pendant shimmered in the refraction of the chandeliers. My nubby grey herringbone jacket brushed up against her exposed powder white skin. "Now just take your mind off those Stepford wives and their silly boyfriends," I whispered in her ear. She let out a wicked laugh. Other couples watched us – we were the animated ones.

Eerie and hypnotic, the song played on. Time vanished; almost ceased to exist. Spinning, almost sailing, round the floor we lost track of our periphery. I was rehearsing to become the leading man I envisioned I should be, the one I never auditioned for or even wanted.

But I liked Mary Kathleen. I understood her frustration, about not fitting in, wanting to be different from the rest and resenting the pressure to conform, while still trying to make a go of life. I could forgive her impatience. I placed my chin on her solid shoulder. The pull of the song's melody fashioned a soft, gentle curtain protecting us from the hurts and confusion of our lives. For now, we had each other, and that was enough.

***

THE final weeks of 1979 flew by like the pages of a movie magazine with Farrah splashed on the cover and purchased by RJ and me. For months RJ and I had awaited the dawning of an exciting new decade. We were dreamy-eyed teenagers, and we sensed life shifting in a new direction. The next year I'd head to college. RJ's mom gave birth at Christmastime to his sister Charity, the first little girl in a family of four boys. As New Year's Eve approached, we talked about how we might ring in the new decade.

"How about a big party with costumes and music? Something we'll never forget!" RJ said.

"Roller skating," I suggested. "What about roller skating? We can make our own party out on the floor."

Several days later, Mary Kathleen pulled into the driveway and gave her characteristic two toots of the horn. Tonight, just the three of us would roller skate into a new era, a new decade, nobody else on our coattails. With the intense popularity of disco fading, New Year's Eve 1980 sealed the music we loved forever in our memories. Our own Three Musketeers, we headed to the Brook Park Roller Rink where we donned lace up skates and silly party hats ready to ring in the new decade at a roller disco party.

RJ wore his Jordache jeans and a dress shirt, while I sported painter's pants and my favorite hooded sweater. MK, in her sparkling ruby red off-the-shoulder top and tight black spandex pants, set many a guys' tongues a-wagging. Her outrageous sense of style drew attention that we were more than willing to exploit.

At the stroke of midnight confetti fell from the rafters, and we tooted our party favors. The Village People's new release "Ready for the 80's" blasted from the speakers energizing the crowd. I flew around the rink belting the lyrics like I'd discovered my new theme song.

RJ would turn sixteen in two weeks and I seventeen in June. MK was to graduate in the spring. The three of us stood on the threshold of a decade that would see us leave home and grow up. Aware that change was ahead, all we wanted was to enjoy this one happy, carefree night and make it last forever. We skated round and round the rink to the sound of all the last year's beloved hits.

With RJ leading the way, we formed a conga line to acknowledge "We Are Family," cracked the whip releasing our inner divas while "It's Raining Men" poured from the sound system and pleaded "Won't You Take Me to Funkytown" in shoot-the-duck fashion. Donna Summer's "Bad Girls" provided the climax for our evening thanks to the Blender, which brought us to our knees in howls of laughter as we switched skating directions every few minutes going every-which-way.

In between our belly laughs I watched RJ begin to teach MK on skates some of the dances Shelley had learned with him over the last three years. "Slow down," she pleaded. "I'm going to have to take a roller dance class to keep up with you."

***

WHILE RJ continued luring her onto the dance floor, MK and I cemented our friendship in the world of theatre. In March, tryouts for *Once Upon a Mattress* took place. Mr. Molina cast Mary Kathleen and me opposite one another in the supporting roles of Queen Aggravain and the Wizard. When I saw the casting sheet, my heart sunk.

"I can't believe it," I complained. "This role has no singing part, I'm a mute."

"Hon, he's giving you the chance to do a character role. It's a fun part. You'll be able to play off me after all."

"Yeah, but I'm a singer. Do you think he thinks my singing is awful? Oh God, this is depressing."

"How about we look at it as an opportunity?" she said. "You can delve into this role and have another chance for a better role next year. You're only a junior." I wasn't appeased. For several days I thought about quitting the play.

"RJ, this sucks. I think Molina hates me--this is a punishment for sure. Someone told me he'd wanted to cast me in *The Three Musketeers* and was pissed I didn't try out. Doesn't he know I like musicals?"

He reached over and kneaded my shoulder. "Jack, relax, it's not the end of the world. Come here."

I slid over on the couch and rested my head against his chest, the thump of his heart echoing in my ear. He wrapped his arms around me.

"I wanted to let you know I'm going to invite Mary Kathleen to my sophomore dance. Is that okay with you?" RJ asked.

"Sure, why would it matter?"

"Because she was your friend first. I don't want you to think I'm stealing her away."

"No, no, it's fine. Don't worry about it. I'll let you know if something bothers me."

He reached over, brushed back my hair, and kissed me on the lips.

"I'm not sure I'm comfortable with that."

"What do you mean?"

"Shouldn't we try to date girls? I mean, I'm not sure what's happening. I feel guilty when we have sex. I feel awful and I don't like the way I look at you the morning after."

"We don't have to have sex if you don't want to. But I like it."

"I do too, I just don't know what it means."

"Like what, are we gay?" he asked.

My head was spinning. "I don't think I'm gay, I don't identify with any of the gay guys I see. I don't want to be girly and limp-wristed."

"Maybe we just like to have sex with each other."

I leaned into him and took a deep breath.

"It's okay," he said. "Nobody needs to make a decision today."

Relief flooded in. Maybe I just needed more time to meet the right girl. Once I fell in love, everything would work itself out. I would know, she would know. It would feel natural. She would understand me and be patient, and not expect that I fulfill a role. I was sure of it.

And yet no girl made my heart flutter. No girl made me feel out of control. No girl reached into my jock igniting any sort of burning desire. I felt lost. I couldn't see any future besides the one mapped out by my parents, with a wife and children and obligations that stifled and suffocated me. Like a boa constrictor wrapping tighter and tighter around my neck.

***

Mary Kathleen was right. *Once Upon a Mattress* offered me the opportunity to play against type, a great vehicle and challenge for a guy who considered himself first and foremost a male romantic lead. MK and I vowed to chew up the scenery and heighten the comic elements between Queen Aggravain and her loyal accomplice, the wily Wizard. Thanks to a script full of bawdy double entendres we imagined a bubbling, under the surface romance for the overbearing Queen Mother and her nattering right hand consort.

I loved playing opposite MK. Her volcanic reactions on stage pushed me to delve further into my character's dark side. Like disco dancing with RJ, I immersed myself into an entirely new role. I dug deep into the mercurial and scheming persona of my character. I donned the large purple Wizard's cap and robe, all emblazoned with stars and satellites. Disguised behind a long gray beard and mustache, my hunched over body served as counterpoint to Aggravain's haughty posture. For the first time I could imagine what infirmity and old age might feel like.

And in the musical number "Sensitivity," I seized the opportunity to talk-sing a duet, a la Rex Harrison, with the fabulous Mary Kathleen, who'd never ever carried a tune.

"Jesus Christ, I've got to sing a solo," MK confided to me the day after we were cast.

"Hey, you're going to be terrific. The music director will work with you, and I can help."

"I'm freaked. What if I can't do it?"

"Think of it as a challenge, a growth opportunity," I winked, remembering her invaluable advice to me.

Mary Kathleen lost whatever fear she'd accumulated the minute she stepped onto the stage. Her rendition of the song captured the gleeful, manic energy of the arch villainess she loved to play. During performances I'd lock eyes with her as she repeated the opening lines of her solo, the lyrics revealing more than just her character.

"You inspire me," I told her one spring night after the final cast party. "You take risks, and don't really give a damn what people think. I wish I could be more like that."

"Hilovsky, just hang around me a while longer. You'll start doing the same. A lot of girls at Mag's think I'm a loudmouth. I say fuck 'em." She lopped her arm around my shoulders as we walked under a canopy of blossoming magnolia trees.

"Well, you're not what's expected, that's for sure. But I love you for it."

"Oh, honey, that's so sweet." Her blue eyes twinkled, and I leaned in to kiss her under a flickering streetlight. MK sighed and blushed. For a moment my heart fluttered. I was safe in the company of a good friend. Nothing else needed to happen. I was happy with this closeness.

That's what I loved about Mary Kathleen. She was multi-dimensional and complicated: gentle and kind mixed with rage and resentment; elegant and familiar; sweet and sour. She gave me permission to be imperfect, even moody, and she allowed my underbelly to show. Maybe I could bitch and moan a bit, maybe even hiss, right back at the boa constrictor trying to choke me.

Mary Kathleen accepted RJ's invitation to Lakewood High's sophomore dance. During his sophomore year he'd begun to focus more on fashion design and illustration. His final project entailed designing a piece of women's formal wear. So, he crafted a gown for Mary Kathleen to wear to the dance. They met for a fitting, and he gathered her measurements.

Three weeks later, the outfit was complete. Made of black chiffon, the voluptuous bodice featured a white asymmetrical ruffle that climbed over one shoulder while diving underneath the opposite arm. The gown narrowed below the waist with a daring side slit that revealed MK's shapely legs. An upswept hairdo a la Betty Grable and a pair of stiletto heels accentuated her dramatic look. Dressed in a white tuxedo jacket, RJ easily stepped into the role of matinee idol.

"You two are drop-dead glamorous. You're gorgeous!" I exclaimed after seeing the pictures. "Did anyone ask for your autographs?"

"No, but we caused a stir on the dance floor," Mary Kathleen giggled. "RJ spun me, dipped me, and draped me. Thank God my dress didn't pop off with all the seesawing we did."

"Hey, you were marvelous. You didn't blink," RJ responded. "Everyone complimented us on how well we danced together, like we rehearsed. And they thought we made a great looking couple."

I delighted in their growing closeness. Because whatever stirring I felt toward Mary Kathleen wasn't of the romantic kind. I harbored little jealousy for the time they spent together. RJ craved a dance partner, and Mary Kathleen loved the intensity of his attention. Now that Tricia had graduated from high school, Mary Kathleen was the heir apparent.

While they hit the dance floor, I dreamed about a summer of lifeguarding at Lakewood Park and capping my senior year with a plum role in the high school musical. Deep down I wanted to distinguish myself. If only I could convince Molina to take notice and cast me. Determined nothing would get in my way I prepared for the endgame.

Chapter 15

Breaking Away

Me, a budding Perry Mason? Well, my mother thought it was possible. The summer before my senior year I secured a part time internship with a downtown law firm, which I juggled with my poolside duties. Except rather than the criminal law Perry pursued, my firm Sidwell, Sidwell and Barker, specialized in, ho-hum, bankruptcy. Mom encouraged me to explore the law thanks to my godfather Hugh's successful career as a legal executive with a life insurance firm.

For my part, the only thing I liked about the profession was getting dressed up and enjoying the luxury of an air-conditioned office with a glorious view of Lake Erie and Downtown Cleveland. During my lunch hour I'd stroll to the Cleveland Public Library, find an empty patio chair in the outdoor courtyard, unbutton my dress shirt and work on my tan. I much preferred daydreaming in the sun then working inside the law office.

Halfway through July, RJ called. "Hey bucko, where've you been? Wanna go see *The Blue Lagoon* tonight?"

"I'd love to, but I've got plans after lifeguarding. How about later this week?"

His voice sounded disappointed. "Okay, call me and let me know when." I didn't call back. I was busy setting a new course; I had priorities that didn't include RJ.

I spent more and more time with my new friends at the pool. They'd introduced me to alternative music, and we attended concerts headlined by The Police, Blondie, and Hall and Oates. I saw less and less of RJ and the friends from our disco days.

I hoped hanging out with my lifeguard posse would help me create a cooler persona. Dirk, Henry, Scott--they seemed all so relaxed and comfortable in their skin as if no extra effort was required. They were acceptable as they were whereas I felt like I had to prove something, make them like me by being clever. Yes, I had earned the lifesaving certification, but now I had to build a reputation. The certification wasn't enough.

One afternoon in late August, a small girl dove off the diving board. She was a good swimmer but suddenly I read panic in her face as she paddled to the side of the pool. When I saw her begin to struggle, I jumped off the lifeguard stand and reached out with an extended arm to drag her in. Even though she made no cry for help, I had anticipated her need and my simple rescue had prevented her from sinking.

Chills crawled up my back. What if I hadn't been watching? What if I'd been distracted? What might have happened? One of the female lifeguards, Terri, had noticed my maneuver and patted me on the back. My chest swelled that day for I knew that, thanks to my vigilance, I'd made a difference and possibly saved a life. Even though Terri had been the only witness, I knew the truth. I had met the highest standard of any lifeguard.

My confidence bloomed. I felt like a hero who, in just a few seconds, had earned his medal of honor.

Despite my self-assurance, I found it harder to deny my feelings of attraction toward male co-workers, especially Dirk with his sculpted swimmer's build. After swimming lessons, he'd ride the little kids' banana bikes on deck and perform wheelies. During rest breaks he'd cannonball from the high board soaking guards and sunbathers alike. I laughed at his goofy antics, his reckless abandon. I dreamed of feeling that free.

Scott was working his final summer. His clever wit, curly blonde hair, and tan muscular legs drew me to him. He embodied the "surfer dude" ideal I'd dreamed of as a boy. He was the male equivalent of Farrah, only with an even goofier sense of humor.

When Dirk, Scott and I arrived for our afternoon shifts, we crammed into the lifeguard locker room to get ready. "What's up?" a groggy Dirk mumbled as he banged the locker door open to extract his swimsuit. Scott chirped "Mornin'," his bright eyes dancing as if a joke would cannonball off his tongue any second.

I narrowed my focus to their faces to avoid any suspicion as we conversed about swimming lessons, or the weather, or our plans for that weekend. Fleeting glimpses of Dirk's white buttocks or Scott's triangular vanilla tan line aroused me and became a rotating slide show in my brain. But I refused to act on my desire. These guys were my friends, my co-workers, and I struggled not to objectify or to respond to their beauty.

But I couldn't help noticing it-- their bodies and my natural attraction to them. I loved their masculinity, their hair, their muscles, the softness, and hardness that began in one place and ended in another. I began to see my own body as a mirror to theirs. During rest breaks, I swam laps and took pride in my expanding chest, arms, and shoulders. I wanted that kind of body to enjoy for my own pleasure. I looked forward to disrobing with them; to me it was pure and organic, like they were my brothers, yet they weren't. I'd no choice but to shove my desire down.

I'd forced myself to live in denial. Denial that loving other young men was even possible. While I appreciated the beauty of the same sex, I pushed those feelings down into a hidden chamber. I couldn't act as I had with RJ. By doing so I believed that I would poison my life and would forfeit any reasonable future. Not that I even knew how I wanted to move forward in my life.

My seventeen-year-old mind erected a barrier protecting me from even considering same-sex love. I'd grown up disciplined in my studies, disciplined in my piano and voice lessons, and disciplined in my exercise and weight training, running, and swimming. I would discipline myself to not love men. I might appreciate them, even desire them, but I could not, would not, love them. Loving them could only lead to shame, rejection, and loneliness. After all, the only gay men I'd seen in public were effeminate, limp-wristed stereotypes like Billy Crystal on the nighttime adult comedy *Soap*. I wanted the real thing, a man who acted like a man. But I saw no way of getting what I wanted without losing myself in the disapproving eyes of my parents, my religion, and the entire community.

Rather than embracing RJ and holding him close, begging him to help me, I chose to create distance between us. Even though I joined him a week later to see *The Blue Lagoon*, I had made up my mind. The die was cast. Consciously, sub-consciously, I began pushing him further away.

***

THAT fall MK left for Catholic University to major in English. Before she left, she told me her parents planned to get a divorce. "It's kaput, Hilovsky," she said. "My parents are calling it quits. It's over between them." I felt sorry to hear the news knowing with six kids it would cause a big impact.

Meanwhile I pleaded with my mother to allow me to study voice. "This is my dream," I confided to Mom one afternoon en route to my piano lesson. "I want a leading role in the spring musical, but I'm worried the director doesn't think I can sing."

My mother flashed me a look of fierce determination. "Sweetheart, if this is what you want to do, I've heard Koch School of Music is the best. We can set up an appointment to meet one of their instructors and see if they'll work with you."

I'd studied piano at Koch starting in second grade. I knew I could sing but my voice needed polishing. "Let's do it," I said.

Several days later we sat down with Norma Ringali, a mezzo-soprano trained at the Cleveland Institute of Music. She'd sung with opera companies and symphony orchestras. She strode into the room with her dark good looks, pitch-black hair, and forceful voice, like an empress of opera. She was the great hope!

"You've got the makings for an excellent vocal performer," she observed as I sang through the octaves while she accompanied me on the piano. "Now promise me you'll agree to study voice in Italian in addition to singing the pop songs and musical numbers for the plays. This is where you'll build a rich vocal timbre you can carry with you anywhere you go."

I nodded my head and promised I would commit to the Italian while holding firm to the goal of winning my dream part.

"Good, good, now let's start again Eee--Aayy--Ahhh--Ohhh--Uuhhh," and she began to play the scales. I repeated them after her.

Dutifully following her regimen from autumn through late winter, my confidence in my singing ability bloomed.

I memorized Monteverdi and Figaro in tandem with "If Ever I Would Leave You" from *Camelot* and "Try to Remember" from *The Fantasticks*. Then once St. Ignatius announced the spring musical would be *My Fair Lady*, we began rehearsing for my audition, committing to memory the song that would dominate my dreams, waking and sleeping, for three months: "On the Street Where You Live." I'd go to sleep and wake up with the song's preamble floating on my lips, in my imagination, all around me.

Like a love letter, I'd sing the rest of the song before bedtime every night. Drunk with the spirit of romance; the spirit of the leading man on stage, and in life, I wanted to become. I'd played the Tin Man in *The Wizard of Oz*, Prince Charming in *Snow White*, the White Rabbit in *Alice in Wonderland*. Those were all children's roles in children's plays. I'd weathered the supporting roles at Ignatius: the arrogant party boy Reggie in *Where's Charlie?* and the scheming Wizard in *Once Upon a Mattress*. I had no interest in playing the pompous, persnickety Professor Henry Higgins. But the role of the young and charming Freddy Eynsford-Hill? That's what I prayed for every night; that's what I dreamed of.

RJ continued to labor on his portfolio. He'd sit for hours at his drawing board and couldn't imagine a more enjoyable way of whiling away the hours: alone in solitude with his creative work. I dashed in the opposite direction. Active and on the run, keeping myself busy. Unsure of my calling, what sort of profession I might want to pursue, I felt like I was running on borrowed time, clinging to the familiar. I'd magnified our differences to separate us. Despite convincing Mom to let me take voice lessons in hopes of nabbing a lead role in the spring musical at St. Ignatius, I still pegged RJ the artist and me the jock.

One rainy Saturday he called. I hadn't seen him since *The Blue Lagoon* last summer. "Hey, wanna go to the movies this afternoon?" he said. "I got my license so I can pick you up, okay?"

We drove to a matinee showing of *The Shining*. It was like old times all over again. We devoured buttered popcorn and dissected red licorice. We screamed when Jack Nicholson bellowed, "Here's Johnny!" We jumped at the sight of the murderous twins and their Redrum admonitions. And the hair on our necks stood at attention during the final chase scene in the snow-strewn labyrinth.

Exiting the theatre, RJ let out a huge sigh. "Oh, my God. My heart's thumping a mile a minute. Talk about a freak show." Still quaking in my boots from the last image, where Nicholson's face emerges in a photograph on the wall from 50 years earlier, I responded, "That movie scared the shit out of me."

Afterward we drove to a nearby TGI Friday's restaurant. "I don't think I've felt so wound up in a long time," RJ said still clutching his chest. "I'm not a fan of Jack Nicholson, but I'll give him credit. He was one scary madman."

I took a deep breath. "If there's a sequel, I'm not going."

The fries, cheeseburgers and chocolate shakes arrived on a large serving tray delivered by a blue-eyed waiter who flashed his big smile and winked at me.

"He liked you, if you didn't notice."

"You don't miss a beat, do you? A friendly wink doesn't mean a thing… does it?"

"Jack, why don't you own up to the fact you notice other guys? It's okay, you don't have to push it away or hide it from me."

"Hey, I thought we were going to let that topic rest."

"You've been avoiding me, trying to pretend you aren't, but I'm not thick. Why don't you fess up to what's on your mind? What's really been bugging you?"

"God, do we have to get into a deep heavy conversation?" I lowered my voice. "Can't we keep it light? We just saw an intense movie."

"Yeah, and like Jack Nicholson, reality isn't looking so pretty. It's easier to keep on running, lifting weights, or performing some other physical fitness routine to distract yourself."

"I don't have a choice," I shouted. A long uncomfortable silence sat between us.

I whispered, "I've got to go to college. They've already said if it's not in Cleveland, they're not going to pay for it. Can you imagine if I told them what I'm thinking, what I'm feeling?" My heart sank further into my stomach.

"Jack, you don't have to tell your parents anything. Maybe they already know. Don't you think when your dad barreled into your bedroom, he suspected something was happening between the two of us? That he suspected I was bonking you."

"No." I paused looking behind me. "Maybe. I don't know." Tears flooded my eyes.

"But he almost caught us having sex. If you hadn't pushed me away, he might have."

"Shhhh--what if someone hears us. What if we know someone here?"

"Suit yourself," RJ interrupted. "You've got to be true to yourself, otherwise you'll never find true happiness. Maybe watching *The Shining* again will scare some sense into you or you'll find the courage you think you're lacking. Like I said, I've never cared much for Jack Nicholson, but I went anyway, to be with you." Tossing his napkin along with a twenty-dollar bill on the table, he got up and left.

I sat there with my head in my hands before standing to pay the bill. A light rain soaked my jacket while I walked the 20 minutes home. The cold, wet autumn winds, as unwelcoming as the suffocating snow-bound hotel featured in the film, had begun to blow. And I felt like I was headed into a lonely, wet desert, unsure of everything that senior year demanded from me.

CHAPTER 16

Do You Know Where You're Going

My mother dug the wooden spoons into the bowl and began tossing the green salad. Outside the window a few desperate leaves still clung to the bare trees, the countdown to Thanksgiving only a few weeks away. "Sweetheart, have you made a decision yet? Your father and I wondered which college you might be leaning towards?"

Stone-faced I sat at the kitchen table between the two of them, Sunday dinner surrounding us. Every other weekend, Dad liked to broil T-bone steaks, which also included the usual baked potato and overdone broccoli.

"How's the steak, is it cooked through?" Dad inquired as he dug into the charbroiled slab on his own plate. He was always worried about under-cooking meat, and as a result nearly cremated it.

"Delicious, Dad," I responded, cutting into the well-done flank. "I don't mind a little pink."

I continued. "If I choose Baldwin Wallace College, I don't...."

"Oh, honey, that's perfect you can live at home."

"Mom, what if I don't want to live at home?"

"Well, the school is only 10 minutes away, darling," she picked at her salad rearranging the tomatoes. "Don't you think it would be foolish to pay all that money for room and board when you could have your own room, home-cooked meals, and laundry privileges here at home?

"I don't care about the extra money. I think part of the college experience is moving away and becoming independent."

"Well, honey, you can attend any college you want to attend as long as it's right here in Cleveland. We don't want you getting involved with the riff-raff or brainwashed into a cult."

I slammed my fork down on the table. Silence. *Good God, I was the perfect son. No trouble with the police, or drugs and alcohol. Why couldn't they let go?* Mom flashed an innocent smile. My jaw tightened.

"If you go to Cleveland State, you could commute with me on the Rapid," my father added. "We could come home together at the end of the day, like last summer when you worked at the law firm."

I took a bite of the steak and swallowed hard. "Okay, I appreciate your wanting to help, but I'm gonna make the decision on my own. In fact, I'm changing my first choice from Baldwin Wallace to John Carroll University. You know why?"

My mother looked at me confused across the table. "Why dear?"

"Because I want to live as far away as possible, and it's my decision." I could feel my hand trembling, my blood pressure rising.

"And," I added turning to my father, "I'm not going to commute on the bus or transit. I don't want to travel cross-town. I want to live in the dorms with a roommate."

"Son, are you sure you're making the right decision? Wouldn't it be better to save the cost of room and board like your mother suggested?" He bit into his burnt steak.

"It's the right decision. I can come and go as I please. I'm not liable to anyone. I don't have to tell you where I'm going, or when I'll be back…"

My body felt red hot, and I got up from the table to clean the dishes. As we cleared the plates, I turned to my father, our faces a breath apart.

"Look, Dad. You know I'm not a troublemaker. I've never done anything to let you down. Can't you just trust me a little?"

He reached out to touch my shoulder, but I pulled away. Then he shook his head, that full head of silver-gray hair, and looked me straight in the eye. "You do what you want, son. We may not agree with you, but it's your decision."

I dumped the dirty dishes, pots and pans in the sink and began scrubbing them.

Of course, I didn't have a clue how to apply, even though the college admissions office mailed the instructions. Like most big-ticket purchases, my parents believed in shared responsibility. They'd contribute half the cost of my education, so I'd need to take out loans for the rest of the tuition, room, and board. I never challenged their stipulation I must attend college in Cleveland, never sought out scholarships or grants for out of state schools, failed to inquire about opportunities outside the box of my family's comfort zone. Part of me wanted to escape, another part feared leaving home and the safety of the familiar.

But Mary Kathleen had gone before me, and I knew next year RJ would take flight from Cleveland to pursue his dreams in New York. I needed to leap from the nest, now or never. My future depended on it. If I only had a clue how to steer my ship, where I should go, what I should do, what I even really wanted to study. I had no idea how to be and live in the wider world, a world that increasingly felt pressured and antagonistic. Instead, a gray, indistinguishable cloud blocked my vision. I couldn't see my future. And it scared me.

I washed the last dish, placed it in the rack, and beelined to my bedroom. Behind closed doors, I pulled out my Panasonic tape recorder, the one on which I'd sang "Don't Go Breaking My Heart" with Philippa and inserted the tape cassette. In preparation for my audition for *My Fair Lady,* Miss Ringali had recorded a rehearsal tape. Her encouraging words, travelling through my headset, served as a prelude to my own voice singing "On the Street Where You Live." Lost in the music, I dreamed of the role of Freddy Eynsford-Hill, one of the male romantic leads, and about tomorrow and tryouts soon to come.

***

DESPITE the excitement of the musical, as senior year accelerated, I faced a pressing decision: where to attend college. I identified three options I wanted to explore and scheduled visits in January.

First, there was Baldwin-Wallace College, known as BW. It was a 15-minute drive from home tucked into a small-town, bucolic setting. BW offered both a well-regarded theatre department and a top-notch business school. But I hesitated. Despite the charming atmosphere it felt too close to home and a good number of the student body commuted. I wanted to explore my independence.

Next, I visited Case-Western Reserve University (CWRU), which offered a more urban setting in the cultural hub of downtown's University Circle. Brilliant minds in math, science, and law wandered the campus, many students looked like geeks, bookworms. Surrounded by cement buildings that reminded me of Cold War era bomb shelters, CWRU didn't offer the pleasant milieu I'd always dreamed college would provide. I crossed the school off my list.

My last, best hope was JCU, John Carroll University, on Cleveland's east side near Shaker Heights. Forty minutes from home by car, the suburban Jesuit school sat on a sixty-acre campus surrounded by trees and open space. I was 3 blocks away when I first saw the handsome, landmark Grasselli Tower, which beckoned like a lighthouse. A feeling of history pervaded the place with brick dormitories encircling a sprawling quad perfect for playing Frisbee and touch football. Overnight bag in hand I arrived on a Friday evening in the purple dusk.

On the front steps of ivy-covered Pacelli Hall a group of upper classmen, our hosts for the weekend, awaited me and other visiting high school seniors. Emily, a student from Detroit, asked my name, glanced at her clipboard, and checked me off her list. "You made it all the way from the West Side?" she teased. My heart thumped with nervous anticipation; my only response was to nod and shake her outstretched hand.

She reminded me of a character from *The Official Preppy Handbook*, a petite brunette wrapped in a green and black plaid kilt with knee high socks and a crisp, white Peter Pan collar shirt. The penny loafers only accentuated the Girl Scout image. Over the past year, I'd been cultivating my own look, largely influenced by the cool, popular guys in my senior year of high school. With my button-down blue and green plaid shirt, bone-color cords, and Docksider boat shoes, I felt right at home. I fit.

Emily led me on a twilight tour of the campus. "You'll like it here," she said. "We have a commuter population, but the school attracts kids from all over: Pittsburgh, Detroit, and Chicago, and other places in the Midwest. It's quiet during the week when everyone studies but on the weekends we party hard." I could hear Pink Floyd blaring from a dorm room across the quad, and students were milling outside the chapel.

She added, "The Student Union throws mixers, and we're a popular stop for popular touring bands. Two years ago, Springsteen came. Last year we hosted Dave Matthews." Emily was trying to impress me with these big name draws, but I had no interest in hard rock. After all, RJ had introduced me to the joy of disco, which despite its fading fortunes, still occupied prized territory in my heart.

Her running commentary continued. "There's also lots of fraternities and sororities, if you're into that kind of scene." She smiled as if she knew I was on the verge of making a big decision, and she was right.

I looked up at the warm glow emanating from the resident dorms and tried to imagine myself settled in one. A feeling of awe, and fear, overcame me. Could it be true I might have the opportunity to live on my own here, independent, and free of parental influence? Could I handle college life with all its academic and social pressures? And what about girls? How would that fit into my puzzle after four years at an all-boys' Catholic school?

"What do you think?"

I shrugged. "I like the feeling of being away from home. Kind of exciting, you know."

After the short tour, which included the chapel, cafeteria, and gym, we headed back to her dorm. She introduced me to her circle of friends--all juniors--who looked to me like they were well-adjusted in their college world. I wanted to be that comfortable as a college student too!

One guy, David, a marketing major with ruddy complexion and curly blonde hair, quipped, "Watch out for the preying female coeds. They're hunting for their MRS degree." He snickered at his own joke. Emily rolled her eyes. "I'm sorry to say, good old Dave will be your host this weekend. Better be careful about those roving females," she winked.

While I knew they meant well with their good-natured teasing, I wondered if anyone from JCU even had the courage to be outwardly gay? Maybe in the theatre department, I thought, but JCU's theatre program was not of the same caliber as Baldwin Wallace's. Even thinking about majoring in theatre felt like a huge risk. How would I make a living? I could hear Dad saying that out loud.

I swallowed hard and resolved above all else that I must fit in. I had to avoid dropping any hints that I might be different because I found guys attractive.

I shared a bunk with Dave, a mild snorer, and woke early the next morning to further explore the campus on my own. The soft, glowing sunrise and early morning quiet helped sooth my nerves. I smiled when I heard the birds chirping – as if to serenade me.

The campus felt like a New England prep school. I passed by small neighborhood shopping districts. Restaurants and movie theatres dotted the landscape.

I could walk to all these places. This is cool. This feels like it might be my place.

I arrived back at the old-fashioned bell tower. The benches scattered across the campus appeared to say *Come. Rest here.* I could hear them whisper *Stay awhile.* I sat on one and dreamed about what it might be like to experience this beautiful setting every day. I inhaled the fresh morning air, the smell of evergreens, and closed my eyes to let happy college possibilities flood my imagination.

Dave invited me to attend a school basketball game that evening, and then we headed to Pacelli for a party. I observed more friendly kilt-skirted girls, kegs, and guys who acted uptight and serious until they chugged a beer or two. Despite his corny sense of humor, my host Dave sang the praises of JCU. "Excellent education, and the girls are cute. You don't have to marry them if you don't want." *Here we go again*, I thought. He laughed and gave me a gentle jab in the ribs.

I wondered about Dave's frequent comments about girls. Was he putting on an act? Was he gay? Was there something about me, my quiet, gentle demeanor that made him think I was gay? I felt a little guarded and decided to let his jokes go without comment. I smiled and nodded.

On Sunday after I said my goodbyes to Dave and Emily, I drove home musing about my visit. Considering the limited choices my parents gave me, I was convinced JCU was my best option for getting far enough away from the home nest. I could experience a whole new world. More distant locales would beckon once I graduated; for now, I liked the intimacy of the campus with its handsome Gothic architecture. I envisioned sharing a dorm with a college roommate; we'd become great friends and knock around campus together. And I could still visit home if I got the urge. I had made my decision. I applied to John Carroll with Baldwin Wallace College my backup choice. I crossed my fingers and waited.

Three weeks later I received an acceptance letter from John Carroll with the offer of a small scholarship to offset the annual $6000 tuition. I immediately responded that I looked forward to attending in the fall. I called Baldwin Wallace to let them know of my decision; they were unable to match the scholarship John Carroll offered.

A door had swung open. I now had a direction, a port of call.

CHAPTER 17

The Audition

IN FEBRUARY MR. Molina posted an audition sheet for *My Fair Lady*. For three months I'd prepared my solo. With a stomach full of butterflies floating up my throat I took a deep breath and tried to relax. When Molina called my name, I took my place on center stage under the bright spotlight of the school cafeteria, our makeshift auditorium.

Sprawled on top of a lunch table, he lit a cigarette. Smoky plumes curled like a halo circling his head.

"Okay, Hilovsky, you can begin anytime," he nodded, scratching his disheveled salt and pepper hair, and pasting a nonchalant smile on his face.

The accompanist winked at me and started to play.

My mouth opened wide, and a rich, hesitant baritone emerged. *"I have often walked. Down this street before...."* Like a melodious river the lyrics resounded in the near-empty auditorium. I completed the introductory verse and continued. I could feel my heart opening, sailing forward, and all I could sense, notice, feel, understand is that the words meant something. I'd reshaped them to make my own love song. And the memory of Mary Kathleen last year performing with me on this stage cheered me on.

Everything disappeared except for her exuberant face, a shadowy mirage, rooting for me.

"Nail it, Hilovsky," she whispered. "Go for it, goddammit!" I'd reached the core truth, one that contained my hidden secret. *I wanted to be a performer. An actor.* Make communion with the stage lights, the nicotine halo, and the rush of that melodious river. *"Let the time go by. I don't care if I...."* I dove for the final note and reached it. *"Can't be here on the street where you live."*

Breathless, I stopped. Quiet. Bright lights and ringlets of smoke circled the stage. My heart pounded, jubilant. A few students clapped and then quiet resumed.

"Thank you. Mr. Hilovsky. Lovely tryout," Mr. Molina announced in a monotone voice. "We'll post the casting results tomorrow."

***

The next morning, I couldn't contain my anticipation and made a beeline to Molina's office before classes started. Scaling the six flights of stairs of the Ignatius Administration building my heart matched the quickening pace of my stride as I rounded the corner of the hallway to his office. When I reached the door, there was no piece of paper, no cast list posted. "All right, no news is good news," I told myself. I turned only to come face to face with him.

"Good morning," he said. "I suppose you've come to see the results from auditions yesterday. Congratulations, you've been cast."

My face lit up. "Wow, thanks, that's great news!" Like an eager child about to unwrap his Christmas gift, I watched him tape the type-written sheet to his door.

Then he turned to me and said, "Rehearsals start Monday. I'll see you then." He smiled and walked away.

I stared at the sheet. At the top listed in big black letters were the two leads: Henry Higgins and Eliza Dolittle to be played by Benjamin Caine, football player and student council President, and Maria Valmont, the beautiful soprano featured in last year's *Once Upon a Mattress*. My eyes ran down the list until landing on Freddy Eynsford-Hill. I looked for my name, only to discover an imposter's: Tim Freeman's. A frickin' soccer player!

I swallowed, and it was all I could do to keep my heart from spiraling down six stories into the dark underground of the building's basement. Betrayal. He cast someone else. He congratulated me but cast someone else in my role. The role I invested six months of my life to train for, that I coveted since last September, was given to a soccer player. Gone, into thin air. Whatever made me think I could've outsmarted Molina, the bastard!

I scanned the sheet. My eyes traveled to the bottom of the page. There sat my name under Chorus/ Cockney Men. I didn't even warrant a character name--only listed as one of the generic street people.

Tears burned down my face as I descended the stairs and emerged into the blinding morning sun. As I crossed the quad, cold air pummeled my lungs. Still February, still winter in Cleveland.

Anger infiltrated every pore of my being, a rage my tears failed to quell. How could this happen? I'd wanted Freddy, I'd dedicated myself to studying voice with hopes I'd prove I could sing better than anyone else on that stage. My efforts weren't enough for Molina. I'd failed to impress him. I never had a chance in the first place, competing against the popular crowd, the goddamn jocks, like Benjamin and Tim. They used theatre to enhance their college application and impress the chancellors at Notre Dame or Harvard with their well-rounded extra-curricular achievements. Big whoop; they could do more than chase a ball down the field or run a few miles in no time flat.

The unfairness, the injustice, infiltrated my stomach like acid rain. Freddy was my role. My part. I found an outdoor bench and plopped down head in my hands. I didn't know where to go, what to do.

I thought about the sacrifice I'd made and considered throwing in the towel, quitting the play. I'd wasted so much time, only to fail. Then from across the quad ambled Mick Toscavich, a smile on his face, light as a feather floating in the air. He sat down on the bench and gave me a nudge. "Hey, we made it, we're both Cockneys in the Chorus. I saw the list. Good for us."

My foot crushed loose gravel beneath my feet. "Yeah, yippee for us. I thought I had a real chance at one of the lead roles. But I'm stuck in the background again."

"Hey, man, I wanted a meaty part too," Mick chimed in. "If not Higgins, I would've loved to play his sidekick Pickering. But this wasn't our year." He sighed looking over his shoulder. "Let's face it. Molina's got ideas about casting before he even holds auditions. He picks the show based on his talent and jocks are part of the mix. This year Benjamin and Tim were in the running. Fair or not, we may as well make the best of it."

I kicked some loose stones. "Yeah, well I think it sucks."

"We can make these roles something more. Build them into flesh and blood characters. Ever heard of a drooling, lecherous Cockney?" he joked.

I smiled and bit my tongue. "You're a dope, Toscavich."

"A persistent dope," Mick countered. "One of these days, you'll find yourself in the lead role. Don't give up that easy." He nudged my shoulder again, and we headed to first period.

***

By early February rehearsals for *My Fair Lady* were in full swing. Denny, Don, Mick, and I comprised the Cockney quartet. We studied after school with an exacting dialect coach who taught us how to sing with a proper Cockney accent. We needed to sound as convincing as possible when we accompanied Eliza Doolittle on "Wouldn't It Be Loverly" and her dustman dad Alfred in the barn-busting "Get Me to the Church on Time."

I convinced my grade school friend Philippa, now at an all-girls' high school, to audition. She was cast in the chorus too along with several other young women I knew from previous Ignatius plays. In between scenes Don, Denny, and Mick would crack jokes. Stealing a line from the Ascot Gavotte scene, Don would shout "Move your bloomin' arse," whenever he saw me in the crowded hallways. Philippa howled with laughter.

Unstoppable Mick would parrot Eliza, "I'm a good girl I am." The Cockney accent became our adopted M.O.: a way to make fun and joke around and blow off steam from a stressful day while losing ourselves in the creative swirl. At times I missed RJ--his sarcastic wit, and especially the way I could talk with him about anything--but I avoided picking up the phone to call. I made this show--this cast--my everything while anticipating high school graduation and a new life at JCU. RJ's charisma wouldn't overpower me this time. I wanted my own star to rise and shine.

A month into rehearsals for *My Fair Lady*, Marvin, a junior and new chorus member, and his friend Hope, also a junior from a neighboring Catholic girls' school, burst into my world. Little did I know Marvin would intersect my life in the future while Hope would play her own mesmerizing role.

Knee-deep in getting fitted for costumes, Marvin turned to me and stuck out his hand. "W-w-what's your name?" he stuttered. "I'm M-M-Marvin." Dressed in a pink button-down oxford cloth shirt, navy blue cords, and suede buck shoes, he cut a meticulous, slim figure. Despite his snappy dressing I felt sorry for him, that he couldn't stop sounding like a scratched record repeating himself over and over. I also in a small way related to him, recalling how the acne on my face made me feel self-conscious, and how a stutter could draw just as much attention as an unsightly facial blemish.

"D-d-did you hear about Mr. N-Novak?" he asked with an all-knowing, mischievous grin on his face. George Novak, a red-faced, heavyset man who wore loud blazers and served as assistant coach of the football team, taught me sophomore year geometry. "H-h-he invites football players back to his house for dinner, gets them drunk, and challenges them to wrestling matches in their underwear." Marvin snickered as he relayed this tidbit of hearsay shortly after our first meeting.

No fan of the boisterous Mr. Novak, I laughed along with Marvin. When it came to gossip, who didn't like hearing dirt on an intimidating teacher who took pleasure in flunking students when they failed his difficult exams then chided them for it in front of their classmates?

"Let's call him 'All Hands on Deck' Novak," Marvin quipped. I overheard him ridicule several other classmates behind their backs calling them "losers" because their style of dress didn't match up to his own.

Marvin befriended two other juniors involved with the play that I didn't know--Dylan and Luke, both on the swim team. One thing I did know is I was attracted to them too. Dylan sported cute freckles on his dimply face, gorgeous blue eyes, and a tight swimmer's build, while Luke, lean and lanky with a square jaw, reminded me of a teenage Christopher Reeve, the late 1970's Superman.

I would have welcomed getting to know Dylan better since he was gentle and kept to himself other than the moments he'd steal a glance at me with those soulful blue eyes and long lashes. Philippa struck up a conversation with him and soon discovered they shared similar musical tastes. I imagined he and I might have more in common than swimming and musical theatre. Observing him play the clarinet in the pit orchestra, I'd fantasized about making out with him, though I didn't tell Philippa, who also had a crush on him. Dylan appeared less confident, more vulnerable, and shyer than RJ.

Marvin often got bossy with Dylan, interrupting our conversations with his constant stutter sounding like the rat-a-tat-tat of a machine gun. During rehearsal breaks I felt uncomfortable approaching Dylan for fear Marvin might resent it and start dishing dirt about me. Despite all the confusion about myself, and with little more than a gut feeling, I'd begun to surmise not only Dylan, but Marvin too was gay.

But Marvin's determination to introduce me to this girl who worshipped Elvis Costello broke through my ironclad reserve. And while wary of his motives I had to admit he had a way of making everything seem more thrilling by virtue of exaggeration.

"She's here, you g-g-gotta meet her. You g-g-gotta meet Hope." Marvin's hands were all aflutter, which they almost always were when he had something exciting to report.

I sat up and snapped to attention. He had told me about his friend from St. Augustine Academy, who might be helping with makeup and costuming during the run of the show. His green eyes lit up in wonder when he had described her: "She dresses alternative and is devoted to Elvis Costello. She's a b-b-blast."

"J-j-jack, meet H-h-Hope." There she stood in the green room, right behind him, carrying a large black makeup case that looked like my father's toolbox.

I first noticed her long and lean figure, athletic yet feminine, in a white linen blouse and short denim skirt, a heather green sweater slung over her shoulders. Her chocolate brown hair fell to the nape of her neck in springy waves that curled forward. Her electric brown eyes met mine.

I was speechless, and just kept smiling. She didn't look that alternative to me, just preppy in a "not trying too hard" sort of way. I wasn't sure why Marvin had singled me out to meet Hope, although I suspected he was showing her off to everyone, as if she were a badge of honor.

"H-h-hi!" I stuttered in a poor attempt to avoid tripping over my words.

A flip smile lit up her face. "Hey, where's the dressing room? I've got my brush and plenty of powder. I'm ready to go."

"There is no formal dressing room, we're in it," I blushed throwing my hands up in the air and rolling my eyes. "I'm willing to be your first experiment. I'm a Cockney so I could use some ash and a smidge of color on the cheeks. After all, I'm back on the bottle," I joked, winking at her.

She giggled while tucking her wavy curls behind her ears, which caused my heart to flutter like a butterfly poised for flight. Then she sat me down in a well-lit corner of the room. I took a breath and tried not to stare.

"Well, let's look at you. I've no problem wallowing in the mud and dirt of the lower classes." She took out her brush and started applying a light foundation. I observed her artful concentration and decided I liked this girl. She was both clever and distinct, yet not caught up in her prettiness.

"Marvin tells me you like Costello," I said.

Her brown eyes met mine again and slam, we connected. "Yeah, he's fantastic. But so are the Talking Heads. I like the British." She let out a girlish chuckle. I looked down and her metallic flats, which matched her glittering fingernail polish, caught my attention. My eyes followed her long, coltish legs enveloped in white hose as she leaned over her makeup box, rustling around for an eyeliner pencil. I tried to stay cool, but she drew me like a magnet--her style of dress, her vibe--made my heartbeat race.

She applied some dark circles under my eyes and a smudge of red on my nose and cheeks, which she skillfully blended. "I think you're about ready for your close-up, Mick," she whispered with a bolt of confidence. She lowered a mirror in front of me to reveal the transformation.

"Kinda looks like Jagger, doesn't it?" she said with a puff of pride.

I nodded and looked into her all-knowing eyes, detecting a hint of vulnerability. This girl intrigued me. She'd cast her spell.

CHAPTER 18

High School Musical

With opening night for *My Fair Lady* fast approaching my excitement grew by leaps and bounds. The majority of the first act, the Cockneys were outfitted in ragged shirts and breeches. For the second act, which opened with the Ascot Gavotte, costumes got brighter and more dramatic, accented in black, white, and red with a hint of pastels. The sets and backdrop curtains recreated mid-20th Century London. And the gorgeous, funny, romantic score swept us all off our feet. This would be the most accomplished spring musical St. Ignatius ever presented!

After the first dress rehearsal the supporting cast headed to Heck's Café for a burger and late-night gossip. We laughed about how the male lead, Benjamin Caine, had taken to scribbling his lines on his wrist.

"He constantly looks like he's checking his watch for the time," Denny blurted taking a chomp out of his burger.

"Hey, remember," Mick chimed in, "our success depends on Benjamin's success. If his Henry Higgins flops, so does the play. We should do more to support him."

"What do you m-m-mean?" said Marvin. "He's a football player not an actor. Anyone could do better."

"Cut the guy a break," I said. "He's doing the best he can. Molina encouraged him to audition and gave him a great opportunity. At least he's trying." Marvin's undermining was beginning to irk me more and more.

At rehearsals, Hope continued to show up with her makeup kit in tow clothed in her latest preppy-punk look. Hair pulled back in a chignon, she powdered all the Cockneys before giving us a dash of red on the lips and cheeks and some dirt smudged on our brow. She'd now and then assist Maria who played Eliza in her multiple costume changes.

Observing Hope from a distance made my heart dance to a staccato beat. While Mary Kathleen, with her dramatic flair and love of the spotlight, reminded me of the upstart kid-sister I never had, I was smitten with the mystery of this new girl. I wanted a part of her: her effervescence, her confidence, her way of embracing the world as a gigantic playground to explore. All these qualities enamored me. In her denim miniskirts and troubadour blouses, Hope cut an impressive figure among the other girls on the stage and crew. Her style stood unique. When my gaze lingered too long, her eyes met mine in mid-glance.

"Some people consider staring rude."

"What if it's meant as a compliment?"

"Well, you're giving me a lot of compliments lately," she chuckled before turning away to complete a makeup job.

Her quick wittedness, like Mary Kathleen's, made me smile and find her even more appealing. That combined with her embrace of all things new, especially music.

When she discovered my love for disco, she jumped into the fray. "The Bee-Gees and Donna Summer are so yesterday," she pontificated. "A new sound's arriving." She invited me for a spin in her white Jetta so she could play me a tune from *The Clash* cassette tape.

"All right, Miss Know-It-All, you need to tell me what will replace disco once it goes away. Is there a grand scheme awaiting in the wings?"

Hope smiled. "New Wave. It's already here. Blondie, Elvis Costello, have you heard of the Eurythmics, and Boy George and Culture Club? If you haven't, their wave is crashing on British shores."

"But," she said, "there will always be the King."

"What do you mean? Elvis is dead."

"No, silly, not Elvis."

She hopped out of the car and began playing a game of Charades. With unmatched zeal she cavorted in front of me her tongue drooping out of her mouth and hands glued to her hips, doing the most hypnotic, God-awful impersonation of Mick Jagger I had ever seen.

"Love him," she said. "Worship the ground he walks on."

***

CONSUMED by my infatuation with Hope, I'd all but forgotten RJ since last fall when we saw *The Shining*. I had allowed myself to put him aside, to immerse myself in greater distractions, convince myself if I found the right girl, I could be straight. And now with the arrival of Hope I felt a kind of heart-stirring excitement and possibility. Hope's spell enveloped me in its hypnotic bubble. Maybe the last four years with RJ didn't really mean that much after all. Maybe it had all been an experiment that I would somehow outgrow.

I worshipped everything about Hope: her humor, intelligence, fashion sense and inimitable style. But I was also scared about what that meant for me. How do you love a girl? Is it the same as loving a boy? And when do you get more intimate with someone you like? Mom had warned me about pre-marital sex; she'd spoken harshly of cousins who got pregnant without being married. That was a cause for shame and embarrassment in our family, at least in Mom's eyes. But I didn't need to worry about pregnancy with RJ, much less the whole notion of premarital complications. I liked sex, but was I in love with him? And what about Hope? Was I in love with her? Maybe I was confusing love and lust and infatuation. So far there was no reason to worry.

"Hey, you, I've got another song for you." Hope pulled up in her White Jetta to pick me up for our final dress rehearsal. "Y-y-you're gonna love this," Marvin said from the passenger seat, Ray-Bans perched on his head. She cranked up the radio and rolled down the windows. Guitars and bass and drums burst forth in a melodic explosion, a bevy of female voices harmonizing in the background.

Hush my dar~ling, don't you cry, qui~et, angel, forget their lies. Zipping out of the driveway, we sped down Story Road. Hope shifted into second gear, Marvin on her right, and me stretched out behind them. The peaches and cream of her shampoo captivated my nose.

"Okay, they're new, right?"

"Our lips are s-sealed," Marvin joked.

The lyrics grew darker in tone: *Spread~ing rumors, so far from true, dragged up from the underworld, just like some precious pearl.*

I closed my eyes and relaxed while the wind whistled through my hair. I could barely decipher Marvin expounding some story about Dylan and Luke on the swim team, but all his words got blurred by the breeze and the blare of a hot new girl band called The Go-Go's.

***

OUR production of *My Fair Lady* opened on April 7, 1981. Pins and needles excitement flooded my veins as I pulled on my mussed up Cockney britches and plopped on my cap. We'd spent three months making this show the best it could be, now the grand finale of my senior year.

Springtime was in the air. An entire year had come and gone since sharing the stage with Mary Kathleen in *Once Upon a Mattress*. I'd come to accept my lot in the chorus with my Cockney pals; after all, Denny, Don, and Mick got the shaft and lost out on lead roles too. On the upside my old friend Philippa and I had a chance to spend more time together thanks to the countless rehearsals leading up to opening night. In addition to our singing in the chorus, we each had a character role: I in the Cockney quartet and she one of the chambermaids.

Anticipation, like the scent of buttered popcorn at the refreshment counter, wafted through the air. We opened with the elegant overture, followed by "Wouldn't It Be Loverly" and soon thereafter the bawdy "Get Me to the Church on Time." The audience went wild.

The hubbub during intermission bubbled as we hurriedly changed into our costumes for the opening number of the second act, the Ascot Gavotte. While the boys donned morning coats, ascots and top hats, the girls slipped into corseted gowns and showy bonnets. Last-minute nerves abounded during the backstage rush.

Hope peeked from behind the curtain and winked at me. "We need to give you a little more powder, big guy," she said. "Your face looks a bit shiny." She dabbed the applicator on my forehead, cheeks, and nose then blended my lips.

"Will you always be my makeup artist?" I sighed with an adoring expression.

"You'll have to start paying me a retainer," she joked.

Yes, her lighthearted one-liners, like tennis lobs to my side of the court, were all I needed to take the bait. Hope was a mystery. But I resolved that I would solve her. She shared similarities with Mary Kathleen but minus the volcanic anger at the world. I wanted to reach for Hope but every time I took a step closer, she stepped back.

"Now you're perfect," she said patting my cheek before disappearing. The overture for the second act with its piercing strings and rapid-fire trumpets had begun.

The curtain opened on a pickle-faced parade of spectators dressed to the hilt for a day at the horse races. When everything is brought to a halt following Eliza screeching at the horse to "move your blooming' arse," the audience succumbed to howls of delight.

Then Tim Freeman, the soccer player Molina had cast as Freddy emerged on stage in a dapper gray tux and top hat. When I saw him a gnawing sting squeezed my insides. But I watched from the curtain as he began to sing my song, "On the Street Where You Live." Tim's shy face and blue eyes gleamed as the tender words trickled from his thin, vibrating lips. His voice captured the tune's emotional core and scaled the first peak. He continued, strolling across the stage, more confident and relaxed as he approached the final crescendo. For a moment he caught my eye before I turned away. His voice crested, and he slammed it home.

The audience roared its approval. I bit my lip. It was lovely indeed. Maybe the role had gone to the right person after all.

CHAPTER 19

The Prom/Playing the Part

As THE DAYS ticked down to senior prom Denny, Mick, Don, and I decided our quartet would attend as a group: Denny asked Petra, the yearbook editor from St. Joseph all-girls' school, Mick escorted my childhood friend Phillipa, and Don brought Lisa, a *My Fair Lady* chorus member from Beaumont, another girl's school.

I'd invited Mary Kathleen, home from D.C. for summer break, to join me. I informed her I planned to ditch my gray herringbone suit, worn to her Christmas Ball, for an ivory tuxedo. When she greeted me on her front doorstep dressed in a lace hoop skirt with spaghetti curls straight out of *Gone with the Wind*, I blinked twice suspecting my eyes were playing tricks on me.

"What did you expect?" she said with a characteristic upturn of her eyebrow.

"Nothing predictable. I'm happy to play Rhett Butler to your Scarlett," I said extending my arm. After all, on stage and off, we were celebrities in our own mind.

En route to my parents, who wanted to see us before we headed to the dance, she announced a surprise. "Hold on to your dashboard, Hilovsky. Come fall I'm not returning to Catholic University."

Before I could respond she screamed, "I'm moving to New York to study acting!"

Speechless, I touched her cheek with my free hand before summoning the words, "That's great. I can't believe it." I shook my head knowing RJ would be moving there also. Now I'd have two good friends leaving me behind and headed to the Big Apple. While excited for them, I hoped my decision to attend John Carroll would provide me with a new beginning and fresh start.

When we pulled in the driveway my parents greeted us on the front lawn. We emerged from the car like a married couple in shades of creamy white.

My mother beaming from ear to ear reached out to embrace Mary Kathleen. "You look like a Hollywood starlet, dear. Vivian Leigh couldn't compare."

"Oh, thanks, Mrs. H.," she said with a meek shoulder shrug.

"Well, son, you've got quite a looker here tonight," Dad said wrapping his arm around MK's bare shoulders.

We stood in the backyard near my father's vegetable garden, while my parents snapped photographs. Like a bride and groom on top of a wedding cake, I wrapped my arms around MK and gazed in her eyes, even orchestrated a dramatic dip, an homage to our disco days. After all, this is what boys did when they went to prom. It was all about romance. I had to play my part. But to what end?

The trees and lawn glittered with the golden light of the setting sun. The sweet fragrance of roses my father had planted danced through the air while red plump cherries were ready to burst forth from the backyard tree. Soon Dad would scale the ladder to pick them. Mom would bake delicious tart cherry pies and strudels. He would make his famed cherry brandy to serve at Christmas.

As we pulled out of the drive, Dad called out, "Have a great time. And don't stay out too late." He smiled and winked while Mom waved.

While I didn't touch an ounce of liquor, everything about that night seemed fuzzy and in slow motion. Denny, Don and Mick, my Cockney trio, crowded round us when we arrived at Stouffers Inn at the Square in downtown Cleveland. They fawned over our Scarlett-Rhett apparel. Each of the couples posed for pictures on a dramatic circular staircase. We scarfed down our rubber chicken dinner. We boogied to the sounds of a forgettable band that played old Beatles' music.

Afterwards Mick and Phillipa invited Mary Kathleen and me back to Phillipa's house. In the downstairs recreation room, I kicked off my shoes and propped my tired feet on the coffee table. Philippa switched on the radio to KISS-FM.

"I can't believe we're graduating from high school. It's almost over. That's scary but I'm excited."

"Hilovsky," said MK, "you're gonna miss high school, but it's a pain in the ass. College is where the action is."

Phillipa, always under the watchful eye of her protective parents, un-tethered her up-do, shook out her blonde locks and exclaimed. "I'm ready for any change. Just get me out of this house."

"Okay, okay," Mick said, "enough of this college talk. Let's play a game." He met my eyes, and we laughed. "Truth or dare, anyone?" I proposed.

Mick volunteered. "I'll go first. Truth or dare, Mary Kathleen?"

"Truth," MK blurted out.

"How many members of the *Once Upon a Mattress* cast have you kissed?"

She looked over at me and then did the math work. "Three," she responded. "Lou Novak, Joe Mahoney, and Hilovsky."

"Okay, Mick, it's your turn, smart aleck," MK said. "Truth or dare?"

"Dare."

"I dare you to kiss Phillipa."

He leaned over to where she sat on the other side of Mary Kathleen and planted a kiss on her cheek.

"That's way too sedate," MK observed. "Try again on the lips."

Phillipa, who'd dated little during her high school years, leaned back as Mick planted a lingering wet one on her lips. "Whew, that was some kiss," she sighed.

Before I knew it Mary Kathleen and I were in a kissing match with Mick and Phillipa. While MK's lips were soft, pliant, and welcoming I could feel my spirit pull away as if my true self were floating above watching the unfolding spectacle. My body felt disconnected, lost, from my mouth.

In the background radio static, Gilbert O'Sullivan gently crooned his singular hit, "Alone Again, Naturally."

***

A week after prom I graduated from St. Ignatius High School. The ceremony took place at The Front Row Theatre where famous Cleveland talk show host Mike Douglas aired his syndicated hit before relocating to New York. In our blue and gold caps and gowns, 250 young men stood in line waiting to be seated in the red carpeted theatre. When the President of the school, Fr. Walsh, called out my name, I strode to the stage to receive my gold emblazoned diploma, then shook his large ruddy hand.

"Congratulations, Mr. Hilovsky. Job well, done." I smiled and with a lilt in my step returned to my seat. Once the last diploma was presented all the parents, from the comfortable and affluent to those who struggled and sacrificed to send their son to Ignatius, rose to their feet and applauded.

I looked out past the bright lights but couldn't locate Mom or Dad. But I knew they were proud of me, and my heart swelled.

Fr. Walsh gave the benediction. Then a sea of graduation caps sailed into mid-air. Release. Yes, release and utter relief. Four years of an all-boy's school forced me to learn how to relate to the same sex with the endless guy talk, focus on sports, and one-upmanship. It really wasn't me. Yes, I'd cultivated my inner jock and thespian, but I felt unknown by the very classmates who knew me the best. I had to subvert my attraction toward other guys in class to survive, to avoid getting beaten up, like the cast-to-the-ground sophomore with the leather handbag, ridiculed for just being.

I felt like a fake but was reassured by what MK had said: high school was over-rated. College promised something better.

As my class left the theatre an overwhelming sadness washed over me. I couldn't get RJ off my mind. He was to complete his junior year at Lakewood High this month. We'd not communicated since his birthday in January. I wondered if he would have liked to see me graduate. My self-enforced separation from the friend who knew me best had led to a lonelier road. I looked forward to lifeguarding and palling around this summer with the friends I'd made over the last three years at the pool. But none of them rivaled the friendship that RJ and I had forged. All the memories flooded back. I forced a lid on them.

RJ was probably angry with me for not phoning him. I didn't call because I was afraid. I didn't want to turn into a gay person, and when we were together, we inevitably got physical, which led to more feelings of guilt and shame. How could I mature into a real man if I liked having sex with men?

The weekend after commencement my parents threw me a graduation party. On a sunny Sunday afternoon, we sat around the backyard picnic table welcoming guests, taking cover under the protective shade of the cherry tree. Hope and Marvin surprised me with flowers. Phillipa and Mick showed up with a book of poetry. Aunt Virginia from Columbus sent an alarm clock so I wouldn't miss my early morning classes. My godmother Fran and Cousin Liz drove from Michigan to present me with a watercolor of a sailboat my godmother had painted just for me. Above the boat in handsome calligraphy, she inscribed "I am the master of my fate; I am the captain of my soul." I felt liberated by that message of self-possession. That I could do anything I wanted with my life. Could I?

RJ didn't join the festivities because I left him off the list. When Mary Kathleen arrived, she asked what went wrong. "Hilovsky, you and RJ are good friends. Why are you ignoring him?"

"We've drifted apart." I'd explained half-heartedly. "I'm not sure we have anything in common anymore."

Hoping to sever my past from my future I realized that bringing RJ along would only complicate matters.

CHAPTER 20

Lost Summer

W ITHOUT RJ THE summer of 1981 turned into the summer of lost memories. After graduation my attention turned toward preparing for college but other than settling on John Carroll University, I didn't really know where I was headed.

I could rely on the Panasonic digital alarm clock from Aunt Virginia to wake me up in time for calculus. I'd recently begun reading Lisa Birnbach's *The Preppy Handbook* and started to stockpile a collegiate wardrobe. Was I even a preppy, or more of a wannabe? I wasn't born into a lifestyle of sailing, rugby, and polo. But I liked parties and enjoyed looking good. All I desired was a new identity, a new image, something different from what I'd known over the past 4 years. At Ignatius, other than with the theatre crowd, I'd felt confined. How did I escape this feeling of claustrophobia?

On June 5, 1981, the day before my eighteenth birthday I sat in a hair salon and while skimming *The Cleveland Plain Dealer* my eye landed on an article about the first reported cases of a deadly pneumonia sickening the homosexual population. Gay cancer, or gay-related immune disease, afflicted a small group of young gay men in Los Angeles. Symptoms included night sweats, weight loss, and what a month later would be reported by *The New York Times* as a rare skin cancer called Kaposi's Sarcoma found in forty-one gay men in New York City and San Francisco.

As I digested the scary details, my breathing grew shallow while my mind raced. Even if I wanted to test the waters of gay life, why would I ever risk exposing myself to a plague-filled existence? Gay disease further intensified my internal struggle. Haunted by the threat of annihilation, the doors of my own closet closed tighter. I wanted nothing to do with this pox; the haunting details infiltrated the deep recesses of my mind.

Instead, I focused on the more immediate world of lifeguarding. For a third year I returned to Foster Pool with the goal of building swim endurance, perfecting my tan, and just plain having fun. By now I'd reached senior lifeguard status along with dreamy Dirk Fresca for whom my crush continued! I tried to avert my gaze in the locker room, even though his creamy-skinned, swimmer's body tested my every resolve. He'd traipse into the changing area, throw open his locker door, and strip down to his undershorts all the while engaging me in mundane conversation.

"So, you're headed to college in the fall," he said one hot afternoon.

I looked up from untying my sneakers. "Umm, yeah, in September. Not that far away. Have you heard of John Carroll?"

"I've heard they've got a good swim team. I'm looking at schools outside of Cleveland. Muskingum, Oberlin, Stoney Brook. If one of them offers me a swim scholarship, the decision's made. You know what I mean?"

"I bet you could easily qualify. I've heard you've got quite a backstroke." I removed my shorts and fumbled in my backpack to find my swimsuit.

"Well, I've competed a lot in it. My fly is pretty decent too."

While we slipped into our suits, I could feel that same tingle below my belt. *Oh, please God, not an erection, not now!* Thankfully whatever arousal materialized subsided as we left the changing room and emerged on the pool deck into the perfect blue of another day. No sweat. Embarrassment averted.

Around the Fourth of July Mary Kathleen and I met. She updated me on her parent's divorce. "All I know is Mom is leaving in August and moving into an apartment in Cleveland," she said while we sat on my front porch drinking lemonade.

I felt sad to hear about the breakup. I really liked Mrs. Cassidy. I remembered how she wore stylish designer dresses, fashionably belted at the waist, her hair pulled back tight from her face like a European film actress. I half expected her to talk with a British accent. She liked to smoke Virginia Slim cigarettes, and when she answered the door when I came to collect my newspaper money, her eyes looked sad. No longer would I be collecting for the paper route since I was leaving for college in the fall. The money I'd earned the past ten years would help pay for my first year's tuition. Mom and Dad and a Pell grant would help with the rest.

After a long silence I asked Mary Kathleen, "Don't you want your parents to stay together?"

"Yeah, if they loved each other." she sighed. "But they told all the kids they hadn't loved each other for a very long time. They said they got married too young and hadn't really thought about raising a big family. When Dad's company started to take off, Mom felt even more alone. She felt like she didn't deserve all this money."

Mr. Cassidy, a successful entrepreneur, had built a tool and die business into a financial empire. He'd invested in the New York Yankees and the Bonne Bell Company, a Cleveland based cosmetics manufacturer. Mary Kathleen and her brothers and sisters enjoyed alpine skiing trips, Caribbean vacations, and Saks Fifth Avenue presents for birthdays and Christmas. Not to mention the four cars hogging the driveway. Their material success knew no bounds.

"He told Mom if she wanted a divorce, she'd need to move out," Mary Kathleen said. Her eyes looked red and blotchy. I could feel her vulnerability. I wanted to take her into my arms to reassure her it would be okay. But I didn't know if it would.

We huddled together on the porch chairs, my bare toes touching her pale white legs, while dusk turned to night. I mused that this was the same chair in which my mother in nice weather sat watching for me to return home from school, a waiting place, a spot where love and awareness grew.

I felt sorry for Mary Kathleen and recalled my own fear of my parents divorcing. Thanks to the Catholic Church's Marriage Encounter retreats, they'd found a way to improve their communication. Would their marriage last or would I come home on break from college to find that they, too, would be splitting up? I shuddered at the thought, wrestled it from my mind, and leaned in closer to MK.

In another month, my parents would drive me crosstown to University Heights to begin a new chapter in my life, separate but still in the shadow of their influence.

CHAPTER 21

John Carroll, Ready or Not

Wᴵᴛʜ ᴛʜᴇ ꜰɪɴᴀʟ box loaded, Dad slammed the trunk door shut. "No turning back now," he chuckled.

It was a sultry August day when I left home for my freshman year of college. We'd stuffed the Monte Carlo with two suitcases of clothes, a box of brand-new towels and sheets, my oversized beanbag chair, a lamp for my dorm room desk, and a few posters to decorate the walls. I removed the poster of Farrah in a red bathing suit from the back of my bedroom door and rolled it into a cardboard tube. Now five years old, it felt like a relic from a bygone era, like my relationship with RJ, and I left it behind along with the scrapbook in my closet.

Prior to moving into the dorms, I took a personality test so John Carroll could match me with a roommate that would be a good fit. The test also screened smokers versus non-smokers. I stepped foot on campus with great anticipation that sunny August day, tanned and relaxed in a striped rugby shirt and St. Ignatius gym shorts.

My parents and I arrived at Bernet, a handsome brick building and oldest residence hall on campus. We took the elevator to the second floor and walked down a hallway painted a dull gray with carpeting to match. Fluorescent lights flickered overhead. A propped open bathroom door revealed private stalls and a gang shower, all in gray and white marble. I felt a little disturbed by the starkness of it all. There was no sense of warmth, just functionality.

"It reminds me a little of the army," my father let slip from the side of his mouth.

My mother put on her best face. "Jack, you're going to have a wonderful experience here. Dad and I are so proud of you."

"Maybe they'll renovate the place soon," I said inhaling a deodorized scent that failed to disguise the puke-like smell of the carpeting.

Further down the hall we cracked open a door to discover a bright room, about 250 square feet, overlooking the campus quad. Here's where I'd be living for the first time away from home. Excited and a little scared at the same time, I took a deep breath and exhaled. On the left side of the room bunk beds were stacked against the wall. A guitar case rested on the top bunk. A radiator occupied the space underneath the window. To the right of the entry sat one wood desk and lodged against the left wall sat another one. Each desk came with a chair. Two dressers crammed against the wall were open and empty.

"Wow, looks like basic training," Dad turned to me and placed his hand on my shoulder. "Sure, you don't want to come home and live, son?"

"Oh, Frank, Jack's going to do just fine here. It'll take a little adjustment, but once you hang your posters and unpack your clothes and towels, you'll start to settle in."

"Uh, hi there, I'm Victor." A tall, skinny guy with short curly black hair and pale complexion appeared in the doorway. He stuck out his hand to shake my father's.

"Pleased to meet ya," my father responded. My mother reached out to introduce herself and flashed a cursory smile.

"Hi Victor, I'm Jack. Well, I guess you've met my parents, haven't you?"

He blushed for a moment. *God, he's kind of cute,* I thought. In his black t-shirt and black jeans, he resembled Bruce Springsteen.

An awkward moment as my mind whipsawed around. "So, do you play the guitar?" I asked pointing my head toward the case on the upper bunk.

"Oh, yeah," he nodded.

"Jack plays the piano," my mother interrupted and turned to me. "Honey, maybe you could practice together."

"Later, Mom," I responded tartly.

"Well, I'm still unpacking the car," Victor announced.

"Did your parents come with you?" Mom interrupted again.

"Oh, no, I drove myself from Chicago."

"Cool," I said. "Can I help you?"

"I'll be fine, be right back." Victor faded into thin air as quickly as he appeared.

"Seems like a nice enough fellow," Dad said.

"All the way from Chicago," my mother repeated. "That's a far way from home."

I hugged my parents goodbye. Climbing the back steps, I carried the final two items: my beanbag chair and a clown marionette, a gift given to me by Delores, a cherished family friend. During high school I mowed her lawn and washed and waxed her Cadillac for $50/week, a generous contribution to my college fund. Her advice last summer over iced tea still resonated in my ears: "Your mother needs to let go. And you need to go out on your own and find your way. Become a man, Jack. Get as far away as you can." I was attempting to do just that, I thought, as I placed the red, white, and blue puppet on top of the bookshelf on my side of the room.

I fell into the lower bunk and surveyed my new environment. I'd wait to claim a desk and dresser after Victor returned.

Yeah, Mr. Springsteen, my guitar-playing, Chicago-native roommate.

***

"YEAH, yeah, that's the ticket," he replied when I suggested a new layout for the room. "You're good, ha-ha, with interior design." Victor's Chicago accent grew more pronounced the longer I spent time with him. His cadences were rushed, and he talked most of the time in a soft, nervous whisper of a voice, like a gangster on the run. Whenever he entered the room, my stomach got queasy. His nerves unleashed my own.

We agreed I'd stick with the lower bunk since all my classes fell on Monday, Wednesday, and Friday starting at 8 am, and all Victor's began in the afternoon. I took the desk against the right wall and the dresser next to it, he claimed the desk and dresser on the opposite side of the room.

I told him I'd really wanted to live on campus and experience dorm life with a roommate. He snickered and said, "Are you sure you know what you're getting into?" That might have been the first clue.

By the second week, I realized I was in big trouble. There was a reason Victor scheduled all his classes for the afternoon: he then had the freedom to go out drinking and arrive home plastered at midnight just as I had fallen asleep. I'd wake up to banging doors and fluttering overhead lights.

"Hey, what the hell," I'd say as I opened my sleep-filled eyes to a grey cloud filling the room and a huge sucking sound.

"Oops, sorry man, I just need to take a hit." He was smoking pot, for God's sake!

"Hey, can you do that somewhere else?"

"Not really," he'd reply and then inhale before turning off the lights and scaling the ladder to the top bunk.

In addition to his marijuana habit, which wasn't a match-up question on the student lifestyle survey, Victor also brought girls back to the room during the week. One school night in October I'd turned out the lights after studying for a calculus exam. I awoke to giggling and "Ohhh, ahhhh, oohhh, aaaahhh, Ohhhhhh!"

The bunk bed started to rattle and shake. "Victor, who the hell is up there with you?"

"Go back to sleep, guy."

"Victor, if you don't get her outta' here, I'm gonna get up and turn on the light."

"Relax," and the moaning and rattling continued. "Ohhh, ahhhh, Oooo...."

I jumped out of bed and switched on the light. "Out!" I screamed, averting my eyes from his perch.

When I looked up, I saw Victor wrapped in his blue blanket with a frizzy-haired, freckle-faced girl whom I recognized. *Oh my God, it's Kathy French, who played the church organ at my grade school, St. Angela Merici.* She smiled back and waved, her braces glittering in the overhead fluorescent light.

I stumbled into the hallway in my t-shirt and boxer shorts and headed toward the blinding-white bathroom, which reminded me of a mental hospital ward, especially in the middle of the night. The place smelled of beer and urine.

I returned to find the church organist gone, and Victor splayed on the top bunk, his scrawny white legs hanging over the edge.

"Why'd you have to do that?" he said angrily.

"I share this room with you, you didn't even tell me you were bringing anyone home. That totally sucks when I have a test tomorrow. It's two in the morning."

"You're not my parents," he sneered. "This is my room too. Couldn't you have kept your mouth shut? It would have been over soon enough."

"Oh great, I get to lie in the bunk below while you fuck the girl who plays the church organ. Lucky me!"

"You little faggot," he murmured and swung his legs over the bunk, turned his back, and crawled under the covers.

The words washed over me like he had dumped a bucket of mud over my head. His calling me a "faggot" didn't sound like a literal insult, but it cut like a knife.

My stomach in knots I slapped the light switch and plopped down on the lower bunk to digest his rant. *Fucking idiot*, I thought to myself.

I took the calculus test the next day and despite the interrupted sleep, I remembered all my algorithms and formulas. And when I needed an overnight break from Victor's late-night hijinks, my old high school friend Don, who lived at home and commuted to Carroll from 2 blocks away, invited me to use the foldout bed in his parent's study. "You're always welcome here," Don's mom offered, placing a tender hand on my shoulder. "You don't even need to let us know you're coming." She put a house key in my hand. "Thanks," I gulped, tears filling my eyes.

Just around the corner loomed Homecoming Weekend with Halloween following on its heels. I'd visited my parents on several weekends during September and October, a built-in excuse to see Hope Mantello, escape my roommate, and do my laundry, which Mom insisted she could handle.

I'd avoided sharing with them my difficulties with Victor because I didn't want them to say, "Come home, it will be different here." I loved my parents, but I was determined to carve my own path and learn my own lessons. Maybe I could still make the roommate situation work.

When they arrived in late October for Homecoming weekend, we walked to Heck's Burgers for dinner.

"How's it going with your roommate? Dad asked.

"I think his parents flew in from Chicago and he's picking them up at the airport," I said. "His dad's a pilot for United."

"Honey, have you met his parents yet?" Mom asked.

"No, but he must have been born in a barn. He doesn't clean up after himself and he brings girls into the room after hours."

My parents sat there in silence.

Then Dad spoke up. "Well, Jack, talk to him. It's your room too. Make sure he knows you're not trying to criticize but you're there for school and not parties and girls."

I smiled. *Yeah,* I thought. *I'm sick and tired of everyone trying to pigeon-hole me. Oh, yeah, there's Hilovsky. The square...the fag...the mama's boy...trying to act straight as an arrow when we know otherwise.* It's not like I didn't want to loosen up and have some fun in college, I just wanted to feel safe in my room and be able to study there with a roommate that tried to be nice to me.

"Maybe I need to pledge a fraternity and get out of this dorm. I don't think it's working," I said, shaking my head. "He brought Kathy French home the other night."

Mom looked shocked, not so much Dad. They both knew her from the church. Whereas my mother didn't like to talk about sex Dad at least seemed to get that young people might have it. He served in the Army after all!

Dad sighed, "Son, maybe you need to toughen up a bit. Develop that shell I told you about. Don't let things get to you so easily. Have a beer now and then."

And with that, my father called the waiter and ordered me my first Guinness Stout, five months after my eighteenth birthday.

***

As Victor continued to screw any girl that showed interest and willfully ignore me, I sunk deeper and deeper into denial about my sexual desires. To compound matters, the dreaded facial acne returned. I called Dr. Zorn for a tetracycline fix and returned to using the UV sunlamp when I came home for visits. While less severe than high school, the outbreaks were upsetting and sent me back to the mirror to examine the damage. If only I could have stopped looking. The mirror only magnified my distress.

"No," I'd say to myself. "Leave it alone." Hands clenched at my side, I tried to avoid looking all together. But I was like a dog with a bone. I couldn't put down my obsession. I wanted to squeeze every pimple and blackhead, which only made matters worse.

To compound my sexual frustration and paranoia, I heard rumors about a student in the theatre department. On Friday and Saturday nights he'd loiter in the front of the campus waiting for drunken college guys to return from Heck's Burgers. He'd hang out near the bushes by the campus parking lot and proposition them. I was titillated by the story yet afraid I'd come face to face with him some day. Would he read me; know I might have similar desires? I never dared to find out. I avoided that part of campus thinking if I didn't see him, I could avert confronting my own loneliness, my own desires.

One night I returned to my dorm room only to find my side trashed. My desk had been shoved to the middle of the room and on it lay the clown marionette from Delores shredded in bits and pieces on the hanger. Its hands and feet were mangled, the head torn off, the body lacerated. Vaseline was smeared over the entire surface of my desk. The can of petroleum jelly sat on the top of the bookshelf along with the ruler used to slather it. Books were strewn everywhere. A note taped to the shelf above the desk in big, black, blaring letters read *Grow up, faggot.*

Hot tears streamed down my face. I envisioned our family friend Delores on her crutches the day she'd given me that silly creature made of Styrofoam and wood. It was an assault on me; an invasion, and there was no way to take it other than acknowledge the wound. I knew Victor was in on it, likely aided by his smarmy friends from the Bernet dorm.

I sat down and began to sob, the memory of the security I felt when at Don's house juxtaposed with this violent moment. The sun set on the quiet campus. It was a Saturday evening, and everyone had gone to the Rathskeller or out to Heck's for a burger. My head shaking, I wiped my wet face with my sleeve. I didn't even act in the least bit like a fag. But they wanted me to be one. I'd arrived at college craving to start a fresh chapter in my life and release the fear of being discovered, committed to doing anything to avoid suspicion. I would show them. But first, I needed to make a permanent escape from this room and a roommate who despised me.

CHAPTER 22

Something Good

THE PHONE RANG on a cold, windswept day in January. Outside my dorm window a white blanket covered the ground, and I could hear the crunch of snow underfoot. Cold air blew through the leaky windows while the old radiator cranked heat into the damp spaces.

"Jack?"

"Yeah," I said pausing to realize the tentative voice on the line was the best friend I'd willfully ignored for over a year, determined to push him out of my life.

"Oh my God, RJ, it's been ages. How did you find me?"

"I called your mom, and she gave me your phone number."

Another pause. The digital clock hummed on my desk. It flashed 1:43 pm.

"You know, I really gave some thought to whether I should call you..."

"'I'm glad you did," I interrupted.

"No, listen to me. I'm not sure what happened, or what I did to suddenly have you cut me off the last year. But my mother said forgive and forget, forget about who did what to whom and just call. So, I'm calling."

I cradled my head in one hand as I held the phone with the other. "RJ, I'm sorry. I needed some space."

"But you could have told me at least, rather than letting me hang out to dry all this time."

"I didn't know, I thought you'd be busy with your senior year and getting ready for college."

"Bullshit, you avoided me. You dropped me like a hot potato to go off with your lifeguard friends and then you didn't even invite me to your graduation party last summer, all because you didn't want to deal with it. You didn't want to deal with being a homo."

"That's not true," I said clasping the receiver to the corner of my mouth. "I wanted some space, some breathing room from you. I felt claustrophobic. You the great dancer, you who got the girls--Janice, Marlis, Shelley, you who had the drawing talent, and the family that let you be yourself, the family you didn't have to please."

I feared Victor would come in at any moment. He had a psychology class that ended in 5 minutes. I stood up to lock the door.

"Well, it's a terrible way to treat a friend," RJ responded his voice trembling.

Gargantuan tears flooded my eyes. They fell on top of my desk, the same desk Victor slathered with Vaseline at the end of the year. I reached for paper, Kleenex, anything to staunch the stream.

"Jack, are you alright?'

"No, no, I'm fine, it's just," I blew my snotty nose. "I've had a sucky first semester here with an idiot roommate who hates my guts and likes to fuck with my mind. We have nothing in common. I don't know why we ever were assigned each other. He brings sluts back to the room and stays out all hours, then comes back and wakes me up with his big mouth and his music." I sniffed. "But that's all going to change. This weekend I'm switching to another dorm. I'm starting over."

My thoughts drifted to my transfer to Miller Hall and my new roommate, a friendly upperclassman named Dave Bonaventure, whom I'd stayed with the weekend I'd first visited John Carroll. Serendipity brought us back together—his old roommate graduated one semester early leaving an available space. We'd kept in touch, and he offered me the slot. Plus, he had lots of friends--good friends--who knew my name and said, "Oh, you'll have to join Dave at our parties." It made me want to cry, the fact they wanted to include me compared with the thugs in my dorm.

RJ broke the silence.

"I'm sorry for what I said."

"I can handle it," I sniffed, wiping my nose and eyes. "Maybe my life will improve once I escape this dorm. It can't get any worse."

"Well, if you need me, you know I'm here. I've always been here. By the way, I got accepted at FIT (Fashion Institute of Technology) so I'm off to New York in September."

I smiled. "That's great news. I knew you would. Let's try to get together when I'm next home, or over Spring Break."

As we hung up the phone, relief and regret overcame me. Relief that RJ had allowed bygones to be bygones and picked up the phone to call. And regret that I'd avoided him and treated him like a pariah my last year in high school. He deserved better. I'd acted like a coward.

***

THE next weekend I made the switch and left Bernet behind for good. Down came several posters: The Talking Heads (a gift from Hope), Olivia Newton John's "Physical," and John F. Kennedy on his sailboat. I'd packed suitcases full of clothes before I left for Christmas break, so I'd be ready to hightail it to Miller the minute I returned. My towels and sheets, comforter, and toiletries, all boxed and taped. School supplies in a pile along with my notebooks, lamps, and the Panasonic alarm clock from Aunt Virginia.

Victor stood in his long black wool overcoat as I emptied the room. "Don't ya think you'll miss it here," he said with a sour laugh.

"Ha, Ha," I responded. "Not a chance. But nice knowing you." Dave and all his friends had come to Bernet and one by one carried a box to neighboring Miller so I wouldn't need to make multiple trips.

Before heading out the door I stopped. "Ya know, I really had high hopes for getting along, but I've learned you can't force people to like you." I reached out to shake his hand. We exchanged a cool, clammy farewell, and I walked out into the sun of a brightening afternoon with a yearning that college life would hopefully get sunnier.

***

WITH Mary Kathleen in New York, Hope Mantello became my de facto muse and girlfriend. Except, I had more interest in worshipping her elusive persona than making love to her lithe, boyish body.

I'd always enjoy pretty girls with charm, smarts, and grace. My obsession with Farrah made that clear, and her career and personal life trajectory, like mine, was in transition mode. No longer with Lee Majors, she was now dating Ryan O'Neal, Lee's former best friend. Her movie career was on hold after three consecutive flops. But she'd soon return to television in *The Burning Bed* and *Murder in Texas*, playing victimized women who rose to confront their attackers. Maybe I could learn from her moxie how to fight back.

In the meantime, I couldn't help but focusing on Hope. How I adored her. Mary Kathleen exerted a down to earth gravitational pull on me, in addition to making me laugh and relax. Hope made me feel crazy and out of control. I wanted to get closer to her, know her better, but she only let me in so far. I suspected Marvin, who had introduced us during *My Fair Lady*, kept his finger on Hope to ensure she remained in his orbit. One weekend she came to visit the campus and stayed with Philippa at her neighboring all-girls' college. We continued to see each other when I came home that fall. And I accompanied her to her Snowball Christmas Dance over the holidays.

If I were honest maybe I loved the idea of Hope rather than the girl herself. Her carefree fashion sense—preppy and punky—her flirtation, her outrageousness, her love of music and dancing, all of these coaxed me out of my shyness into a universe where I could explore possibilities for myself, how to live life with more gusto and abandon.

During her visit we watched her brother Phil, a quarterback on the opposing football team, play against the John Carroll Blue Streaks.

"Football bores me," Hope said as we sat in the stands on a sunny fall day. "But I do like the social part."

Later that evening we walked to Heck's for dinner. "I have so much fun with you," I told her as we strolled through the campus holding hands. "Can't we see each other more than once a month?"

Hope looked me straight in the eye with those chocolate brown eyes I adored. "I'm not ready for anything too serious. Especially since it's my senior year, and I'm going to go away to school. I want to be open to dating other people. Can't we just have fun?"

I bit my lip. I knew it was over if other guys were in the picture. My heart craved more, and yet I didn't know how to be with this girl. I wanted more than a buddy, a playmate. Either way, she'd be leaving. And so, I let go, and we drifted apart from each other without even a final goodbye.

***

MOVING into Dave Bonaventure's room in Miller Hall felt like escaping a juvenile detention center and arriving in the Promised Land. After four years of attending an all-boy's high school, walking into Miller where the sexes weren't segregated brightened my outlook. I no longer felt hostage to the male adolescent mentality rampant in my former dorm. Just having girls around, I observed, made guys act in a more grown-up way. In the nick of time, I'd been rescued from cohabiting with cavemen and now lived in the civilized world.

Miller smelled different. No stale, sour odors fouled the hallways. Clean and bright, the floral scent of air freshener permeated the place. Fewer freshmen populated the dorm; the student lottery system allotted many of the rooms to upperclassmen. Men resided on one wing of the three-story red brick building while women resided on the other. Common areas bridging the two wings allowed the sexes to comingle day and night.

On Friday afternoons following his last class, Dave would invite his upperclassmen friends over for beer and pretzels. He always included me in his weekend social events and made sure I had a cold beer in my hand and introduced me to the parade of pretty women he knew. He welcomed me to play my own music on his Sony turntable. Often, I waited until he left for class, before queuing up the stereo with songs such as Billy Joel's "Songs in the Attic," or Diana Ross' hit single, "Upside Down."

"What do you want to do with your life after graduation?" Denise, a free-spirited sociology student, asked me during one of those late-night beer parties where we sat around listening to Dave's Leonard Skynyrd record collection.

I responded with a "who me?" wide-eyed, confused look and shrugged my shoulders. "Work in an advertising agency. Maybe go to law school?" I replied.

Denise put down her beer can. "No, really, Jack, what do you want to do? That sounds like your parent's answer."

Fact is, I didn't really know, or I didn't want to admit that I knew. Like my fear of the gay world, I held performing as a career at arm's length. I'd come to John Carroll intending to major in business thanks to the school's well-known program. But I wasn't at all like the twenty guys from my high school graduating class, many of whom decided to attend Carroll, study business admin, and then assume the reigns of the family trade. A desire to please my parents, despite insisting I'd make my own decisions, influenced the equation. But as I continued fulfilling core courses for my business major, I'd begun to hate the rote memorization of management principles. The coursework felt stilted, unimaginative.

"I'd like to run for public office," I mused with a big, naive smile.

Her face lit up. "Now there's an answer. Are you going to be the next JFK?"

"Who knows, it's a long way off. I better concentrate on passing this semester before I set my sights on the White House." I laughed and tried to imagine myself with a wife and kids boarding Air Force One. An applauding press corps filled out the background. Like JFK, I knew I loved my country and wanted to make a difference. But we already had an actor in the White House. On so many fronts in my life, I hadn't figured out how to get from here to there.

She asked me if I planned to watch the new *David Letterman Show*, did I own a personal computer, and did I think Reagan wanted to bomb the Soviet Union? I loved Denise's curiosity and that she cared enough about me to dig deeper.

***

MY first week in my new dorm I met Patrick Francis, Head Resident Assistant of Miller Hall. God, he was beautiful. Wavy brown hair and warm brown eyes danced above a bright, white toothpaste model smile. A returning sophomore and captain of the diving team, Patrick ranked nationally both in Toledo where he attended high school and at the college level. I immediately liked his natural, homespun way of relating to people.

"Welcome to your new digs," said Patrick, peeking through the doorway. "I thought I'd stop by and introduce myself."

Slouching in my boxer shorts I jumped up from the couch. "Sorry for the mess, I'm still unpacking."

"Don't worry about it. Your roommate told me you moved your stuff over the weekend. I'm Patrick, your R. A."

His hand felt warm to the touch as I shook it. So did his smile and everything about him, feel warm, that is. I wanted to cry because I finally felt safe and protected after enduring Victor for an entire semester and not knowing whom to trust and whom not to trust. I knew I could trust Patrick.

"If you need anything, I'm down the hall. I'm usually in class during the mornings and I have diving practice in the afternoons. But I'm back on duty in the evenings."

I visited Patrick often those first few weeks in Miller, lingering in his doorway during small moments of conversation. He listened about what happened with Victor and followed my brown eyes with a patient focus. "Freshman year, it's a big adjustment," he said. "Give yourself time. It will all fall into place." A psychology major, he understood human relationships. His presence calmed me.

I also took steps to widen my social circle. I wanted friends separate from my roommate's. I'd relied a lot on sunny Hope my first semester but now she stood in my rearview mirror. It stung that she didn't want to get more serious. I adored her but it seemed futile to chase her now that she decided to attend college out of the area. I needed to get to know my peers on campus.

One day Patrick introduced me to his best friend, Brooks Lawson, a talkative marketing major and the recent Homecoming King. His blonde good looks and easygoing personality charmed everyone on campus. After our first meeting, he'd greet me with a "Hey, Pal, how's it going?" whenever I'd see him. I wasn't sure if he knew my name, but it didn't matter. Just radiating in his sunny orbit was enough for me. He knew everyone on campus, drove a red Miata convertible, and sported a year-round tan. I was enamored.

I soon learned that both Patrick and Brooks identified as born-again Christians. I didn't hold it against them since I knew RJ's mom, who also practiced Catholicism, considered herself in the same league of believers. Besides, they weren't lecturing me or trying to brainwash me in any way, shape or form. Thanks to Patrick and Brooks, and their intoxicating personalities, other ideas began to percolate in my head about how to shake up my life, make new friends and lay the groundwork for a fresh beginning. Any other questions, I could save for later.

Something needed to change. Something good needed to happen.

CHAPTER 23

The Pledge and the Fraternity

M<small>Y WHOLE LIFE</small> I'd wanted a brother: someone to teach me the ropes, advise me how to live my life so I could avoid screwing up and making mistakes.

My second semester freshman year tall, blonde Brooks Lawson asked me a simple question: "Hey Jack, ever thought of joining a frat?" I had visions of an out-of-control *Animal House*; despite my fears I convinced myself I needed to take a chance. I'd escaped Bernet Hall and now craved a new summit to scale.

Besides the desire for a brother figure, three reasons influenced my decision to pledge the Kaps: 1) the frat's reputation for throwing fantastic parties; 2) their commitment to community service; and 3) the good-looking brotherhood.

When my dreamy R.A. Patrick said he planned to pledge, I took the plunge. Our class included a ragtag group of sophomores and juniors: loud-mouthed wise guy Ted Silvers, who tutored underclassmen in math but upon first impression resembled the JCU version of John Belushi; Brendan O'Malley, the red-headed shy fellow who enjoyed cracking jokes that fell flat and always seemed headed to a party; Greg Malone, the philosophy major who lived across the hall from me and often could be found feet up on his desk and cigarette in hand reading Kant or some other great philosopher; soft-spoken Patrick, the diver and R.A.; and me, eager to please, ambitious to cultivate a new circle of friends, and the only freshman pledge.

***

THE phone rang Saturday morning at 8 AM. "Hilovsky, Goddammit, get your ass out of bed and bring me some breakfast." I threw on a JCU hoodie and sweatpants and flew down the dorm stairs to the Student Services cafeteria. I piled a tray with a plate of eggs and sausage and added a bowl of fresh pineapple fruit salad before bee-lining back to Miller Hall.

Breathless, after climbing three flights of stairs, I shifted the teetering tray to one hand, knocked with the other, and slowly opened the door to discover Pledge Master Sam Smith sprawled on a beanbag chair with his latest squeeze. Sam sporting only his boxers, she on her tummy in black lace panties and nothing else. Their bodies were entwined in a loose-fitting knot.

I'd never seen a girl revealing this much skin, lying there topless. I stood frozen in the doorway. My already red cheeks turned a deeper shade of crimson.

"You can just place the tray next to Brenda," Sam chuckled, enjoying my discomfort. "Thanks for the door-to-door service."

Later that morning another frat brother Jeff Peters called for my services. His two pierced ears with gold jewelry were a source of fascination for me (what did they signify, was he gay, bi, or what?).

"Dude, what's up? Come to my digs pronto," he squawked before banging the phone down on the receiver. Down the hall I scurried before encountering him spread-eagled on his leather sofa spitting a mouthful of tobacco juice into a copper kettle on the ground next to him. He pointed to it and said, "Empty this shit in the toilet and clean it out." Disgusted with the smell I carried the stinky pot into the shiny, new bathrooms and flushed the contents down a virgin white toilet.

Serving my brothers humbled me. All for the greater good of the brotherhood, I kept reminding myself despite the condescension and verbal abuse. It was all a means to an end, at least that's what they told us pledges.

***

ONE night the Kaps threw a keg party in Pacelli Hall. Since fraternity houses were forbid on campus and nearby suburbs, frats hosted parties in the dorms where the brothers would often claim a wing of the floor by virtue of many of the same frat settling there. A brother by the name of Lizard hosted the gathering in his room. The captain of the rugby team, and proud of his prowess with women, Lizard showed off his latest flame, a cheerleader with shiny red hair.

"All right hosebags, let's get this party going. Beer Bong time." He uncoiled a long hose attached to the beer tap. "Who's up first?"

I stepped to the front, and everyone began chanting, "Hilovsky, Go, Go, Go." Lizard tapped the line and the liquid refreshment coursed through the tube and exploded down my throat until I thought I might gag. I waited another few seconds before raising my hand.

"Fuck, that was fabulous," said pierce-eared Jeff slapping my back. "I didn't know you had it fuckin' in you."

I wiped my mouth with my hand, stumbled into the hall, and heaved open the door to the Pacelli bathroom. Chunks of my last three meals flew into the toilet.

Then I promptly passed out on the cold bathroom floor.

***

HEAD throbbing, I awoke on the lower mattress of a bunk bed that wasn't mine. I blinked in the semi-darkness. Brooks sat in a chair directly across from me with a faint reading light illuminating his pink lips and warm blue eyes. God, he was handsome.

Each time I encountered Brooks Lawson, my blonde, gregarious fraternity brother, I'd get all fluttery and thought for sure my knees would buckle under me. I felt like an enamored teenager encountering his fan magazine idol, something a guy would never admit, but that's how I experienced him.

"Where am I?" I blinked. "What the hell happened?"

Brooks put his book down, came over to where I was laying, and knelt beside me. "Bud, you fainted in the upstairs bathroom. You're in Pacelli in my room. Smith and I carried you down here."

"What time is it? Did anyone see me?" Frantic I scanned the room.

Brooks nodded to the clock radio. "Almost midnight. No, we snuck you down the back stairwell and managed to avoid most of the partygoers. Are you feeling okay?"

"Just a little queasy." I rubbed my stomach and rolled over to my side.

You looked pretty pale, but I wasn't too worried since you'd tossed most of your cookies before you hit the ground."

I started laughing. "Oh, God, I never imagined myself getting so sick, or wasted that I'd pass out." I tried to get up and felt dizzy all over again.

"Stay down for a while longer. You can crash here tonight if you like. Besides, it's starting to rain." Thunder rumbled in the distance. The wind whistled against the dorm window.

"Thanks for scraping me off the floor and bringing me down here," I said, embarrassment creeping into my cheeks.

"You needed a hand, bud."

"Sometimes I think I need more than a hand. I feel like I might not be cut out for this fraternity thing. Smith's so unpredictable, always asking for some crazy thing."

"Hey, we're brothers, that doesn't mean we get along 24/7. And Smith's gotta be tough. Remember he's the Pledge Master, the ringleader of the group. He's going to throw you some attitude. You're handling it pretty well, I think." He gave me a light jab on the shoulder. "Do you want some water before I turn out the lights?"

I nodded, and he brought me a glass. The room went dark, and Brooks climbed into the top bunk though I'd wished he'd stayed face level with me. My body tingled -- I felt both safe, nestled here with someone who treated me with such care and concern, and slightly aroused.

"Do you have any brothers or sisters?" I asked in the vacuum of the night.

"One younger sister, back in Detroit. She may come here next year. You're an only kid, right?"

"Yeah, that's me. The one and only. But I have a large extended family, lots of cousins on my mom's side.

"Where do they live?" he asked, his voice a whisper in the darkness.

"Oh, here, in Cleveland and Indiana. My cousins Jake and Kent are landscapers. They love the land and working with the soil. I really admire them for following their passion and doing what they love, no matter what."

Brooks rustled under the sheets. "Aren't you doing that?" The thunder and lightning crashed outside his bedroom window.

"I thought I wanted to study business, now I'm not so sure. I am really liking political science and my professors there. Maybe I'll get involved with politics someday. Work on a Presidential campaign, or run for office myself."

"Wow, that's great. I'll sign up to be your campaign manager."

I smiled at his gung-ho willingness to believe in me and felt warmth ripple through my entire body. "Brooks, what made you become born-again?"

He paused. "That's a complicated question. I guess I felt...lost. I grew up in a comfortable existence. Didn't really struggle for anything. Could have any girl I wanted. Nice clothes, car, vacations with my folks. The works."

"Yeah, what's wrong with that?"

He shifted his bodyweight and looked down from the top bunk on me lying beneath him on the bottom rung. More lightning flashed in the sky. "Jack, I knew there had to be more. It was all too easy. I didn't want to keep having a good time and losing sight of what's to come."

"What do you mean? What's to come?"

"Judgment Day. We're all going to be called to account on how we've behaved and treated each other. How we've conducted our lives."

"Yeah, but don't you think trying to live a good life in the here and now, being honest, not stealing from others, treating others as you would like to be treated is the answer. That way we're always living in the light."

"But you need to commit your life to Christ. Make Him the reason for living. That's what it means to be born-again."

"I think I can be a good Catholic, a good person, and still make Christ the center of my life without declaring I'm born-again." At least that's what I hoped; that God loved me regardless of my nature, regardless of my attraction to other guys.

Brooks didn't answer back. I lay there listening to the rain for a moment and felt an incredible loneliness pour over me. I thought about his legs--long, muscular, and slender. About his smile and blue eyes, his easygoing, light-hearted personality, the little red Miata sports car he drove around campus. Why did he bring me here? Why did he insist I stay? I didn't have the guts to test the waters and reach up to touch him.

Soon I heard a gentle, soft snore coming from above me. I turned over quietly and hugged my body. I clutched the blanket and tried to release my unsettled thoughts. I couldn't go on like this forever, wanting something I couldn't have. I tossed and turned until settling into the sound of Brooks inhaling and exhaling above me.

Separate but together, I felt comforted by the rhythm of his breath. The warm covers around my shoulders were as good as I could get, and I soon fell fast asleep.

***

"Hello, hello, Jack?"

I paused for a moment. Silence. "RJ?"

"Yeah, long time no hear, what're you doing?"

"Oh, God, I'm pledging a fraternity. The Kaps. Talk about crazy times."

"Whatever possessed you?" I could envision his head wagging in disbelief on the other side of the line.

"I really like the guys in the frat. They're smart, good looking, and popular."

"Do any of them suck you off?" he inquired with characteristic glee and his usual sarcasm.

I laughed. "That's not the reason I'm pledging, jughead. What've you been up to?" I asked, hoping to change the subject.

"Well, I'm having my graduation party in early June. I'd like you to come if you're available."

"I'd love to." I took a deep breath and closed my eyes. "Thanks for thinking of me. I know last year was difficult with us."

"That's history; don't worry about it. I'm glad you can make it. Don't let those fraternity boys tar and feather you, okay?"

My face broke into a grin. "That won't happen. Maybe they'll instead dip me in chocolate sauce."

"Promises, promises. Oh, did you hear Farrah and Lee are officially divorced?"

"No, I've hardly read a newspaper."

"It's kind of sad."

"Do you still have the scrapbook?

"Is the Pope Catholic? We'll have to update it when we see each other this summer."

"Yep," I smiled. "I'll call you when I get home in a few weeks."

My heart skipped a beat, I felt happy, expansive, just hearing the familiarity of his voice. Same old RJ. He always managed to keep me on my toes. Outside my window the bright orange sun made its final descent behind Grasselli Tower, and a quiet dusk settled on the campus.

***

MAY arrived and with it the beginning of Hell Week, the grand finale of pledging a frat. Wild-eyed and cranky Lizard spit out commands from the head of the cafeteria table. "Okay, hosers, now that you've brought my grub, I'd like you to take the redhead here for a walk on the leash."

Relieved I wasn't suffering that humiliation I attached a dog collar to his neck and escorted red-headed pledge brother Brendan O'Malley out of the cafeteria.

We circled the Quad passing all the dorms and Admin Building. "Oh, great," said Brendan, sweat pouring off his brow. "Now my teachers think I'm an idiot, leashed like a stupid mutt."

***

"HILOVSKY and Francis, your First Hell Week challenge is plain and simple," said Pledge Master Sam Smith with a twinkle in his eye. "I want you to streak across the campus, gonads and all. Then follow it up with a panty raid in Murphy Hall. Bring back a pair of Brigid Gurley's lacy underwear, got it?"

Right there in the school parking lot, Patrick Francis and I eyed each other with goofy grins before stripping down to our tennis shoes and passing our clothes to Pledge Master Smith for safekeeping. "On your mark, get set, GO!" he screamed.

As we sped through the heart of the campus girls hanging out the window of the second floor of Miller Hall waved, screaming "Whoo-hoo, hello cutie patooties."

We breezed past a group of Chinese exchange students, one of whom took out a camera and snapped a photo of us mid-stride.

All balls and cock, we bounced up, down, and sideways across the lawn. It was dusk, getting colder, unlike the summertime heat RJ and I in adolescent zeal experienced while blazing through the alfalfa fields in Michigan.

We bolted into the lobby of Murphy Hall as Brigid emerged from a study lounge. Her blue eyes lit up, and she covered her mouth as Patrick and I ran toward her. Breathless, I wheezed, "It's Hell Week for the Kaps, and we need your underwear."

Brigid eyed our posteriors, led us to her room, and handed over a pair of lavender bloomers with a lacy waistband from her dresser door. "Here, take these, all for the good of the fraternity." She winked, opened the window, and we scrambled onto the lawn. Her roommate, Peg, adjusted her eyeglasses and began to scream as we scrambled away.

"Come back again, you can have a pair of mine next time," Peg yowled into the night.

Panting and red-faced we arrived back to Pledge Master Smith, who returned our clothes to us. "God, I can't believe we just did that," Patrick mused shaking his head as we hurriedly dressed in the purple of the night.

My arm wrapped around his shoulder, I laughed, barely concealing a growing erection in my shorts. "It couldn't have happened to a nicer pair of guys," I said before turning to conceal the evidence.

***

SAM banged his fist on the hardwood desk. "Men, your final task leading up to your initiation ceremony is Mission, a road trip all brothers take prior to our acceptance into the fraternity of the Kaps." He removed a large manila folder and laid it on top of the desk. "Here are your instructions. Your journey will take you to Erie, PA, Buffalo, and the Canadian side of Niagara Falls. There's no turning back now" he chuckled. "Be back by Sunday night. You've got 72 hours."

***

"RISE and shine, you homos," roared Ted in the early morning, like it was *Animal House* all over again. The five of us sped down the highway in Ted's Impala until we arrived in Erie, where we spent the night at Greg Malone's parent's house in the suburbs. That was the first time I recalled hearing him use the word homo, which was unusual considering all the cussing we'd grown accustomed to during the 5-month pledge period.

I decided to ignore his slur, but it nagged at me. I'd endured the hostility and hurt of my cousin Jimmy calling me fag in middle school until I fought back and punched him in the nose. While I witnessed taunting of weaker boys in high school, few threats were directed towards me. Yeah, I'd messed around with my best friend, and I'd suffered crushes on other boys, even yearned for their bodies while changing for gym. But since RJ nothing sexual had happened between me and other guys.

And yet there were indications all around that I chose to ignore and shoved under life's rug. I'd developed feelings for Brooks Lawson after he rescued me from my drunken stupor the night of the frat party, and I couldn't deny the heightened fondness I felt for my R.A. and fellow pledge brother Patrick. My life felt frozen like I couldn't move forward, and I didn't want to return to the sexual relationship I'd had with RJ because it would confirm my worst fear: that I was in fact homosexual. My throat grew tighter, constricted, like I was going to choke, or worse suffocate, if I didn't find a way to relax, free myself, and breathe.

I wanted closeness with another man. What did that mean? Was I gay? Were any of the men I had feelings toward even curious about exploring it? Did they have feelings for me? The questions frightened and excited me at the same time. How would I know? How could I find out? All these conflicting desires and contradictions battled inside but I refused, steadily ignored, unearthing them. I didn't identify myself as gay, and I sure as hell didn't want AIDS. I didn't even know any "normal" gay people, whatever that meant. I felt trapped, no way in, no way out.

***

"OH, my...Jesus," I whined surveying the wide expanse of green at a golf course somewhere in Buffalo.

"Oh, c'mon Hilovsky," said red-headed O'Malley, "we'll cover for you if you're caught. It's just a prank, after all."

So, I gulped, cracked the car door, and with one eye on a golf cart 1500 yards in the distance hightailed toward the Ninth Hole. Once there, I glanced in all four directions before taking another gulp. Grabbing the tee flag, I dashed back to the car.

Ted revved the engine, the door flew open, and the escape began.

"Holy shit, I can't believe I did it." Within a moment's notice a police car emerged from behind, flashing cherry red lights blazing.

"Oh, crap," said Ted as he pulled over.

Sweating bullets in the backseat, I wiped my forehead. The officer's eyes met mine. "It's my fault, officer, they put me up to it, I mean, my fraternity is on a mission."

The officer chuckled and said he'd have to take us into the station. When we arrived the judge dressed in a black robe with madras golf pants peeking out sat at his imposing desk. He lowered his bifocals and peered at us. "All right, gentlemen, I'm going to make this easy. Do any of you deny that an hour ago you arrived at South Park Golf Course and one of the occupants of your vehicle walked onto the Ninth Hole, removed the tee flag, and absconded with that property in a 1981 Pontiac LeSabre?"

"No, sir," I stuttered. "I don't deny I committed such an act. But I hope you'll consider it was a prank; we were told by our fraternity we needed to bring the #9 flag back from this course."

"Judge, we're all guilty just the same," interrupted Patrick. "We put him up to it, nobody else had the guts." I smiled at Patrick, reveling in his defense of me.

"Yeah, sir," Ted said. "We're all responsible. But we were told not to return without proof we swiped it."

The judge chuckled. "I know what it's like to pledge a fraternity. In fact, I'm a member of Alpha Epsilon Pi, Class of '51. But I can't let you take the flag. That's rightful property of the South Park Municipal Golf Course. I can however let you take a photo of the flag as proof you absconded with it, until the law intervened."

"Hey, judge," Brendan O'Malley, the redhead interrupted. "How's about we get a shot of us holding the flag with you in the picture?"

I penned in my journal: May 17, 1982. Jack Hilovsky, caught red handed in thievery, stealing the #9 tee flag from South Park Golf Course. Judge agrees to drop charges, pose for picture, we are released, no bail required, tee flag returned to rightful owner, apology accepted. I realized the brothers I had so wanted rallied around me in my moment of need. I'd proven myself, and they'd stood up for me.

***

AFTER our meeting with the judge, Ted, Brendan, Greg, Patrick, and I blew out of Buffalo and drove across the border to Niagara Falls. Around dusk our ragtag team pulled into the Canadian tourist station. With no time to spare before closing we dashed to purchase tickets to board the Maid of the Mist boat tour. Our to-do-list demanded a picture of all five of us in raincoats on the fabled tourist attraction.

The rain stopped and a breathtaking rainbow emerged stretching from the American side all the way to where we stood in Canada. We paused to drink in its brilliance while the ear-pounding drum of the Falls cascaded into the cavernous infinity below.

The majesty of it all was mesmerizing. My thoughts drifted to Mom and Dad, their story of how they met at a CYO dance, and their honeymoon at Niagara Falls.

I smiled to myself remembering how when I was a kid, I thought my parents had a pre-arranged marriage because Dad first asked my grandfather's permission before popping the question to my mother. Both my parents had waited a long time to tie the knot. It seemed like a fairytale arrangement with old-fashioned customs.

Mom and Dad took me several times to see Niagara: once in 1974 before our Cape Cod/Provincetown trip, Dad took a picture of Mom and eleven-year-old me skipping through the parking lot like innocents from *The Wizard of Oz* en route to see one of the great wonders of the world. The photo captured the utter joy of carefree abandon, as we basked in the late afternoon's orange glow.

The hoots and hollers from my pledge brothers jolted me from my reverie. They gathered at the bow of the ship as we approached the voluminous waterfall. Spray and chill and mist and light collided. I squinted to observe the towering waves twenty stories high.

Deep in my thoughts, I knew I needed more distance from my parents and going away to college had started the process. How would life change once I became a brother in this fraternity? How would I change? Would I grow more confident, more independent, consider leaving Cleveland for an adventure in another place? Contemplating a move felt exciting but scary.

Patrick walked over and nudged me. "Earth to Jack. Lost in space?" He smiled that adorable wide smile I loved so much, his eyes crinkling along the edges. He slung his arm around my shoulder, and we sauntered over to the less crowded side of the boat. *Oh God, if he only knew,* I thought to myself as we approached the others. But at least now we were brothers, and this warmth and affection soothed me. I'd never misinterpret it and expect more, yet why couldn't I have this in a love relationship? I wanted to melt into my attraction and never leave.

After our sailing adventure and a rushed dinner, we returned one last time to the Falls and found a secluded Canadian viewing spot. After a quick glance both ways we dropped our trousers on a perch overlooking one of the 10 Wonders of the World. Five white luminous asses emerged to satisfy the final demand of our relentless Pledge Master: a true "moonlight serenade."

"Smile," Brendan winced, as he set up the tripod and hit the flash button that recorded the shot of our milky behinds.

**

AFTER mooning the Falls, we returned to Buffalo to spend the night. Greg Malone contacted a friend from his high school days, who was studying to be a priest at Christ the King Seminary, a theological college in the historic part of town. We rang the rusted buzzer. Adam answered the door of the two-story duplex.

We all stood there with our duffle bags, like Mary and Joseph looking for room at the inn.

"Greg, man, how are you?" Adam, tall, athletic, and in his twenties, embraced our wider, and a bit shorter, pledge brother. Greg glowed.

"We need a place to stay," Greg shrugged.

"The other seminarians left for an overnight retreat so we can have you camp out in the dormitories."

My heart leapt when Adam gave Patrick and me a room to share. After settling the others, he led us to our dorm. We showered and unpacked our bags after a long day.

Wrapped in a thin blanket, I sat across from Patrick and tried to get warm despite the damp surroundings. "Sometimes, I think I'm not meant to join a fraternity," I said.

He looked at me, puzzled. "What do you mean? Are you thinking of dropping out?"

"No, I'm just not much of a poser," I admitted. "I wanna be honest and not turn into a dick."

Patrick laughed. "Well, who's saying you need to change? We all join for different reasons. I thought it would be fun to have a brotherly connection, I missed that growing up."

"But don't you have an older brother?"

"Yeah, but we're still competitive," he replied. "I always wanted friends with different interests so we wouldn't compare ourselves."

"I know what you mean," I said. "Sometimes when I see guys who are better than me in tennis or some other sport, I get jealous. I want to wipe them out."

RJ came to mind, and how I distanced myself from him. I knew I could never match his dancing talent. I felt like I lived in his shadow. Even with girls I assumed the role of his sidekick, his swiveling hips drawing them like bees to honey.

Patrick had fallen asleep before I returned from brushing my teeth. He looked so beautiful with his soft eyelashes resting on his cheeks, like a dozing prince waiting to be kissed. My heart skipped. What to do with all these feelings of desire mixed with confusion about who I was and wanted to be?

I fell asleep to the sound of Patrick's endearing snore.

The next morning Adam served us sausage and pancakes. He told us how he and Greg had attended an all-boys' boarding school. They'd shared a room during high school. They knew each other's patterns, the rhyme and rhythm of each other's lives.

"We were close," Greg remarked. "We smoked together, until Adam decided to get into better shape two years ago. We trusted each other."

Adam nodded in agreement. "We're like brothers. That will never change."

I looked at Adam and Greg. They were comfortable in each other's presence. "Do you think you'll ever share a place again?" I asked.

"It depends." Greg said. "I still haven't ruled out returning to the seminary and becoming a priest."

"Dude," Ted Silvers and Brendan O'Malley lamented, "don't say that. Priests don't have any fun. Too many rules. Besides, you'll give the fraternity a bad rap."

"Oh, I'm not there yet, guys," Greg replied. "Give it some time."

I smiled. My Aunt Mary, a devout Catholic, always said I'd make a good priest. "Have you ever thought of serving our Lord, Jack dear?" she'd ask countless times when Dad and I visited her during my years in high school. I adored my aunt, didn't want to disappoint her, but had to be honest.

"I don't think so, Aunt Mary," I'd shrug. The thought made my stomach queasy. I never could make all those sacrifices: the vow of poverty, a life of chastity, married to the Church.

I looked at Patrick and saw another reason. I'd begun to uncover, even comprehend, why I'd had such difficulty through the years. Trying to be good, trying to please, trying to be the best son, or do the right thing. Maybe the time arrived to stop trying so hard. Could I let go and just admit I loved guys? Admit that I had a crush on my own frat brother, Patrick Francis? He represented everything I desired in a guy—athleticism, intelligence, gentle-heartedness, and boy-next-door looks – and he turned me on.

Adam blessed our travels and sent us on our way, with a big bag of apples, oranges, and Pringle's potato chips. I could see how Greg might enjoy staying here with Adam, to enter this place of serenity and quiet. The seminary felt protected, a place where I could think big thoughts and uncover major truths. Like the answer to the eons old Ontological Question, who am I? I watched the two men embrace and wished I didn't feel so jealous. I had no idea the extent of their relationship, whether they'd shared sexual experiences, were gay, or not. All I knew is they were close, and I wanted that for myself.

My five pledge brothers and I arrived in one piece back to Cleveland that Sunday in May. The following week on a sunny Friday evening we were inducted into the brotherhood of the Kaps fraternity. Sam Smith, Lizard Orman, and Brooks Lawson, along with the rest of the brothers, handed us our wood-carved fraternity paddles. They were inscribed with the fraternal crest on the front and on the back included each pledge's fraternal bloodline. Holding my paddle, touching the inscriptions, I gulped with pride and reflected on the bumpy road I took to enter this crazy quilt of a frat. I belonged. I knew I belonged. I'd earned the right. A lump grew in my throat, and I blinked back tears, praying nobody could see.

CHAPTER 24

RJ Graduates and Heads to NYC

I'D ALWAYS APPRECIATED the ritual and symbol of my own Catholic faith—it gave my life purpose and provided a calming sanctuary in stormy times. And so, as the spring semester ended, I completed my finals and turned in my term papers, including one I found most challenging and rewarding on Native American shamanism for my Alternative Religions class. Exploring various faith traditions unique from my own opened a window into how others practiced and believed. I decided there was no right or wrong path to God.

Scrambling down the stairwell with my suitcase and duffle bag I greeted Dad in the dorm lobby. "You ready, kiddo?" he said tapping me on the back. "Yep, I'm done," is all I said, leaning into the crook of his arm. I wasn't going to tell him about the hijinks with the golf tee and the judge in Buffalo. I didn't want him to worry that I broke any laws. We piled everything into the trunk of the Monte Carlo and headed back home.

While my father cruised down MLK Boulevard and merged onto the Shoreway, I rolled down the window to soak in the light breeze, closed my eyes, and relaxed, relieved that the ups and downs of my first year of college now appeared in the rear-view mirror. Free of Victor and newly inducted into the brotherhood of the Kaps, I looked forward to welcoming a new roommate, Robby, in the fall. And this summer I'd have my reunion with RJ. Life seemed in perfect order.

I gazed north. Seagulls soared in the distance. A warm, June breeze blew off the water and tickled my neck. I inhaled the familiar, fresh, and fishy smell of Lake Erie thanks to an early morning thunderstorm. In two weeks, I'd celebrate my nineteenth birthday. And it was strawberry season. I loved strawberries almost as much as I loved my birthday. The red-ruby color, the sweetness, the juice made my tastebuds water.

I arrived home to a completely renovated kitchen. "Surprise, what do you think?" Mom declared pirouetting in place like a showcase model on *The Price is Right*. I looked around with big eyes; my mother had always sought my opinion about decorating but this time she'd gone her own way with Dad's handy help. No longer a 1950's pink, with red countertops, the new kitchen was painted a cheerful yellow and accented with daisy wallpaper. New appliances—a harvest gold fridge, stove, and dishwasher—complimented the yellow décor, along with a white kitchen table and lime-colored cushy chairs with chrome accents. I nodded my approval, knowing it meant the world to her that I liked it.

That weekend RJ hosted his high school graduation party. My stomach turned to butterflies when I realized we hadn't seen each other in over a year's time. "What if I don't recognize you anymore?" I joked over the phone. "I haven't changed that much, silly," he replied. Mom and Dad entrusted me with the keys to the Monte Carlo.

As the car zipped along, I felt a rush of freedom and beamed as I turned on the radio. Michael Jackson's "Rock with You" exploded through the speakers. Rolling down the window, I sang along at the top of my lungs. My hips gyrated against the seatbelt. My butterflies continued bringing me back to RJ. What would he look like? How would he react to me? Would I feel any leftover attraction toward him?

I climbed the front steps and rang the bell. In a turquoise peasant blouse and white jeans Mrs. Fallon emerged from the kitchen and peered through the screen door. "Oh, hi honey," she said in the most nonchalant manner, as if she'd just seen me yesterday. "Everyone's in the back sitting in the shade. I'll bring you a Coke," she smiled.

I rounded the corner only to discover RJ standing alongside the above ground pool, chatting with an assortment of friends and relatives. He turned briefly to see me and then returned to his conversation. My heart leapt. He looked great--tanned, relaxed, and content. I drank in the scene, the pool, the people. Relief washed over me.

A warm hand, connected to a friendly voice, touched my back. "Hey, what a surprise! I'm so happy you're here." Shelley Lundgren hugged me; her hair, now a sunny blonde shade and tied back in a crisp ponytail, brushed my face. My heart fluttered seeing her so happy in my presence. My high school crush on Shelley had never abated. Standing here now in front of her, I felt like dancing, aware that I was a different person from before. My shoulders brimmed with confidence.

I hugged her again. "God, I'm so glad you're here. I haven't seen you since..."

"Since RJ began dancing with Mary Kathleen," she nodded.

From behind, I felt a tap on my shoulder. "Long time no see, stranger." There he stood in his white designer suit a la Travolta with a lilac shirt opened at the neck. For a fleeting moment I stared at him, my mouth agape like an idiot.

"What's the matter, cat got your tongue?"

"No, I just wasn't expecting to see you...."

"Looking so good?" he smiled with that trademark, loveable cockiness.

"How can you say that? You always look good," I replied flustered.

"Well, you'd never know," he sniffed, "since we haven't seen each other since you left for college." His brown eyes looked square into mine.

After the verbal touché, he glanced over his shoulder, allowing me a moment to regroup, though his critique hit a sore spot.

I grabbed RJ by the elbow and steered him to the driveway. "Can we talk?" I murmured. At wit's end, I'd reached my tipping point. "You know, things have changed. I'm not a puppet to your puppet master anymore."

"I never said you were a puppet," he snapped. "I think you imagined I was manipulating you or something," he whispered in a defensive voice.

"Well, you had the limelight. I needed to catch a breath, get out from behind your shadow. So did Shelley."

"What shadow?"

"Your dancing and all-encompassing shadow. I couldn't be myself. I needed to uncover my own talents, and how I wanted to be in the world."

"I never held you back."

"No, but maybe I held myself back. I craved your approval and the attention that followed basking in your glow."

"Well, times have changed."

"Yeah, they have. I'm glad we took a break." My jaw softened, and I felt empowered having released the buildup of resentments I'd avoided verbalizing for far too long. I glanced into his eyes. "But I'm glad to see you again. I'm sorry about the missed parties and graduations. Thanks for inviting me to yours."

"If my mother hadn't told me to do the right thing, to call you, I don't think you'd be here right now," RJ said. He wiped his upper lip, and I could see the hurt in his eyes.

Embarrassed by my actions and drawn to his vulnerability, I gazed at him and then looked away. I wanted to kiss him, but I couldn't. I felt conflicted knowing I'd created distance so I could find myself and avoid continuing a sexual relationship I couldn't allow myself to enjoy. And yet we shared a history I wanted to reclaim.

I couldn't provoke that kind of intimacy, not in front of everyone. So, I reached out and ran my hand through his soft, gorgeous, feathered hair. Not once, but twice. He pulled away.

"Why the attention?"

"I don't know," I shrugged. "I don't know." A big splash sent a huge wave in our direction dampening my shirt and our combative posture.

Friends from our little theatre days and from RJ's high school class came by and offered him congratulations and bon voyage to New York. I felt separate from RJ but connected to him even more now that we'd completed our confrontation. Our relationship felt different from high school but had retained the comfortable familiarity I'd yearned for, and missed, at John Carroll University. RJ's grandmother and his Aunt Mimi, who threw my sixteenth birthday party, came over and wrapped their arms around me. I felt at home, at ease, at my best.

"I want you to meet somebody." RJ took my hand and dragged me through the crowd. We found Shelley along the way, and she followed.

In the corner of the yard stood a strapping guy over 6 foot tall wearing a red Speedo bathing suit and whispering sweet nothings into the ear of Tricia, the girl who, thanks to her braces, bloodied my teenage lips the night I turned sweet sixteen.

"Darling, you're back," Tricia mewed. "It's been ages." She threw her arms around me tracing my spine with her long red nails.

"Meet Rick," RJ said, as he placed a firm hand on the hunky guy's shoulder. "Rick and I hung out senior year at Lakewood. He's an art major too."

"Pleased to meet 'ya. I've heard a lot about you, all good things." He gave me a firm handshake and looked me straight in the eye. I felt intimidated, and awkward, and a bit jealous that he got to spend an entire year with RJ that I didn't, even though I chose to distance myself from my best friend.

"RJ's told me about your vacation one summer. When you ran buck naked through the fields in Michigan." He smiled revealing big white teeth that reminded me of Farrah.

Rick continued. "And your disco dancing days. You guys were quite the trio, right?" he said glancing Shelley's way.

"That was a long time ago," I said. This guy really had the lowdown. Growing more uncomfortable by the minute I wondered what else he knew.

"What do you think?" RJ whispered in my ear.

"He's cute and talkative, nice butt." I looked back behind me at Rick noting his towering height and folksy attitude. Had I been replaced in the best friend department? I could feel the jealousy coursing through my veins. I should feel happy that he found another guy that liked spending time with him. But I also felt possessive; RJ was my friend. Maybe if Rick weren't such a hunk, I wouldn't have felt threatened. Maybe deep-down what RJ had, I wanted too. Was Patrick, my pledge brother, RJ's replacement? I was unsure what he was other than a long-simmering crush.

As the afternoon wore on, RJ cued one 45 after another on the jukebox, many of them our favorite songs from the 70's. The Bee Gees' "More Than a Woman," followed by "Still the One," followed by Andy Gibb's "I Just Want to Be Your Everything." The music brought back memories of our visits to Leonard's Deli, our time vacationing at my godparent's lake house, sleepovers, and YMCA dance parties. It also reminded me of the conflict I experienced wrestling with the guilt and shame of our relationship, struggling with what it meant for my future to be involved with a guy rather than a girl. And then, like the final act of a play, the happy and carefree feelings returned. The music, a touchstone, brought me home to the good times we'd always shared.

We sat in the sun and talked about RJ's acceptance at the Fashion Institute (FIT), and Shelley's plans to study music at Oberlin in the fall. RJ grew passionate as he talked about the classes he planned to take in sewing and couture. Observing his excitement about his future triggered a sense of pride and amazement in me. He'd spoken of his dream to work in the fashion world when we'd first met at Lakewood Little Theatre and now he was making it a reality. I knew how much he loved clothing, design and art. He dedicated himself to his drawing, a talent I'd witnessed unfold since we were 13 and took charcoal drawing classes.

After a dip in the pool, Rick, RJ, and I changed in the downstairs laundry room. While RJ showered, I caught a glance of Rick's beautiful smooth body and muscular legs from behind. He swung around to reveal a generous, uncut penis with a tuft of brown pubic hair. He smiled catching me observing him. Embarrassed I felt a slight tremor in my groin and quickly averted my gaze slipping into my shorts. I couldn't deny my attraction. I liked men, I liked dick, and I still felt guilty about it.

When would I accept the truth of my own desire? Could I just allow myself to relish in the beauty of this moment, appreciate that my friend had found a new love interest, and be happy for him? Could I let go of the sense of doom I felt and ponder a future where I might pursue a special someone?

Stuffing my feelings, I hurried my goodbyes. A relaxed RJ stood by the backyard gate lying in wait as I headed out.

"Don't be a stranger, stranger."

I smiled staring into those dark brown, familiar eyes. "I won't. Maybe the beach next week?"

He nodded, and we embraced. His chest against mine, I inhaled the memory-laden fragrance of Farrah Fawcett Shampoo in his hair.

***

ONE week later, RJ and I returned to Huntington Beach, where we'd spent summers sunning ourselves on the gargantuan rocks jutting into Lake Erie. We found a private place on a smooth, flat stone and spread out our beach towels. White caps danced on the water's surface. The wind tousled our hair. Despite the crashing waves and seagulls overhead, the beach felt quiet, deserted.

"So, tell me more about this new guy," I asked

"Oh, we're just getting to know each other. I met him at an art show. He's kind of quiet, but God, what a body."

I envisioned Rick at the party. His beautiful, lean, muscular physique in the red Speedo. I also remembered how I had turned away when he caught me gazing at him. I'd begun to live with the tensions of this no man's land. On one hand, allowing the pull of my attraction to beautiful men; on the other, containing it for fear of rejection by society and family.

Then I asked what I really wanted to know. "Have you had sex with him?"

"Not really. He's stayed overnight, but we haven't gone that far. I'm not sure whether he's into guys. He dates girls."

RJ shrugged and rolled on his stomach. The blazing sun emerged from behind a cloud. I straightened my towel on the rock's uneven surface and pulled out my paperback copy of *The World According to Garp*. With RJ and me, some things never changed. Our conversations always veered toward sex, while evading the topic of how we felt about each other, until we hit a boiling point, and then the feelings burst forth. Like after we saw *The Shining* when he asked me point blank at TGI Fridays if I was gay.

But I didn't want to go down that road. I didn't want to fall into a sexual relationship with RJ because it would just confuse matters, confuse me even more. I felt helpless because we had shared so much in our growing up years, and yet now I felt mired in my lonely struggle to come to terms with my desire.

I feared intimacy, and I feared being alone. I feared AIDS, and I feared even associating with guys thought to be gay. I also was terrified that if my parents ever found out about RJ and me they'd ban him from my life, or throw me out of the house, and I'd lose all financial support.

My crush on Patrick was likely to go nowhere. I began to sense that despite our closeness, he wasn't gay, or if he was, wouldn't give himself permission to explore it. A battle royale waged inside me—thanks to the warring signals—desire and repulsion—that refused to reconcile.

I realized I wasn't reading *Garp* anymore, my thoughts returning to RJ's party and how much I missed his companionship. I missed disco dancing, I missed our daily chatter about Farrah's latest escapade, I missed the care-free times we shared sleeping over at each other's houses, and sunning on his backyard pool deck. I just didn't want to have sex with him anymore. But I craved the closeness we shared.

Despite his prodding me to face my true nature—neither one of us was in a hurry to "come out" or define our sexual identities—RJ accepted my desire to remain platonic and not jump into a physical relationship again with him.

All the same I continued to wrestle with the demons of same-sex allure, and yet felt like the very friend who had initiated me, needed to be protected from my angst.

If we did get physical again, I feared he'd point to our continued sexual encounters as proof I hadn't changed at all, that we were now headed down a path of no return, that we were homosexuals, gay—words we never used to describe each other.

I closed the half-finished chapter I'd begun in *Garp* and rolled on my back, cupping my eyes from the overhead glare of the sun.

***

I spent the summer of 1982, between my freshman and sophomore year of college, chasing the same routines of the past three summers: lifeguarding and teaching swimming lessons at Foster Pool in Lakewood; bumming around in the off-hours with my fellow Foster Pool co-workers; and when time permitted sneaking off to the movies with RJ. We loved musicals, romantic comedies, and horror films and that year *Annie, The Best Little Whorehouse in Texas*, and *Poltergeist* lit up the screen and fueled our imaginations. I couldn't envision getting scared out of my wits with anyone else but RJ. Maybe it was that feeling of tension building up to the scary part, and then the release when the monster or spook sprung from nowhere and frightened the living daylights out of us. Like our earlier sexual encounters, climax and all, the movies bonded the two of us.

In mid-August, RJ left for the Fashion Institute of Technology in New York. In the dorm roommate department, he fared much better than I with his new roomie. Frank, a theatre major from Pennsylvania, loved late night conversations, musicals, and dancing. On weekends he and RJ explored the city's nightlife. By the second weekend of school Frank confided to RJ that he was gay and introduced him to his boyfriend, Tony. When RJ told me about Frank, I was envious, imagining what it might be like to have a gay confidante at JCU.

In the meantime, Philippa, my middle and high school friend, had returned from a trip to Europe with her parents and brother. During her visit there, she had made plans to meet the cute swimmer and clarinetist Dylan from our *My Fair Lady* days. Once the show closed a year ago in May they'd spent some time together before Philippa left for college and Dylan started his senior year at Ignatius. Now with Dylan graduated earlier this summer they had renewed their interest in one another.

"We had a great time in Vienna," Philippa sighed. "We walked hand in hand along the ancient boulevards and visited the Opera House. It was romantic."

Remembering my own crush on him I listened in rapt attention. From the pictures Philippa shared, Dylan was stunningly handsome with his full lips, blue eyes and doe-like eye lashes. "Sweetie, I'm happy for you two," I said.

"I'm concerned though," Philippa continued. "Marvin and he had a falling out. Now Marvin's spreading rumors about Dylan and his team-mate, Luke, insinuating the two of them are having an affair. Dylan said it's untrue. When they first joined the team, they did have an encounter, but they decided to keep it as a friendship."

I sat in silence, unsure what to say, impressed that Philippa had such little judgment concerning Dylan's openness, but burdened by my own fears, doubts, and attractions. I knew Marvin was envious of Dylan and Luke's tight bond. "I guess Dylan should be careful whom he tells," I cautioned. "I want you to be careful too, Philippa."

Philippa went on to say that when Marvin began dating a young woman named Annie his senior year at Ignatius, he remarked that neither Dylan nor Luke had a girlfriend. Then during Ignatius' spring musical, *The Boyfriend*, Marvin began whispering behind the stage curtain to a few members of the chorus: "Di-di-did you know D-Dylan and Luke are lovers? I c-c-caught them f-f-fondling each other in the locker room. They're p-p-pretty boy queers."

I cringed when Philippa recounted this episode to me. Whether it was true, or not, didn't matter. Marvin had no right to plant seeds of innuendo, seeds of destruction, for the sole purpose of sullying their reputations and destroying their privacy.

Soon everyone at Ignatius knew about the alleged pretty boy affair. Luke, the more popular of the two, disavowed the rumor and kept a distance from his swim mate. Dylan, who didn't confirm or deny the allegations Marvin spread, turned into a laughingstock and punching bag for homophobic classmates looking for a scapegoat to mock and take out their aggression. All I knew is it was despicable gossip.

CHAPTER 25

Ch-Ch-Ch-Changes

IN SEPTEMBER, I returned to Miller Hall for my second year in the dorms. With Dave graduated I had invited clean-cut Robby Monaghan to be my roommate. We had met through Christian Life Community, a faith-sharing group I joined during my first semester while living with Victor. Robby hailed from Jersey City. He sported a mop top haircut that reminded me of Paul McCartney in the early days of the Beatles. He said a silent prayer before every meal in the cafeteria and spent much of his time with his tomboy girlfriend Sherri, who greeted us with "Hi'ya Jack, Hi'ya Angel Face." I loved Sherri and Robby for the positive, infectious energy they spread around them. Everybody knew they were born-again, but nobody made a big deal about it.

Robby liked to keep our door wide open, welcoming visitors into our space. With his breezy manner he made friends easily and drew new people into our social galaxy.

"Good morning, sunshine," Sherri warbled when she picked Robby up to walk to class. She sometimes seemed to be addressing Robby and me at the same time, so I'd just smile and soak up her effortless joy.

If loving God made people this content, I thought, maybe I needed to find a little more of Christ myself. When I pledged the Kaps, I'd drifted away from Christian Life Community. I rationalized that the frat had sucked up all my time and energy. I needed some inspiration, like what Robby and Sherri had.

No longer required to serve the frat on bended knee, I explored joining other extra-curricular groups. I attended a meeting of the political science club, and discovered the campus radio station, WUJC, way up in Grasselli Tower. I always wondered what it might be like to have my own radio show and spin records. After an intense semester of pledging, I needed to make sure I kept my focus on academics.

***

"Hu-u-ulo."

There in the doorway loomed Marvin Fortis from St. Ignatius High School. Dressed in madras plaid shorts and a white polo shirt, he sported a Cheshire cat grin like he had a secret tucked up his sleeve. Seeing him close-up at the threshold of my room, my stomach grew unsettled. I blinked as if I'd encountered a ghost. Stuttering Marvin, who'd introduced me to marvelous Hope. What was he doing here?

I jumped to my feet, swaying as I lost my balance for a moment. "Hey, long time no see. You're here; I completely forgot you were coming to JCU."

"My older brother, D-d-Doug, attended here. I'm ca-ca-commuting for my freshman year," Marvin explained.

"Well, that's great. Do you see Hope? Has she left for college yet?" The words escaped from my mouth in a rapid staccato.

"Sh-sh-she's going to O-o-Ohio State. Left yesterday. Su-su-such a fun girl. Didn't you have f-f-fun with her?"

I nodded like one of those bobble head toys, and said I'd missed her. We'd gone our separate ways; she was out of my life. I quickly changed the subject back to him. "What classes are you taking?" My mind flew, searching for topics to keep up the small talk, like what was happening with his girlfriend and him, wanting above all to dissuade Marvin's sharp tongue. "How's your commute… How's Annie? …Oh, you broke up…Oh, she's headed to Ohio State like Hope…."-

But Marvin had an agenda and was persistent.

"D-d-did you know your former roommate Victor left JCU? I heard it from one of my f-f-friends in Bernet," he said with an all-knowing nod, like he'd sniffed around in my business and found a hidden clue to my tortured past.

My throat tightened at the mention of Victor's name and whereabouts. I had no interest in discussing my awful ex-roommate or the clique that purged me from Bernet Hall. Marvin had entered dangerous territory by bringing up this painful part of my past. I broke eye contact with him, shrugged and responded, "If it's okay with you, I've got some studying to do. See you around campus." I shakily closed the door.

Robby and Sherri didn't say a word.

I couldn't let go of my disturbed reaction to Marvin's visit. I felt sorry for him with his stuttering problem and all, but his darker side worried me, how he'd misrepresent people and destroy reputations with his penchant for gossip. I recalled the details of my conversation with Philippa in late summer, about the relationship Dylan had with Luke, how Marvin had humiliated them by his use of innuendo, how he couldn't be trusted.

I sat at my desk with my head in my hands allowing the rage I felt on their behalf to subside. Truth is, I felt impotent to do anything about it without casting a suspicious eye on myself.

Maybe Dylan and Luke had survived the character assassination, but I didn't want to take any chances. I feared if I gave Marvin too much information there was a risk he would use it against me. His mention of Victor set off warning signals that made me edgy and suspicious of him. Yet he would keep coming back, that I knew.

"Earth to Jack," roommate Robby called, extricating me out of my painful reverie. Sherri asked, "Are you okay, sunshine?" while Robby stared at me like I needed an oxygen mask. I wondered if they could feel the hyper-alert defense system springing to life in my body.

I blinked and shrugged my shoulders looking back toward them. "I'm fine. Everything's fine." I could tell they didn't believe me, but they were nice enough to let me be.

***

THE second week of my sophomore year I met Stephen. The air was crisp, leaves were starting to fall off the trees, orange, red, and gold. Of all people, Marvin was the one to introduce us, like he'd introduced me to beautiful Hope my last semester in high school. The guy had a way of drawing intriguing people into his web, but once inside negotiating the territory grew complicated.

"Nice to meet 'ya," Stephen smiled like a bright ball of morning sunshine. From the get-go my heart palpitated as I reached towards him and grasped his extended hand. The solidness of his handshake, the playful glint in his eye, his tousled ash blonde hair, the tuft of fur popping from the neck of his shirt—I couldn't take my eyes off him. Everything about this new guy entranced me. I took a deep, calming breath and just stood still smiling at him.

"J-j-jack's from Fairview," Marvin announced to Stephen, placing his hand on my shoulder. "Just a mile away from where I grew up."

I rolled my eyes because Marvin always mentioned I was from Fairview like it was some sort of status symbol. Truth be told, the bigger homes and mansions occupied forested property, built a decade after my parents settled in our modest home on the main arterial, Story Road. I loved where I grew up but didn't equate it with wealth or privilege.

"I've never even visited the West Side," Stephen said with a squinty, adorable look, eyes upturned and friendly. My blood rushed through my veins like a flooded fire hose. "I'm from Twinsburg," he mentioned. I knew it was a rural woodsy area where they held a festival every summer celebrating identical twins.

"Well, we're even. Until I started John Carroll, I'd never stepped foot on your side of town, except for a visit to Randall Park Mall!"

Stephen laughed and brushed back the hair from his forehead. Over six foot, he stood an inch taller than I. His brown eyes lit up when he smiled. My chest fluttered like a bird in flight just standing next to him.

The next time I saw Stephen was outside the Student Service Center on a sunny fall afternoon. We sat on the steps of the chapel and talked about our Catholic upbringings. "I studied at Holy Trinity my first three years in high school. The priest's life wasn't for me," Stephen confided when I asked him why he left the seminary.

"Why not?"

"I knew I couldn't take the vow of poverty," he shrugged. "Chastity would have really tested my willpower," he laughed. "I like sex too much!"

A brimming smile broke out over my face. Stephen reminded me of my frat brothers Patrick Francis and Greg Malone, both sensitive, soft-spoken guys who coaxed out people's feelings. Feelings I didn't realize lived inside me.

Here I was conflicted about my sexuality while Stephen spoke so freely of his. I loved listening to him. I wanted to be with him, near him, talking with him, running my hands through his tousled hair, and soaking up like gravy all that he had to offer.

Stephen had befriended a group of students involved with Campus Ministry. On a Monday night he invited me to join him at a Christian Life Community (CLC) mixer and introduced me to several of his friends.

"A lot of these folks play at the Sunday guitar Mass. I sing with 'em and strum a few notes," he whispered at the Murphy Hall chapel where we all gathered.

"I used to play the piano but I'm out of the habit," I said. I imagined for a moment what it might be like to make sweet music with Stephen. My heart skipped a beat at the thought.

From a distance I saw Robby and Sherri sitting in a corner chatting with several other students. I waved, and they waved back with their reliable bright-eyed enthusiasm. I introduced them to Stephen.

I shook my head at the irony of it all. I'd just completed pledging a foul-mouthed, practical joke-playing fraternity yet I'd already grown distant from them while finding myself here with these guitar-strumming, soft-spoken Christians. All of them seemed so positive and attractive and radiated an outward glow. There was no bitterness or one-upmanship. No competition about who was tops.

I was happy yet struggling with a lot of nervous energy trying to unpack the roiling waves of my secrets and contradictions and looking for a safe harbor in which to settle. I felt lodged between two worlds: the party hardy, "let the good times roll" popularity of my fraternity tribe versus the contemplative, under-the-radar nature of the Christian students who joined hands every Monday at CLC – not to mention my sexual orientation conflicts.

Neither group felt completely hostile, nor did they feel completely safe. I was certain nobody at CLC would kick me out due to my involvement with the Greek system, but wondered if the Christians would pause if they knew about my same-sex attractions? Would they ask me to leave, give me the cold shoulder? I didn't see one obvious gay person in the bunch. Was there anyone like me looking for a place to fit, searching for a place to exhale and just let go?

Part of me yearned to reveal myself; another part found it imperative to hold back and protect my secret. I continued to struggle with whom to trust or confide in; at least I'd reconnected with RJ and knew if I really needed to talk, I could call him. The certainty of our friendship reassured me. He was my ballast in an uncertain sea.

***

Soon I began encountering Stephen wherever I went on campus. As we got to know each other better, I began to trust him and relaxed my guard. I jumped at the chance to spend time with him. Every opportunity I got.

"Yeah, I'm pretty set on majoring in psychology," Stephen told me one fall afternoon soon after we met. "Reading people, figuring out what's going on in their head, fascinates me. And treating the whole person, not just the physical." He said he was considering a career in mental health counseling. "I'm curious about people's motives and the reasons behind their actions." I nodded and listened.

Later my sophomore year he gave me a written personality test. The evaluation summary read: *"You need to adjust your expectations of others and the world otherwise you'll meet with continued disappointment and frustration."* I felt like a thunderbolt crashed down from the sky. I fretted, asking myself what's wrong with wanting my life to turn out just right. Then I wondered if that dreaded perfectionism was a defect in my character? When circumstances didn't work out the way I planned, I often did get upset. Maybe the test really did have a message for me.

"Look at it this way," Stephen explained. "You've got the power to change your attitude."

I thought about my father's recurring advice. "Keep your perspective, son." Was Stephen's advice counter to my dad's? When I was upset my freshman year with academic demands and obsessed about making the Dean's List, Dad wrapped his arm around my shoulder and encouraged me to worry less, apply myself to the task at hand, and trust if I put in the effort, it would be reflected in my grades. Most of life revolved around maintaining a positive attitude, Dad said, difficult in the face of trials and tribulations. Letting go of my perfectionism and resulting high expectations of others and myself could therefore lead to less angst and upset.

They were both right.

***

ONE night after a CLC mixer, Stephen and I strolled back to our dorm. A luminous half-moon hung in the sky. Autumn was in the air. Leaves hanging on for dear life blew off a towering oak landing with a soft whoosh on the cement walk.

"God, this campus, it's beautiful," Stephen marveled. "The trees and open landscape. It's like we're living in a country club."

I laughed. "Some people might consider that a defect of John Carroll."

"I'd rather live at the country club than the seminary. At Holy Trinity, I didn't have much time for being a happy-go-lucky kind of guy between the routine of prayer, meals, and spiritual discernment."

"Yuck, sounds like too spartan an existence for me."

"Well, I had a posse of other seminarians with me."

"So now you're here to get an education, meet a girl, and settle down?"

"I don't know. Maybe."

Maybe? For a moment, my heart jumped. "You mean you might not get married?"

"Well, I'm not saying that. But I'd like to travel. Maybe join the Peace Corps. Wouldn't it be cool to go to Africa, or somewhere exotic, and help people?" I felt a bit deflated that my fantasy answer wasn't in the cards but we both shared a common desire to make the world better, which made me feel closer to him.

We continued to walk with the moonlight casting a milky glow on our path. Clouds stretched across the horizon, rain threatening for tomorrow. Tonight, humidity and potential hung in the air. I couldn't imagine being with anyone else in such an idyllic setting—Stephen's candor and sweet honesty penetrated my entire being and my defenses evaporated. I felt like I was 16 years old again, my heart fluttering and nervous, my senses even more aware, a yearning and yet fear that I was moving into risky territory with no idea where I stood. This guy wanted a friend, someone willing to lend an ear. I wanted a partner – a sexual partner – a soul mate.

As the months passed in the fall of 1982, Stephen and I spent more time together: we'd grab lunch, sometimes dinner (if I wasn't beholden to the frat), attend Christian Life Community gatherings, or after studying together in the library, down a beer in the Rathskeller, the campus bar. Sometimes Marvin would join us, but I was far happier and more comfortable when I had Stephen to myself.

At times I felt like Stephen's disciple, reveling in his quiet nature, listening to his philosophizing. He eagerly shared his thoughts, dreams, and desires with me. At times I felt like his tablet--a journal--on which he wrote his most private reflections and hopes for the future. I avoided disclosing many of my desires because most of them had to do with the joy I had being in his company and the resulting sexual attraction I had toward him. I didn't want to risk disturbing the serenity of our togetherness. Was this an infatuation? Would I lose myself again like I did with RJ? For now, the relationship with Stephen gave me enough. I didn't need the physical. I could survive on the rush of his special platonic elixir. Admitting I was falling in love with him would only complicate matters.

We discussed politics and Reagan, whose views I'd begun to question despite his popularity on our suburban Catholic campus.

In the classroom my political science professor Dr. Kathleen Babbitt soldiered on, challenging us to examine and defend our points of view. I wrote papers on nuclear disarmament, international trade barriers, and the morality of the death penalty. Dad's pontificating at the dinner table influenced my views too. Like my father, I believed in progress, fairness and equality, and a social safety net to protect the poor and vulnerable. For that reason, my views aligned more with the Democrats although I observed many students at John Carroll, especially the more privileged ones, siding with Reagan. Many, like me when he was first elected, appreciated his optimistic, sunny personality. I began separating the man from his politics.

Ever the contrarian, Stephen wondered whether some of Reagan's positions might be good for the U.S.

"Shouldn't we limit welfare, so it doesn't become a way of life?" he'd say. "Maybe the government needs to stop funding abortions. I mean, doesn't that encourage more of them to take place?"

I'd listen and wag my head, not in agreement or disagreement, but still trying to carve out my own beliefs.

Over the next few months, Stephen dated a few girls from Christian Life Community, but the relationships never seemed to last longer than a few weeks. We both accompanied sorority girls to dances even though Stephen had an aversion to the Greek cliques. I bridged the gap, maintaining a toe-hold in both worlds.

"Beer, oh beer, for Old Delta K," I'd scream into the quad after a night in the Rathskeller. I began to consume more alcohol to dampen my conflicted feelings about guys, and it allowed me to relax more around girls. I liked losing control of my inhibitions.

I was curious about what it might be like to have sex with a woman, to see what it felt like, but wrestled with uncertainty and confusion about the multiple ramifications. Catholic guilt and Mom's childhood lectures about morality and my body being the temple of the Holy Spirit played tricks with my head. What if a girl fell for me, and I was only using her to experiment? What if I didn't get aroused, felt no sense of attraction, with her baring her all in front of me? Would I feel like a failure? Or like Lizard might say, "a fuckin' douchebag?" Worse yet what if I got a girl pregnant? Then what?

Despite Mom's platitudes, I'd already dove into the sexual sea with RJ and tried to reconcile both the enjoyment and the guilt. How would I ever feel normal at this too-small school, worshipping at the feet of Stephen whom I was almost certainly falling in love with despite knowing almost-for-certain he liked girls?

After another night of dancing and playing the oh-so-fun drinking game, Quarters, until we achieved a mighty buzz, I walked back from the Rathskeller with him.

"When do you know if you're meant to be with someone?" I asked out of the blue.

"I guess your feelings tell you," he shrugged. "Or your awakening crotch," he blurted laughing.

"Well, I can't get this person out of my mind. They're haunting me."

"Tell them. Don't hold back."

But I couldn't tell Stephen. I felt confused about what to say, how to explain. Where to begin the story? All I knew is my feelings continued to percolate to the surface although I tried my best to tamp them down because I didn't see any way to express them without at a minimum complicating, or worse threatening, my friendship with him. I felt nervous the more I saw Stephen because I could see the relationship felt unequal, like I was idolizing him and he was just confiding in me like a friend, even though I haplessly hoped – yes dreamed – it might turn into something more.

And always there was Marvin, lurking one step behind, in the background, in the foreground, a shadow, a narrator. "Any new romances to report?" he'd ask with that shifting Cheshire grin, like the invisible cat in *Alice in Wonderland.*

And there was Stephen's roommate, Seth, who'd moved from Atlanta to attend JCU. A blonde, skinny guy with a sarcastic southern drawl, he constantly rattled on about the bad food in the cafeteria, the household help back home in Atlanta, and his Mama's good cooking.

Like both Marvin and Seth, who were drawn to his easygoing, magnetic personality, I couldn't pull myself away from Stephen. Seeing his sweat-drenched jersey after we played racquetball together, I wanted to stick my hand down his shirt and feel his hairy chest, plant my lips on his, but that was a pipe dream.

CHAPTER 26

Melissa

I MET MELISSA in the autumn of my junior year at John Carroll when she wandered into a University Chorale rehearsal. With her strawberry blonde hair, upturned lips, and doe-eyed glances, Melissa Hartrick reminded me of a young Ann Margret, the famous actress who appeared in the movie musical *Bye Bye Birdie*.

"Who are you?" I asked after she flashed me a pert smile and wink. I surprised myself that day with my uncharacteristic forwardness, but I couldn't ignore her unwavering gaze.

"Oh, just a lonesome girl looking to sing a few happy songs," she purred with a saucy, magnetic grin. I laughed and her smile widened.

"Well, you found the right place."

We giggled about the corny choreography we had to perform while we belted out "Going Out of My Head."

"All these arm movements and gyrations," I griped, raising my outstretched hands to my ears, and tossing my head from left to right and back again. "They're a little over the top, don't you think?"

"What's a little dramatic flourish?" Melissa shrugged. "We'll go with it. Just pretend we're part of the Up with People brigade." I choked back a laugh recalling the cult-like reputation associated with that U.S. choral group who traveled the globe spreading goodwill and cultural awareness with campy, patriotic fervor.

Despite singing in separate sections of the Chorale I stood close enough to hear her soprano voice, which blended in a beautiful way with my upper baritone. "Your voice is heaven. It's gorgeous," I told Melissa. I closed my eyes and imagined us making soul-stirring music together, like Freddy Eynsford-Hill serenading Eliza Doolittle in my high school musical.

"You're just feeding me a line," she teased. "I know your kind, telling a girl everything she wants to hear, buttering her up." Truth is, her voice danced in the air, defying gravity, and I got lost in its rhythms and cadences. Maybe Melissa and her charms might be enough to make me forget about Stephen. She'd cast her spell with that voice, that luscious hair and her smart, cheeky rapport. A girl who mesmerized my brain and my heart.

A week after we met, she took me by the arm after rehearsal. "Ya know, has anyone told you how special you are?" My heart pirouetted and sailed past the autumn leaves overhead. Nobody had used those exact words before. Not commitment-avoidant Hope, whom I'd placed on a pedestal, nor Stephen, whom I realized couldn't give me what I really needed.

Special, I marveled. She thinks I'm *special*!

I gazed into her blue eyes losing myself in her beautiful spirit. "You're some kind of girl, the best, heart to heart," I said thumping my chest. Part of me, though I loved hearing her say it, felt embarrassed, awkward, naked suddenly. Like a fraud, because I knew my secret might derail this dream of finding the right girl, one who would understand me and in whom I could confide my own weakness. A girl who might distract me from my lingering attraction to men due to the sheer power of our connection and mutual fondness for one another. These new, mixed feelings danced inside of me.

Is this what I wanted, a relationship with this pretty girl, so fragile and vulnerable and courageous enough to tell me she saw me, she really saw me?

Over the past year I'd spent lunch hours and late-night jam sessions with Stephen but where was it going? I knew I longed for a soul mate, someone with whom I could share my innermost dreams, thoughts, and fears. Maybe a woman, this woman, could satisfy me? I decided to try.

Soon Melissa and I grew inseparable, sharing our most private thoughts and our day-to-day ups and downs. Confidantes, we peeled back the layers of artifice at John Carroll, dissing the cocky bravado of fraternity boys and the eager-to-please anxiousness of their sorority counterparts. We derided the cat and mouse dynamics of men relating with women, and vice-versa. We discovered the confusing awkwardness in our own relationship, which started with a spark and heated up quickly.

The first time we kissed, the touch of her lips felt electric. Intense warmth spread through my entire body. I panicked, feeling hyper-conscious of my emerging erection pushing against my khaki pants. Is this how I was supposed to feel, or was it all heat and flash? No, I thought, this must be it, finally. I am attracted to this girl. She's different. She's special, remember?

I pulled back; my face flushed.

"What's wrong?" she asked.

"Nothing, I'm just...nervous. I'm not used to getting so heavy." She met my eyes and stroked the back of my head. I looked down at the perched tent under my belt, feeling embarrassed, wanting to go forward but fearful of the consequences.

"We can take our time," she assured me. "No need to hurry." We reclined on the bunk bed and sank into each other. I took a breath and relaxed. *Okay*, I thought to myself, *I'm in safe hands. Melissa won't force me to perform. I can go at my own pace.*

Shoulder to shoulder, her breasts felt like down-stuffed pillows. In early adolescence I'd grown accustomed to RJ's chiseled, sinewy anatomy. Melissa's curves felt alien, what's more I feared getting swallowed up in the depth of her emotional pull. While RJ and I shared our feelings, the initial draw with him was a physical one with few emotional demands to satisfy.

Melissa was a communications and theatre major. "I want to be an actress," she announced to me one Saturday afternoon on the quad. "Katherine Hepburn is my role model," she'd say arching an eyebrow and brushing back her luscious, shiny hair. "You can be my Spencer Tracy." I liked the comparison because since childhood I fantasized about what it might be like to become a famous actor and go to Hollywood. My experience with Mr. Molina at St. Ignatius had diminished that prospect, but I still dreamed of a relationship that sizzled with physical and intellectual stimulation, just like Hepburn and Tracy's did.

We talked about her family. She told me about her sister, Kate, two years younger, who planned to attend John Carroll and study something practical, like accounting. Her mother worked part-time for May's, a local department store. Her father, an insurance agent, travelled a lot for business. Melissa's loneliness followed her to college. Her parents didn't understand her desire to major in a creative field, which didn't align with their notion of a proper, reliable profession.

I understood, wrestling with the expectations of my own parents to study a practical subject like business followed by law school. All they wanted for me was to enjoy a more comfortable life than they'd experienced, yet I never felt deprived of anything growing up in our house. My overwhelming need to please my parents, make them proud, resulted in a tightrope walk between my passion for the liberal arts and their soft-spoken wish I settle into a secure, stable profession, much like Melissa's parents hoped for her.

"I always wanted a brother or sister," I told her. "You're lucky to have Kate to confide in." We spoke about both of our family's expectations and the pull we struggled with to appease them since they'd sacrificed, with the help of Stafford loans and Pell Grants, to send us to school.

Melissa wanted to get closer and spend more time with me. She'd drop by my dorm room unexpected, and I'd welcome her freewheeling invitations. Sometimes I feared she was too needy, that she relied too much on me for company because other than her roommate Karen, a studious biology major, I never saw her develop close relationships with other people. And she'd begun chewing her nails, which concerned me.

I knew I wanted closeness too, but unlike all my fraternity brothers who collected girlfriends like trading stamps and boasted about them, I wanted my private life to be private.

"Why don't we eat dinner together?" she suggested. Sometimes we did but I often felt self-conscious bringing her to the fraternity table. Her jeans were plain, and she wore baggy, comfortable sweatshirts while many of the girls associated with my frat brothers dressed in skirts and snug sweaters from J. Crew, L.L Bean, and Talbot's. For our style-conscious classmates, image was everything. At John Carroll, clothing communicated your pecking order, even shaped a person's identity.

I'd accepted the marching orders of this style regimen—after all, I liked clothes, and embraced the upturned collar on the Polo or Izod sport shirt, khaki pants with cuffs rolled, and loafers. But I also knew not everyone could afford, much less wanted, to adhere to the dictates of John Carroll's fashion order, where the prep look ruled if you wanted to grab the attention of the popular people, get invited to the fun parties, and dreamed of a chance to find your photo in the campus yearbook.

While John Carroll was a small, Catholic college, unknown outside of the industrial Midwest, thanks to the influences of a small but influential contingent of kids from places like Chicago and suburban Detroit, we acted, dressed, lived like we belonged in the Ivy Leagues, if not a highfalutin country club.

Melissa was the first woman since Mary Kathleen who intuitively understood me. I didn't have to explain myself, like I did with Hope, or other girls I'd accompanied to dances. She would draw me out if I got quiet or sullen. "What's the matter, Mr. Cranky?" she'd tease. The corners of my mouth lifted and before I knew it, she'd helped me to forget all the worry and angst bubbling inside my brain around my business and stats class.

At the same time extended silences felt comfortable between us. We could communicate with a touch or a look, as easily as words. I loved that about Melissa.

When I was away one weekend, Melissa told me she attended a University Club fraternity party. During the evening she met an upperclassman from U Club who started flirting with her, calling her sweet lips, and patting her ass. Melissa, who loved attention, tolerated the first grab or two. Then the physical attention started escalating, as the frat guy grew more intoxicated.

"Hey, sweetie-pie, come closer and put those beautiful lips to work down here," he pointed to his awakening crotch.

"Fuck you, asshole" she said and turned to escape his cloying reach. He grabbed her hand and forced it toward his lower anatomy. She said she'd kneed him in the balls, ran outside, and couldn't stop crying.

I noticed things about Melissa that were different. She went through periods, hours to days, when she'd be either extremely happy or extremely hopeless. This was foreign to my own experience, and I worried about her.

The more time we spent together, I could see she felt helpless to right her vessel amidst life's unpredictable waves. The recurring bouts of sadness continued but neither of us knew why exactly. The incident at the fraternity party we rehashed again. She recounted how she shouted, "Let go of me, let go of me, you asshole" and used her knee to kick him where it counted.

We both concluded this encounter hadn't led to any sort of depression since she'd fought back, taken matters into her own hands and taught the guy a lesson. Melissa refused to be a trophy, and I think she knew I wouldn't treat her like one.

I thought I could help her, I thought I could make her happy. I'd wrap my arms around her shoulders and say, "Look, you're a beautiful girl. I care about you. I love you."

But she'd wag her head, needing more convincing. "I don't know what to say," she'd shrug. "I need to see more of you, I'm not sure." I felt helpless to convey what she needed to hear.

Yet I continued moving forward in our relationship, despite my concerns about her mental health, due to the fact I'd not met a girl as beautiful, thoughtful, or emotionally candid as Melissa since I'd arrived on campus and didn't want to give up on her. One night in the cafeteria we lingered over cereal topped with ice cream, a student favorite when the main entrée disappointed.

"Hey, guess what," I ventured, "my parents are planning to visit the campus over Parent's Weekend. Want to meet them?"

Her face lit up and her eyes glistened. "I'd love to meet your parents. What a thoughtful idea." She leaned over and squeezed my hand.

A week later we watched John Carroll get trounced by Baldwin Wallace College on our own football turf. The trees almost completely bare on this sunny, crisp autumn day, Melissa sat with my parents and me in the stands.

"Nice to meet you, dear," my mother said, taking Melissa's hand. My father told her she reminded him of a famous actress, but he couldn't remember her name. She laughed, saying "Wouldn't that be my luck, to be famous and still nobody could put their finger on me." He guffawed before saying, "It's Bacall!"

Later in the school cafeteria she treated them like honorary guests at a lavish banquet despite the institutional setting of a student mess hall. She brought them water with lemon, laid out their silverware, and even folded their napkins by their plate. And when she excused herself to visit the lavatory, both my parents leaned over and said, "We love her."

My parents' positive reaction made me feel like I'd won an award at the Ohio State Fair.

***

THE next weekend Melissa showed up at my door out of breath and with a look of fright on her face. "I swallowed some pills mixed with alcohol. I couldn't help it," she whimpered.

"You what? How could you? You could get real sick, even die. Did you want to do that?" Distraught, I took her in my arms and shook her, fearful I'd driven her to harm herself, even though I couldn't think of what I might have done to cause her pain or agony.

I knew I'd fallen into the habit of regarding Melissa's actions as exaggerated, but I took very seriously her feelings of isolation, her frightening experience at the frat party, and her perceived inability to satisfy her parent's expectations. We both shared a similar story when it came to craving affirmation from our peers and approval from our parents. I insisted we go to the infirmary. She needed help.

"You are judging me, and I won't put up with it," she said, a passing reference to the last conversation we had concerning slick fraternity guys and her inability to see past their charm. Her words were slightly slurred, almost indecipherable. "You are so judgmental, a very judgmental person," she repeated pointing her slim finger at me and pulling back her frayed strawberry blonde curls. "And I won't let you take me anywhere with you."

Since she refused to go to the ER, I insisted she stay with me. The temperature that night fell near freezing, and I pulled her next to me and held her tight.

I felt her shaking at times and sobbing at other times, as I drifted in and out of a terrible night's sleep through the early morning and into the dawn hours. I heard her fall asleep around 3 or 4 am as she inhaled and exhaled softly into my chest. I could tell she was going to be okay. Relief flooded through me; I could never have forgiven myself if her overdose had led to her death all because I hadn't taken her to the ER. But I realized I could never again be in this position.

The pills and alcohol episode caused an irreversible rift in our relationship. I felt confused and uncertain how to cope with Melissa's moods, her ups and downs. I knew I didn't possess the mental bandwidth to help her. Hamstrung and uncertain what to do, beyond encouraging her to seek professional help, I began creating distance. We grew apart, seeing less and less of each other, waving politely in the cafeteria or outside on the quad. One day we ran into each other, and I told her "I'll never stop caring about you. I'll never stop loving you." Choking back tears she said, "I know."

I never saw Melissa again and never came to know what happened to her. What I did know is Melissa taught me that you can't control people and you can't fix them. Sometimes people we love are wounded. Sometimes they must face their demons alone, and I had my own demons to face: spending too much time and effort in my head, for one; feeling responsible for others and their feelings, for another, not to mention my desire for men.

Melissa forced me to start living more in my heart; her emotional firestorms pushed me to confront my own feelings. All I could feel at the end of our time together was eternal gratitude.

I liked Melissa's strength, her steely determination to go after whatever she wanted, whether me, or a career in the performing arts. I also loved her ability to share her inner vulnerability, no matter how weak it might make her appear. And it frightened me that I could have such a strong impact on another human being. I knew I had grown in this relationship.

In the three months we spent together, Melissa and I avoided having sex. I wondered if that was purposeful on my part. Maybe I was hiding. Or did I just hesitate diving into the deep end? I told myself that I feared getting a girl pregnant, a continuing paranoia that stemmed from Mom's disapproval of pre-marital sex.

But I also felt like I had no idea how to pleasure a woman; I was most comfortable pleasuring a man thanks to my long-term contact with RJ. I felt like all my peers around me were experimenting, and yet I didn't have any of the proper tools or education to know what to do, or where to go.

My uncertainty extended beyond pure sex education. I didn't know how to envision myself in a loving, out-in-the open relationship with a guy. Whenever I thought about it, I only saw an amorphous and cloudy future. This feeling scared me more than anything else.

I wished I felt courageous enough to talk with someone and lay all my fears and insecurities -- my complete deck of cards -- out on the table.

***

ONE matter I was certain about—I'd grown miserable in the business school at John Carroll. I'd written an op-ed column for the student newspaper on the value of a liberal arts education compared with the rote memorization I encountered in my business classes, recalling the Japanese management techniques I felt forced to regurgitate on my exams. I cared more about social justice, fairness and making the world a better place. Public service motivated me more than profit.

After reading a book on Marx and the exploitation of the worker in my political philosophy class, I viewed business and the thirst to make money at the expense of all else with deep suspicion. Pursuing the common good is what I cared about. I also wanted to harness my creativity but felt uncertain how to go about doing it.

By the end of the fall semester 1983, I'd begun feeling sick to my stomach, a gnawing pang that refused to disappear. After eating I'd experience this uncomfortable acidic feeling rising in my throat from my esophagus. Nausea resulted. Frayed nerves and constant worry over the grades in my business classes made it worse. The campus health center diagnosed acid reflux syndrome and a chronic ulcer.

One weekend in my dorm room studying for a business stats exam, I suffered an emotional meltdown, burst into tears, and feared I'd never stop crying. I called no one, just sat there alone until the outburst faded away. The episode forced me to face that I could no longer push myself into a business career unless I wanted to continue down a road of unhappiness and physical discomfort. I needed to take a hard, realistic look at my life and start becoming true to myself.

First, I admitted how much I detested studying business. I hated the memorization and recitation of technical concepts that inspired little passion in me. I craved a more classic, humanities-based education, grounded in coursework that would teach me how to think and live out the values that I cared most about: people centered values, not profit-centered values.

I decided to go for it: to switch my minor, political science, which did inspire and fascinate me, into my major. I consulted with my academic adviser, who applauded my change of heart and helped me outline my next steps. When I told her about my interest in pursuing an international studies concentration, she suggested a six-week Spanish language immersion program that upcoming summer in Monterrey, Mexico.

I approached my parents about my decision. They expressed hesitation. Children of the Great Depression, they viewed education as a stepping-stone to financial reward and security and didn't want me wasting more time in school. But my godparents Hugh and Fran, always on the lookout for how they might enrich me and encourage me to grow, loved the idea and offered to pay my tuition and registration fees for the Mexico adventure.

They wrote: *We're happy to support you in learning more about the world around you. This experience will change you, and we're one hundred percent behind you.* When I read their note, I jumped up and down like I'd won the lottery. I told Mom and Dad about the gift to bolster my argument it would be a good investment in my future and allow me to position myself in the competitive, new world economy. Mom and Dad finally gave me their blessing.

The day I made my final decision about transferring into the political science department, I visited Dr. Babbitt's office to inform her of my exciting news. Her intelligent blue eyes glimmered with pride. I think she suspected freshman year when I'd taken her *Intro to Political Science* and actively participated in class that I had a greater passion for her subject matter than I did for business classes.

"Congratulations," she chirped, dressed in her trademark red suit and patent leather pumps. "You're now official." She signed the paperwork accepting my transcripts into the Political Science Department. "Feel better now?" she winked. I shook her warm hand and floated onto the campus quad; my eyes outstretched to Grasselli Tower where bells began ringing high above me. I wanted to fly to the top and ring them even louder.

A new beginning awaited me. I'd chosen my path, and while my parents still influenced me, they no longer made my decisions. Thanks to a short round of medication and my new start, the chronic ulcer and stomach problems disappeared in short order.

Adulthood loomed closer, and I was going to own this chapter of my life.

Finally, I was free.

***

WHEN RJ left for New York in August 1982, Mary Kathleen followed close behind him. That fall she'd auditioned for the American Academy of Dramatic Arts (AADA) and received an offer to join the program early the following year.

Twelve months later, a week before Christmas, the phone rang. It was Mary Kathleen. Her voice was barely audible.

"Hey, kiddo. I've decided to dump New York and come home to Cleveland. The Academy hasn't asked me to return for a second year. Goddammit, that place is insane, it's insane living in New York."

My gut churned while my face began to tighten as she continued.

"Would you believe one night I contemplated ending it, I felt so pitiful? I wanted to off myself."

Her voice sounded ragged, tired, despairing. I had no idea she'd ever felt that desperate. My heart raced, remembering Melissa and her crisis. Now Mary Kathleen. When would it stop?

"I couldn't take the pressure of all the classes and the perfection and the bitchy ingénues, knowing I wasn't that way. I never felt good enough."

I struggled to find comforting words. "Babe, you've got acting chops you haven't even summoned yet. Give it time, fuck the Academy."

I wanted to reach across the telephone line, hug her, grab her hand, and squeeze. I knew she'd be okay, MK never stayed down for long. Her anger, the one emotion she knew better than I, powered her forward.

"When are you coming home?" I asked.

"Christmas Eve," she replied. Her voice broke over the phone while I gulped the unexpected tears flooding my eyes.

I pulled myself together and said, "I can't wait to see you!" before we ended the conversation.

My mind raced with thoughts about Mary Kathleen. She'd been so strong and adamant ever since we'd met. I didn't expect that something like a rejection could crush her. I sat alone watching the snow accumulate, flake by flake sailing through the air until each one found an earthly destination.

Is this what it was like in the world, each of us searching for our own place, landing here and landing there, hoping against all odds we fit somewhere? I didn't know what to say, other than I wanted her to know I cared, that the world would be lonelier without her, just like I had felt about Melissa.

***

A week later, gift under my arm, I hopped on my 10-speed-Varsity Schwinn bike and headed to the Cassidy's. I found the white colonial house and rang the bell.

"Merry Christmas, Ms. Cassidy, from your biggest fan."

"Oh, God, Hilovsky, do you have to be so corny?" Her hair knotted in a loose bun; MK flashed me a come-hither grin.

"Anything to make you smile. I just wanted to see for myself you were all right."

"I'm not hanging from the chandelier yet," she said with a mischievous smirk.

I handed her a gift-wrapped copy of Bette Midler's illustrated children's book *The Saga of Baby Divine*, which centered on the story of a tyke with one word in her vocabulary- "More"-and threw my arms around her for a deep hug.

"You'll never guess," she said. "John Carroll accepted me as a transfer student. I start next month."

***

AFTER New Year's had melted into February, I trudged through the snow-covered street to her mother-in-law rental one block from the campus.

At the doorstep of the forest green cottage, I rang the bell and kicked the snow off my boots. The door swung open to reveal a fiery redhead. MK's long brown hair shorn into a carrot-colored pixie. All smiles, the dimples in her pink cheeks popped.

"Hey, look at you, Cyndi Lauper."

Dressed in a blue suede jacket offset by turquoise suede boots, she nearly leapt into my outstretched arms. "Hilovsky, oh my God honey, look at you. Look at that shaggy haircut! How in the hell have you been, sweetheart?"

"I like the look." I ran my fingers through her shiny locks. "I don't think I've ever seen your hair this short much less a shade of Lucille Ball."

"I decided I needed a change after letting it grow out in New York. Hasta la vista to the old me, let's ring in the New Year. Heigh-Ho, 1984! And I love Lucy!"

"No, I really like it. Very new wave." I turned her around and eyed her from head to toe. Just the sight of MK made me happier. The rebel was back in town.

Outside the front window a large chunk of ice fell from the roof overhang and crashed to the ground.

"So now you're at John Carroll for good?"

"Yeah, after the Academy's snub, I didn't want to slink back to Catholic U. with my tail between my legs. Plus, Dad insisted I'd get as good an education here as anywhere, you know he graduated from JCU."

"Well, you couldn't have picked a better school. Your timing is impeccable. I'm now a member of the Kaps fraternity. Bow down and kiss my ring," I teased extending my hand.

"I'll bow down and kiss your ass; I can't believe you pledged a fraternity. How unoriginal of you."

"Oh, MK, give me a break. They're a nice group of guys. Freshman year was rough, adjusting to college life, with my tormenting roommate Victor and all. I wanted to feel like I belonged someplace."

"Yeah, but you've never seemed like the frat type."

I shrugged. "There's a time and a place." I didn't reveal that I'd distanced myself from the brotherhood last year while cultivating my friendship with Stephen and grew even more distant this last semester while dating Melissa.

"So, what did you take away from American Academy's decision?"

"Oh, it nearly killed me. They told me I needed to pull back, that I tried too hard. They told me I over-acted. They told me I couldn't sing. They liked my dancing. We worked on improving some of my weaknesses in the over-acting department. But after a year of training, I think they decided I'd reached my limit. But maybe they'd reached theirs."

Following her into the kitchen I noticed prior to my arrival she'd begun preparing a stew. I shredded the beef in the crockpot and threw in her chopped vegetables. "Maybe they didn't see your true potential, but only looked at what appeared up-front. Don't give up, don't let them decide whether you sink or swim."

I told her about moving to Miller Hall, about the pledge process and how I survived Hell Week. "John Carroll hasn't been all pie in the sky for me either," I whispered. "There's strong pressure to conform. I've had my share of frat pranks and intimidation."

She gazed at me with her wide blue eyes as if to say *I'll beat the hell out of anyone who tries to hurt you.* "You don't need to worry," I laughed. "I made it through the hazing. I didn't lose any body parts." I didn't need to give her the gruesome details.

While I stirred the crockpot, she watched. "I'm going to finish my English degree and then focus full time on performance. I'm here to get the B.A. and get out."

"While you're at it, don't forget to have some fun." I rubbed her neck for a few moments and tried to quell my unease about her even pondering taking her own life. I chose not to mention the subject. The knife she used to chop the vegetables lay on the cutting board, reminding me how easy it is for someone to hurt themselves. I chose to believe that MK didn't have a death wish. She had just hit her limit in New York, and now she'd make a new start.

While we waited for the ingredients to simmer, MK left the room to call her father. I could relate so much to Mary Kathleen and her experience. Her father, like my parents, had high expectations for her. Mr. Cassidy, an industrialist and entrepreneur, wanted his eldest, intelligent daughter to be an attorney. He wanted her to grow up stable, complete her degree, earn a decent income, marry a successful guy, and have kids.

Mary Kathleen would have none of it. She pledged her fealty to birth control and had no interest in children. She wanted to marry a fellow actor who would encourage her pursuits in stagecraft.

I began to realize that fellow actor wouldn't be me, despite our history stretching back to 1979 and *The Rocky Horror Picture Show*. We had relished performing together in two high school musicals, attended her Christmas ball and my high school prom, and negotiated the nooks and crannies of a friendship with RJ. She'd taught me how to stick to my principles, to not apologize for being different, and maybe to be more of a renegade than I might otherwise have been. But we weren't romantic partners; we were buddies, friends, theatre aficionados, and goaders of one another's dreams.

All I knew is I was glad to be in her orbit again. Despite all my questions and fears about my own future, whom I'd become, and what I wanted in my life, her resiliency, her fighter instinct, gave me hope. Hope that I too would emerge on the other side, a victor in confronting my own challenges around identity, independence, and true love.

CHAPTER 27

Awakening

"Who are you?" I felt a friendly tap on my shoulder.

"Are you talking to me?" I said turning around.

It was first period in Dr. Babbit's engrossing state politics class. Right behind me sat a plump, olive-complexioned girl wearing a Princess Diana blouse. I recalled from the previous class she enjoyed arguing a point and answered Dr. Babbitt's questions with a confidence I admired.

She elbowed me. "Yeah, I want to know who all the good-looking guys are in my class. You seem to have a brain too." She stuck out her hand, like a true politician. "I'm Josie."

I cracked a smile and introduced myself. To my pleasant surprise I learned we were both diehard Democrats, and we both loved Dr. Babbitt's dynamic lectures. Josie's father worked in construction, her mother as a dressmaker and tailor for a local department store. Her parents emigrated from Italy in the 1950's before Josie and her sister were born.

I confided in Josie my admiration for the idealistic Kennedys and how one day I dreamed of becoming President of the United States. Now that I was free from the suffocating confines of the business school I was falling in love with the allure of politics. "Well, if you're President, I'll be Secretary of State," Josie quipped. We both laughed.

"You better start planning now, or you'll never catch up to the other go-getters." Facing the reality that someone didn't just get elected President without a political pedigree, I decided a run for the Senate might be a more realistic first step. "By the time I'm ready Metzenbaum and Glenn will be headed toward retirement," I pontificated one day to Josie. As a first step towards that dream, I elected to learn about and get involved in campaigning.

At the time two titans of Ohio Democratic politics represented the state: Senators Howard Metzenbaum and John Glenn, the beloved astronaut, who had recently announced his candidacy for President of the United States. In February 1984, enamored by the prospect of a Democratic hometown boy ousting the Republican standard-bearer, Josie and I rode a bus for fourteen hours to Manchester, N.H. There, during the final weekend of the New Hampshire primary, we canvassed for John Glenn.

Besides our candidate, Fritz Hollings, Gary Hart, Walter Mondale, and Jesse Jackson, among others, all appeared on street corners and in coffee shops. Political buttons decorated lapels and jackets all over town. Campaign literature and posters dotted storefronts, tables, and mailboxes far and wide.

Young, idealistic students like us poured in from all over the country, knocked on doors and expounded on the greatness of their candidate. Slogans on billboards such as *For a Better America, Vote John Glenn*, and *Gary Hart: A New Direction* floated like product endorsements everywhere we looked. All the activity and movement felt so momentous, like life was revealing itself right here and right now. The drama of who would take on Ronald Reagan played itself out before our eyes, and we loved the theatrical intrigue and the cast of players.

As wet snow fell all around us, Josie and I trod the slushy streets of industrial Manchester, canvassing every Democratic household listed on our official printout guide. When they answered the door, we heard the same story: "We like Glenn, and all, but we're voting for Reagan." By the end of the day the moniker Reagan Democrat took on new meaning.

We came to realize our candidate was headed nowhere. Discouraged and downtrodden, we trudged back to the Glenn campaign headquarters and warmed up with a cup of hot cocoa. Other glum-faced volunteers surrounded us, driving home the reality that defeating a popular incumbent President wasn't going to be easy.

Despite the disappointing outcome in New Hampshire, Josie and I returned home to Cleveland from our long weekend, exhausted from our glad-handing, yet euphoric about our firsthand experience in retail politics. I came to realize I liked the excitement, the unpredictability of getting out and shaking hands with people, learning about their concerns and opinions, what drove them, why they liked one candidate over another. I discovered that politics wasn't about strategy alone. It was a people-oriented endeavor that was driven by popularity, likeability, as much as policy. And I had come to these realizations not from a textbook, but from my own canvassing experience, and that was far more valuable.

Back home in our state politics class, I had the opportunity to deliver a State of the State address. As I explained my priorities at a lectern in front of the class, I could feel the electricity, the thrill, of speaking before an audience and an energy exchange, reminiscent of my days performing in children's theatre and St. Ignatius musicals. I glowed inside. No wonder Reagan, a former actor, loved the stage of politics.

It felt natural getting up in front of a crowd and talking about my vision for the future. I believed in the State of the State address I had created: investing in people, health and education programs, and in the future of cities and transportation infrastructure. I believed that the investments I proposed could reap long-term future benefits in a more civil, more progressive society.

As I gave my speech, I envisioned a brand-new horizon, a hopeful future that borrowed from the best of Kennedy's New Frontier and Reagan's shining "city on a hill" metaphor. I aspired to be a true leader, one who got out ahead of the people with a vision and roadmap to get there; a leader who did not appeal to the fears of those he represented but one who appealed to their greatest hopes. I wanted to use my charisma and big heartedness to be a different type of politician, one who led from my heart, gut, best instincts. I envisioned being a gentle warrior.

Josie and I realized that most of our college classmates held opposing points of view. While Reagan's sunny *Morning in America* talk inspired many of them to view him in a positive light, they were blind to what I felt was his true tainted legacy: Reagan slashed social programs that helped the poor, middle class, and the mentally ill; he pumped millions into the military, leaving America saddled with debt. I was able to separate his sunny disposition from the reality of his policy priorities. Why couldn't others see what I saw? My heart sank.

In the back of my head, I also wondered how, if I chose to run for office, I could ever keep it a secret that I was attracted to men. I pushed the nagging thought aside and tried to think about the bigger picture, my belief in public service and how I could make a difference in the lives of average people.

But what I didn't like to think about invaded my thoughts again and again. How would I ever maintain a private life protected from the media's glare? In 1984, there were no openly gay congressmen, at least not that I knew. I'd need to hide behind a photogenic wife and children. I would have to live a lie.

***

"Now y'all need to pack lightly. Ya know there'll be no drinking in the car. I'll be damned if I'm gonna get stopped by the cops and pay a ticket to cover your sorry asses," Beau drawled in his southern Ohio accent. "I expect we'll take turns driving and y'all will pitch in for gasoline,"

Stephen's roommate Seth had invited Marvin, Stephen, our friend Beau, and me to his home in Tampa for spring break. After damp New Hampshire, I was looking forward to sunnier days. Tampa was my ticket.

Beau Bower, a native of Cincinnati, was a consummate storyteller who dressed in punk-ish, disco-inspired clothing. His wardrobe included neon-colored shirts in Day-Glo colors and tight tweed pants cut above the ankle, a nod to Boy George and MTV. He sported a pencil-thin mustache that reminded me of Errol Flynn in the swashbuckler movies. Beau offered to drive us down in his Ford Capri, which comfortably seated four. Seth was to fly home and await our arrival.

On an afternoon in March after our last mid-term, we piled into Beau's car and motored south. "Tampa, or bust," I hooted as the other three woofed in unison. We zipped through Ohio, then Kentucky and Tennessee, before crossing the Georgia border. At 2 a.m., the radio hummed to the restless strains of the Eurythmics' "Sweet Dreams." While the headlights bled into the immense darkness, light fog rolling over the windshield, I squinted and clutched the wheel of the car, wrestling to stay awake. We raced through Atlanta and past the big, bright lights of Coca Cola. While Marvin and Stephen slept in the back Annie Lennox' relentless lyrics lulled me into a hypnotic state. Beau tossed and turned in the passenger seat.

"Hey, wake up." I elbowed Beau in the ribs.

"Huh? Well, what in the hell did you do that for?" he grunted.

"I need someone to talk to. I'm feeling groggy."

"Well, keep your eye on the road. Do you want me to change the radio station?"

"No, I'm fine, just talk to me."

Beau always kept me up to date on who was dating whom on campus. He also liked to play jokes and tease friends. Both he and Marvin shared a dramatic flair for describing situations and people in the most exaggerated terms. Unlike Marvin, Beau's gossiping wasn't of the mean-spirited variety, but a more good-natured exchange of information. I knew Beau wasn't out to hurt anyone, so I never felt on guard.

He stroked his mustache for a few seconds like a magician preparing to pull a rabbit out of a hat. "So, do you think Seth is going to take us to a nude beach, like he said?" My eyes practically popped out of my head at hearing mention of Seth's idea. Raindrops began pelting the windshield, heavier by the minute. The wipers screeched back and forth like the creepy atmospheric music in the *Psycho* shower scene. Titillated by the mere suggestion of our visiting a nude beach, I shrugged attempting to act cool, but I was intrigued. My heart raced. "I had no idea Seth wanted to take us to a nudie beach. I've never visited one. But, why not? We might get lucky."

While I was excited by the possibility we'd encounter naked guys, their bodies lathered with suntan lotion, their penises dangling like forbidden fruit in the warm Florida sunshine, I maintained a façade with Beau. Getting laid meant with girls. Regardless of his object of desire, I had to demonstrate my heterosexual credentials, if not for Beau, for myself, and Marvin and Stephen half-asleep, or half-awake, in the back seat.

Beau harrumphed. "Well, Marvin and Stephen aren't sure they want to go."

"Then let 'em stay back. We'll have the adventure." I envisioned beautifully sculpted, muscular backs and legs running down the beach, like a male version of Bo Derek in the film *10*.

Beau adjusted the passenger seat in the recline position. "That's what I like about you, Hilovsky. You're an unpredictable badass." Our eyes met for a moment until we both broke out in silent laughter. I felt closer to Beau than ever before.

As Beau dozed off, I sat in the driver's seat wide-awake. I thought about his comment. A bad ass? Me? I'd always viewed myself as too strait-laced for my own good.

The idea of visiting a nude beach carried me back once again to the days of cavorting in the Michigan farm fields with RJ. The memory of the two of us running buck naked through alfalfa brought a smile to my face. The guys slept through my ruminating, their snores and murmurs a backdrop to my recollections. I relaxed into my beach fantasy as the wipers cleared the rain from the windshield, a gentle whoosh replaced the screeching. Well-lubricated, they kept tempo, back and forth, back and forth, tick-tock, tick-tock, like a metronome marking time in the dark.

The music transitioned to the familiar toot-toot, beep-beep of "Bad Girls" playing on the radio. My mind drifted back to RJ, our love of disco and every Donna Summer song ever recorded. Those times felt very far away. I wondered how he was getting along in New York without Mary Kathleen to keep him company. I missed him. I wanted someone in whom I could confide, someone with whom I could share these private musings. I missed the close physical contact, sexual and otherwise.

Once we crossed the border into Florida the cold, grey fog lifted and a warm, bright morning emerged. Everything was covered in green, unlike the white snowy blanket we'd left behind in Cleveland. The highway, bordered by mossy trees and swamps, stretched into the distance. Bodies of water and boats peeked out along various byways. Excited by the changing topography I rolled down the window to let in the air and inhaled the floral humidity of a new day.

"You boys made good time," said Mrs. Wales as she and Seth greeted us outside their two-story Spanish-style home.

"Seventeen hours," I said looking at my watch.

"Holy, Moses," Seth whistled. "You must have been racing like hell."

"Eighty miles an hour or so during the wee hours," Beau chuckled like he deserved a merit badge.

Bleary-eyed Stephen and Marvin sat and listened, nodding at appropriate moments and complimenting Mrs. Wales on her homemade muffins.

After unloading our suitcases, we headed for Clearwater Beach, a popular hangout for college kids. White sand stretched far and wide. Little shacks dotted the landscape with restaurants, record stores, and boogie board shops. We parked Seth's VW Bug and headed for the retail district.

A pair of geometric-patterned pink, turquoise, and black board shorts grabbed my attention in a surf shop window. I bought them on the spot.

"No S-Speedo?" Marvin remarked with an arched eyebrow.

"No, I'll let Stephen wear the Speedo," I winked.

Stephen smiled and laughed, "So I'm the one who gets to be teased."

All of us understood my inside joke. Marvin mocked guys who wore Speedos, insinuating they were "girly boys." Even though I wore a Speedo for lifeguarding and swimming laps at the university pool I'd grown aware of people's perceptions toward men who wore teeny, tiny bathing suits.

Crossing the street, we peered out at the Gulf of Mexico, the toasty sand cooking our feet. I inhaled the salty air then raced toward the beckoning waters. I dove into a crystal blue wave and shrieked, "Who-eee!" Marvin, Stephen, Beau, and Seth observed before dipping in their own toes.

"E-e-e-k, it's cold," squealed Seth.

"Oh, don't be such a wuss," Beau huffed. "Look at Jack, the lifeguard."

"Yeah, what about me?" I asked with a fat grin on my face.

"You're like a fish," Stephen said watching me as I showed off my backstroke. "You love the water, don't you?"

I swam over to him. "Yes, and you will too!" I attempted to dunk him but instead we fell into a splashing match. I wanted to get his attention, so I did what came naturally: create a little commotion and act the part of the contrarian. Seth and Marvin and Beau waded over and before too long we were engaged in a game of King of the Hill. Stephen climbed on top of my shoulders and Marvin hopped on Beau's. The contest of wills began. Seth kept count as Marvin and Stephen in mid-air waged arm-to-arm combat.

"No----," I yowled as Marvin pushed Stephen off my shoulders and into the water. I knelt to allow Stephen to climb back on. Soon they were grabbing hands and pushing each other in a playful struggle until Stephen knocked Marvin off Beau's perch.

"Final round," Seth shouted.

Stephen fought Marvin off, while Beau and I made a valiant effort to balance the two on our wobbly shoulders. Marvin plummeted headfirst into the water.

"Yippee, we win!" I yelped.

"Victory," Stephen said raising a sexy muscled arm over his head. I loved this rough and tumble, this physical contact between Stephen and me, the two of us overpowering Marvin. It felt exhilarating, like there was a battle to win even though it was just a silly game.

"You scumbags!" said Marvin wading through the water pointing at both of us. "Wait until I get you. When you least expect it."

"I know, expect it," I laughed.

My crush on Stephen was ballooning. At school we had multiple demands on our time: classes, studying, papers, and the occasional, sweaty racquet ball game. I would see him at Christian Life Community or Sunday evening Mass. Here in Clearwater, we'd have a week of chill, and our lives slowed down. On vacation time, I watched him materialize into the golden boy, his skin tanned, his blond hair lightened, further accentuating that pearly white smile. Ah, if life were a beach movie, I'd have remained in Clearwater forever, playing the male version of Annette to his Frankie Avalon.

Our first night at Seth's, a disagreement broke out over who would share a room with Stephen. Marvin insisted the two of them stay together.

"Beau snored in the front seat of the car all the way down to Tampa," I complained. "It's your turn," I added, looking unflinchingly at Marvin. He shook his head right to left. Marvin had a way of influencing final decisions in his favor on all sorts of matters. He had approached Stephen and Beau ahead of time, suggesting the arrangement as if it were a done deal, like it just made sense. This wasn't a battle I was about to win. I rolled my eyes and agreed to room with Beau.

Once Beau and I settled into our quarters I tucked my pillow under my head and pondered the day's events. "Do you think Marvin has a thing for Stephen?" I asked Beau once he turned out the lights.

"Hell, you can't tell that the old she-dog has her scent for him?" Beau said switching on the bedstand light. He made me laugh with that quirky Cincinnati accent and turn of phrase. "That old she-dog, he's got a scent for Stephen that won't let up," he repeated.

My eyes poked out of my head, and I threw my pillow over my mouth to muffle my laughter. I looked Beau straight in the eye and almost asked whether he liked guys, but then lost my nerve. God knows we all fawned over Stephen, even though he gave us no reason to think he fancied any of us. Seth was his dorm roommate, Marvin his confidante, Beau and I simply friends with whom he enjoyed spending time.

I wondered if Beau knew about my crush on Stephen. I was concerned since I had never alluded to my same sex attractions to any friends other than RJ. Beau talked freely about sex, without identifying the object of his attraction or any specifics. I never broached the topic about his romantic interests because I didn't want him broaching the topic about mine. I was grateful we could discuss the dynamics between Stephen and Marvin; it allowed me to relieve the frustration I often felt around Marvin's manipulative behavior and Stephen's failure to recognize it. Their relationship often affected our group dynamic.

While Stephen fell fast asleep (I imagined) with Marvin (probably awake) in the next room, Beau and I debated everything under the sun. We snickered all night talking about our classmates, the Clearwater scene, and stories we'd never discussed back in cold, shivering Cleveland. I felt relief and a sense of camaraderie that I hadn't shared with Beau ever before. Maybe losing out on rooming with Stephen had an upside in all the laughter and fun Beau and I experienced that night.

Vacationing in Clearwater, my first spring break away from my parents, felt like a dream. Despite the typical tensions that arose travelling with such a motley crew, we were all up for adventure. The five of us devoured delicious tilapia at a local seafood restaurant, downed margaritas at a Mexican watering hole, and danced practically until the morning light to "Rhythm of the Night" and "Jump" at a popular hangout called The Rock Lobster. Stephen zeroed in on a short blonde girl who kept giving him the eye. He just returned the favor but didn't make any effort to engage her. I felt happy he didn't have a need to hook up with anyone. I wanted all his attention. We explored downtown Tampa and drove to St. Petersburg. We never did get to the nude beach Seth had praised to high heaven. The second to last day Marvin and Stephen got into a spat about our dinner plans.

"C'mon boys, we're on vacation," Seth pleaded with a tinge of exasperation.

"What a dick-wad," Stephen muttered about Marvin under his breath. Marvin accused him of being a cheapskate because he didn't want to dine at a reservations-only restaurant on Tampa Bay.

"We're college students, for God's sake," Stephen complained. "Let's go back to the seafood shack."

"T-t-tightwad," Marvin stuttered crossing his arms over his chest. Instead of Seafood Paradise, Marvin's preference, we all landed at The Fish Fry, Stephen's first pick. Sitting on the opposite side of the dinner table Marvin gave Stephen the cold shoulder, but eventually the sulking stopped, and Marvin joined in the final night's rambunctious celebration. "To us, the boys of summer," he said raising a pint of beer.

The last memory of Clearwater I have is the five of us posing for a photo astride Seth's orange VW Beetle in our swimsuits. We sported golden tans, sun-streaked hair, and carefree smiles etched on our youthful faces.

As we drove back to Ohio, I pondered our time in Tampa. Despite the light-heartedness, there were danger signals I could see that threatened to explode in the days and weeks to come. I'd begun to resent the control Marvin employed over all of us. His insistence on certain restaurants, his strong-held opinions on acceptable styles of dress, and especially his critical attitude about people I liked, my born-again roommate Robby, for example, whom Marvin labeled a Bible-thumper and worse.

I had listened, taking it all in, letting him say what he wanted. I made mental notes. I'd begun to tire of his overarching need to manage us all in a way that he couldn't manage his speech. All the warning signs started flashing in big, bold, red letters: tread carefully. A literal twist on the famous Cold War adage of Reagan's: "Trust but verify."

***

As spring sprung my feelings for Stephen grew deeper. I looked forward to our meals together, our weekly walks around the campus, and our late-night talks about philosophy, politics, and the world. My heart raced when he appeared. I grew less interested in spending time with my fraternity brothers, their bravado, like cold leftovers—unappetizing and, at times, tasteless. Often, they acted like overgrown adolescent boys, and I yearned for something more. Stephen provided it. I liked the way his mind questioned the universe and how he would share his thoughts and feelings with me in a way RJ hadn't or couldn't. The confidence he placed in me felt intimate and sacred, and I vowed to myself that I would never betray it.

After our trip to Tampa, we spoke at length about his struggles with Marvin. Over lunch he peered over his shoulder before saying, "I don't like how Marvin gossips about people. My friends from Christian Life Community are believers. What's wrong with that? He makes snap judgments about people depending on how they look or dress. I'm telling you, Jack, I'm frustrated." He put down his spoon and shook his head. "I just think you need to dig under the surface and give people a chance. Not pigeon-hole them."

I nodded as I sat there allowing his words to sink in. My mind raced as I tried to find a way to be honest without badmouthing our mutual friend. "It's not that I don't like Marvin," I said. "It's more about his behavior. If you don't do things his way, you're sentenced to eternal condemnation." I felt relief that Stephen was removing the blinders from his eyes and looking at Marvin closely. Maybe he could confront Marvin's behavior in a way Seth, Beau, and I didn't dare in Tampa for fear of reprisal. After all, it was obvious Marvin invested more time in his friendship with Stephen than with the rest of us. Stephen was the showcase act, while we were the supporting cast of players.

One evening while walking back from the library Stephen stared into the silent starry sky. "There's got to be a Divine Source of all this beautiful existence," he said gazing into my eyes. "It didn't happen by accident. We are here for a reason."

"I don't think anything happens by accident," I replied. "All of us have lessons to learn on earth, and if we don't learn them, we fail to graduate to the next level of awareness. Instead, we need to return to earth and try again. That's what I think."

Stephen laughed and shrugged his shoulders. "I guess I'm learning. Two years ago, I decided seminary wasn't for me, too much orthodoxy and hypocrisy. I'm curious about what makes people tick, just not in the church confessional. I think I'd like to learn more about the human psyche. Maybe I was a failed shrink in a previous life."

Our conversation took me back to spring break in Tampa. I'd read Shirley MacLaine's memoir *Out on a Limb* and began opening myself to her ideas about past lives, reincarnation, and out-of-body experiences. My godmother Fran had enjoyed the book and encouraged me to read it, and I valued her opinion and openness to different ways of thinking. While it sounded New-Agey—all jangling bells and shiny crystals, maybe even a crystal ball thrown in for good measure--after reading the memoir, it left a lasting impression. I imagined if I came back to the planet, reincarnated, it would be as a dolphin. I loved the water, and to me dolphins were both intelligent and friendly. They liked people.

We continued our walk in the night and returned to the subject of Marvin. "I just don't think he gets me," Stephen sighed. "He wants to hook me up with these shallow girls who only care about their looks and clothes and having a good time. What I'm searching for is a soul mate."

I looked away from Stephen and sighed inwardly. If only he knew that's what I wanted too. I desperately wanted to believe that he saw me as his soulmate, considering how much we shared our thoughts, dreams, and feelings. Marvin had other plans—and continued introducing Stephen to girl after girl. They would compete with Marvin and me for Stephen's attention.

I observed and grew jealous over Stephen's daily flirtations with girls, whether it was holding hands between classes or stealing kisses on the quad. My world felt smaller when Stephen invested time with the opposite sex at the expense of our relationship.

And yet I was too chicken to push the idea of me as his soulmate.

***

WITH June fast approaching, rather than continuing to waste time pining, I shifted my attention away from Stephen and threw myself into preparation for my Spanish intensive program in Monterrey, Mexico.

I'd never travelled anywhere outside the U.S. and Canada without my parents and grew excited for the opportunity to see another part of the world. I wanted to slice the strings, the umbilical cord, that kept me attached to my parents. It was time to be my own man.

"Donde esta el bano? Cuanto cuesta? Me llama es," With the help of my Spanish phrasebook I'd repeat aloud while I gazed in the mirror--*Where is the bathroom? How much does it cost? My name is--* until the words rolled off my tongue with confidence.

On the day of my flight Mom and Dad accompanied me to the departure gate. "Call us collect when you arrive, son. And watch yourself." Dad leaned forward to wrap one arm around my shoulder.

"Make sure you eat enough, sweetheart," Mom chimed in. "I wish I were there to make you banana shakes."

I dropped my backpack to the ground and embraced first my father and then my mother. I waved goodbye and ambled onto the plane, not looking back. I had flown only once before with my parents, to Disneyworld, for my 15ᵗʰ birthday. This trip would be the inaugural flight on my own.

Adrenaline pulsing, I gripped the armrest and took a deep breath as the plane taxied along the runway. Then I leaned back while the plane rumbled and began lifting off the ground. The entire aircraft shook as we roared heavenward into clouds and blue sky toward the land of impoverished riches, bullfights, and the Pyramids.

Several hours later, in what felt like a blink, we touched down. As we de-boarded the plane I felt the intense sun on my back and the desert air on my face. My heart leapt at the excitement, and nerves, of being in a new place on my own.

Once on campus I learned that the Instituto de Tecnologico de Monterrey, regarded by Mexicans as the MIT of Mexico, held classes from eight to four. We would learn grammar and vocabulary first thing in the morning, followed by pronunciation. In the afternoon, we engaged in conversation. My head full of verb tenses and conjugations, I would fall into bed at night, exhausted from all the concentration and repetition.-

The most indelible memory of the six weeks I spent in Monterrey was practicing Spanish with Gabriella who would become my Mexican sweetheart. We met my first week at the outdoor swimming pool, she in her modest red one-piece bathing suit and me in my geometric board shorts. I tripped over my Spanish staring into her warm, dancing brown eyes.

"Hola, come esta?"

She laughed, "You mean *'como estas?'* I'm fine, and I speak English." She straightened her black curls behind her ears with her delicate fingertips.

"My name is Gabriella, but you can call me Gabbie." Gabbie took me under her wing and agreed to be my tutor. After class she'd invite me with her friends to El Gallito, a little Mexican bar popular with students.

She loved to dance. In the summer of 1984 Michael Jackson and Madonna ruled the Mexican and American airwaves. After evenings practicing my Spanish aided by her patience and one or two bottles of cerveza, I whirled Gabbie around the dance floor impressing her with my disco dancing technique.

"You're making me dizzy," she'd laugh, switching to English as I spun her into pirouette after pirouette. "Focus," I'd repeat. *"Centrarse en un punto! Focus on a point."*

We collapsed in a fit of laughter, giggling and holding each other up as the lights of the tiny dance floor projected red, green, and blue across our radiant faces, and Michael Jackson continued from one song to the next.

One night we shared an unexpected kiss. My heart fluttered for a moment savoring the touch of her lips on mine, but the feeling got all jumbled and confused. I appreciated the softness, the exoticism, but desired something rougher, coarser, that pushed back against me rather than relinquishing power. I opened my eyes hoping for golden-haired Stephen, only to see Gabbie beaming back at me.

Certain our relationship would remain chaste, I felt no pressure with her, recognizing we were both allowing ourselves the pleasure of a fleeting, and platonic, summer romance. The final night we sat next to one another at a party thrown by her Mexican friends, surrounded by my American classmates, plenty of food, and a Mariachi band.

"Promise you won't forget me," Gabbie whispered squeezing my hand. A warm smile spread across my face. "How could I? You taught me how to order food at El Gallito, encouraged me to just relax and dream in Spanish, not to mention you allowed me to show off my disco dancing technique. You'll always stand out as one of the special girls in my life." I fought a lump in my throat knowing I likely wouldn't see Gabbie again, but I swallowed and hugged her.

Set loose from my Cleveland moorings I'd immersed myself in a new culture and savored my newfound confidence and freedom. After six weeks of studying Spanish, I bade farewell to dear Gabbie and boarded a Pullman train that chugged across the Mexican desert en route to Mexico City. I passed a landscape littered with cardboard houses lit by one electrical bulb hanging from a makeshift outlet. Guilt, and shame, washed over me as I stared out the window, shocked at the living conditions. How could I ever take for granted all the opportunities afforded me back in the U.S.?

Once we arrived in the capital, my classmates and I visited age-old Mexican churches, lingered beneath the green-leafy canopies of Chapultepec, fell in love with the history and poetry of Mexico. We stayed in the Zona Rosa, the cosmopolitan district of Mexico City, where visitors and locals strolled the wide boulevards. We trudged to the top of the famed Pyramids. My eyes soaked in the glory of this land of enchantment, of possibilities.

When my plane lifted from Mexico City en route to the United States, I slumped in my seat and peered misty-eyed out the window as the bustling, polluted capital faded into the distance. I'd be starting my last year at JCU, and already anxiety about the future was setting in. What would I do? Thoughts of law school, the Peace Corps, a move to Boston with its booming economy and historical allure, or someplace else I didn't even know.

Nonetheless, feelings of independence, freedom, and liberation continued to surge within me. My Mexico adventure reassured me I could strike out on my own in a foreign country and survive, even thrive, learning a new language, experiencing a foreign culture, and making friends. Soaring, like the plane, my spirit knew no bounds. When we landed on the Houston tarmac contentment settled over me, along with a sweet melancholy. I was happy to be back in the United States enveloped by my familiar surroundings and language, but I knew I'd always remember what I saw and experienced. Mexico would stay with me forever.

On the ground with my luggage, I headed toward a newsstand and heard the Democrats had nominated a woman for Vice-President. Savoring such a historical moment, I bought *Newsweek* magazine and eagerly read about the rise of Geraldine Ferraro. A wild hope arose in me that the age of Reagan might be coming to an end.

***

I arrived home to find Philippa parked on my doorstep. My childhood friend since seventh grade at St. Angela Merici, and my co-performer in *My Fair Lady* our high school senior year, Philippa had just returned from a trip to Italy with her parents. She'd trimmed her long, unruly blonde curls into a short, modified pageboy, the ringlets framing her kewpie doll face. She'd lost weight since I saw her in June. I thought she looked fabulous.

"Hi stranger, I missed you," she said with a knowing glance as we hugged on the front porch of my house. My arms wrapped around her; I inhaled the lilac scent of Philippa's hair. "My God look at you. Your hair looks great," I said as I ran my fingers through the soft curls. I eyed her black Capri pants and relaxed white t-shirt.

"Somebody went shopping."

Philippa tweaked my cheek. "Now stop flirting, unless you're going to follow it up with some real initiative."

She folded her arm in mine, and we walked to the playfield behind my house and found a patch of grass under the shade of an oak tree to lie down. "I fell in love with Italy," she said. "The people were so friendly, passionate. I felt like I was one of them, savoring their food, their art, their history."

I recounted my Spanish intensive program, my time with Gabbie, and how Mexico changed me. How it made me more aware of my place in the world. "While you sailed the Venetian canals, my Spanish has improved twofold. I can now go to a Mexican restaurant and order from the menu in complete sentences. And thanks to a sweet Mexican girl I learned how to chat about my day, where I went, what I did, and not to confuse the word fish for chicken in Español.

Philippa grabbed my arm and squeezed. "Did you have a summer romance?" I grinned and shook my head no. "Just a friend, but I learned so much by spending time with her and practicing the language. I feel like I could go anywhere and do anything thanks to Gabbie."

As dusk settled and a silvery moon rose overhead, I confided in Philippa for the first time my conflicted feelings over Stephen.

"I kissed Gabbie and opened my eyes half-hoping to see him there," I confessed, my palms sweaty and my voice shaking a little. "What was I thinking?"

"Maybe you needed to experiment," she said. "I had feelings for girls in high school. I thought several girls in my class were gorgeous. I didn't pursue anything physical with them, but we flirted constantly. I admired their looks and didn't feel shy expressing it. Girls compliment each other all the time. They're just like that."

Philippa's encouraging words soothed my discomfort but didn't solve my problem. I knew there were differences in social acceptability between female-to-female versus male-to-male intimacy, especially in the United States where competition in sports and the business world made men rivals of one another. I also knew that the feelings I had for Stephen extended far beyond mere appreciation and verged on lovesickness. I felt like I was floating between two worlds and didn't have the courage or will to cross over to the other side.

"Either way, I'll still love you," she said before embracing me. I held her tight, the soft white moonlight illuminating our faces with twinkling stars overhead. "I know you will," I said. "After all, you're the Kiki Dee to my Elton John." We laughed recalling how in middle school we'd sang the song

"Don't Go Breaking My Heart" into my Panasonic tape recorder. Where did that tape go?

Several nights later Philippa came over again. While I'd always known she had feelings for me, I regarded her more like a sister than a girlfriend. That night we settled in my bedroom with the door closed, something we'd done in middle school to talk privately but this time was different. My parents were away. We crawled into my bed and watched the gathering storm outside. Lightning flashed and thunder rumbled, while we lay insulated in the dark listening to raindrops pelt my bedroom window.

She looked up at me. "Can I rest my head on your chest?" she asked in a whisper.

"Sure," I said with a quivering voice. "That would be nice."

Our mouths touched for the first time. My heart fluttered, both nervous and excited. As the thunder rattled the quiet of the house, I traced Philippa's back and her face with my uncertain hands. My tongue crept inside her mouth. Before I knew it, my fingers began to explore her body, caressing her soft milky white breasts and her tummy. My heart thumped hard. I kissed her neck and shoulders. Knotted in a tight embrace our roving curiosity stopped at the waist. The storm raged outside, a noisy backdrop to our intimate emotion-packed groping.

"How did that feel?" she asked pulling away from me as we paused to take in our experience. Her warm brown eyes searched mine.

"I liked it, I felt close to you," I said catching my breath. I didn't mention part of me felt separate, hovering above the scene, like an actor, watching myself perform a role. But I couldn't tell her the truth—that I didn't really feel any life coming from below my belt.

Her face lit up. I saw the flush in her cheeks. I knew she loved me. And I loved her--just not in the way she wanted.

"Philippa, I'm pretty sure you were right, I have some exploring to do. I don't want to hurt you or harm our friendship. I can't seem to get Stephen out of my mind."

She looked away and then stared into my eyes again. "I thought you might say that after our last talk. But we needed to see how we felt. It's a good thing to do, you know? We now understand better than we did." I squeezed her hand and kissed her on the lips with a gentle firmness. "You are gold to me. I love you," I said before wrapping my arms around her shoulders and allowing quiet to return for a long stretch of time.

***

WITH the month of August left before school started, I returned to my lifeguarding job at Foster Pool. Happy to be back in the saddle, I relaxed into the routine of squealing kids and swimming lessons, suntan lotion and cannonball dives.

One afternoon after her tennis game Mom showed up at the pool to swim and suntan. When my shift ended, she changed and waited outside to give me a ride home. I threw on my t-shirt, shorts, and flip-flops, and hurried to meet her. There she stood by the entrance chatting with a tall, tanned guy around my age. When I approached, she turned to greet me and said, "This is my son, Jack." She then pivoted to the dreamboat and said, "Honey, meet Jeffrey. He's visiting from Wisconsin."

He gripped my hand and said, "Pleasure to meet you. Your mom is a nice lady." His warm smile and firm handshake melted my reserve.

Jeffrey reminded me of Stephen – how I felt about him—warm, twinkling eyes, athletic build with a confident yet gentle demeanor. "This fall I finish my final year of college before heading to New York to start my theatre career. If you're ever in Madison, look me up," he said handing me a small scrap of paper, on which he'd scribbled his name, address, and phone number.

I wanted to run my fingers through his shiny, sun-streaked hair. I wanted to undress him then and there. I couldn't help but imagine him naked in front of me with his muscular legs and broad shoulders. I stood there allowing the electricity to ricochet between us, reserving my private torment, my desire, for later. I denied myself the very thing I really wanted—a shy, hard-bodied, gentle-spirited guy.

As I turned to walk away with my mother, I could feel his parting glance--his smile, his nod--penetrate my body even though we never shared more than a handshake. Hope mixed with regret that I likely wouldn't make it to Wisconsin before I graduated from college. I could have called; I could have written. But I was afraid of what would happen. How would I manage it? Was he gay, or simply friendly? What would happen if I really liked him? And if my mother hadn't been standing there, would I have had the guts to ask Jeffrey out?

Mom turned the key in the ignition. She pulled out of the Foster Pool parking lot onto Lake Avenue. Jeffrey, left behind, a small speck in the rear-view mirror.

***

In September, RJ called from New York. "Hey, bucko, it's 90 degrees in the shade here. How was your summer?"

I smiled hearing his voice on the line. "Tremendous! I spent 6 weeks studying Spanish in Mexico. I met this wonderful girl who helped me with my conversation. I came home to lifeguard. Now I'm back at school."

"Well, you weren't resting on your laurels," he teased. "Guess what, I got an internship in the city. He's a Canadian designer--Alfred Sung."

My face lit up. "I'm thrilled for you. That's fantastic!"

"I'm psyched too. I may be able to get a job with him when I graduate from F.I.T. next year. We'll see. By the way, have you heard the latest on Farrah? She's making a comeback in a TV movie and out on the town with Ryan O'Neal. Finally, our Angel is back on track after those 3 flops at the multiplex."

With her gritty performance in *The Burning Bed*, Farrah landed on the cover of *People* Magazine. Her divorce from Lee Majors finalized two years earlier, she spoke publicly about her relationship with his former best friend, Ryan O'Neal. It was exciting to see Farrah back in the news, but she seemed desperate to please, hoping to reclaim her tarnished image from the affair that ended her marriage. While the media loved to glorify the breakups and reunions of famous people, there was no glory for loving someone of the same sex. Same sex love lived in the dark shadows, undetected by any media spotlight.

While I'd seen very little of RJ over the last year, I continued to dangle promises I would come and visit him in the city. Traveling there took a back seat to my spring break in Tampa and my studies in Mexico. With Mary Kathleen's return to Cleveland, I had fewer motivations to visit the city of my best friend's dreams.

I fantasized visiting Jeffrey in Wisconsin, despite knowing I never would. I wasn't ready to travel the distance, both the physical and emotional miles. It was easier for me to compartmentalize feelings rather than expose them.

Yet slowly I began to unpack, to face, the yearning and desire I'd experienced for Stephen and Jeffrey and other men with whom I came in contact. I couldn't extinguish my hunger or deny my interest and longing. I wanted to connect in a real way. But John Carroll, so small and insular and full of people with narrow impressions of me, kept me in check.

Imprisoned by my fear of "getting outed" and the humiliation and rejection I might suffer, I stayed within my self-imposed chamber. Meanwhile a flurry of emotions battled inside me, all of them bottled and screaming for air. Anger jousted with competitiveness jousted with resentment jousted with love and lust jousted with helpless resignation. They all insisted, like the tragic Willy Loman in *Death of a Salesman,* that attention must be paid. I was on a collision course, and a reckoning must soon occur.

***

THE beginning of my senior year, I slapped a Mondale/Ferraro poster to the wall in my dorm room. It was an act of political courage, maybe even defiance.

"Umm, why are you putting that up?" my born-again roommate Robby said as I smoothed out the poster edges of the Democratic Party running mates, their hands clasped over their heads, at the 1984 Convention.

I shrugged my shoulders. "I don't know. I guess I'm a Democrat." Robby got quiet, and I felt like an underground dissident in Poland's Solidarity movement. I wondered if Mondale and Ferraro's pro-choice views might have something to do with his silence.

"Are you a Republican?" I asked.

Robby paused. "Well, it just depends. I'm inclined to vote for a Christian, or someone who represents that point of view."

I smiled. "Robby, there's a lot of ways even Christian politicians aren't acting very Christ-like."

Like many times before, we agreed to disagree and allow the conflict to pass without getting all hot and bothered.

I thought back to earlier that year when my political science classmate Josie and I slogged through the snow-covered streets of New Hampshire hoping to help John Glenn win the 1984 primary. When Glenn bowed out of the race, we hooked our star to Gary Hart, the senator from Colorado. When Hart dropped out, in late spring, Mondale had amassed enough delegates to clinch the nomination. Not only was he uncharismatic compared with Reagan. He promised to raise taxes. Our last hope was the choice of Geraldine Ferraro to be Mondale's running mate, a decision we dreamed might alter the outcome of the race.

"*Morning in America*" became the theme of Reagan's 1984 campaign. After several years of gloomy economic news and high unemployment the economic tide began to turn. We placed a headstrong grandfather in the White House whose sunny disposition, many of his supporters said, reflected the American spirit of optimism and independence.

The more I read about Reagan, the more I recoiled from his simplistic view of the world: those that worked hard and got ahead deserved the American dream while others who might not have the same opportunity or who didn't follow the script were undeserving or lazy. He saw the world in black and white, while my view involved shades of gray. The world wasn't so simple, and I believed that the underprivileged and the underdogs deserved an equal chance to succeed. Wrestling with my own desire to fit in, and the slow realization I didn't fit in with many of my college classmates, forced me to dig deeper. Where did I fit in with what I believed? Where was my place in the world?

Reagan's popularity among many of my wealthier classmates highlighted class distinctions I'd never examined before. I had assumed my family was smack in the center of the middle class, but then at John Carroll, I noticed how Brooks Lawson's speedy, little red Miata and the Caribbean vacations he took to escape the ice-cold Detroit winters were the result of economic entitlement. Many of the guys in my frat came from more affluent backgrounds than Josie and I did, and they got to participate in the bounty of their parents' success.

Dad used to say the Republicans supported "the fat cats." Now I better understood what he meant. It was naive to assume that people who amassed wealth and privilege deserved it, while others didn't. Being born into money made life easier but didn't mean you were more deserving.

When Mondale visited Cleveland during the final days of the 1984 campaign, Josie and I took the rapid transit to the downtown Cleveland Arcade, a beautiful Belle Artes glass building on Euclid Avenue. Hoping to see the candidate as he emerged from a second-floor shop, we gathered in a crowd assembled along the third-floor wrought iron balcony above. Red, white and blue balloons festooned the bannisters. When Mondale emerged to wave to the audience, I hopped above the shoulders of the crowd in time to capture his friendly gaze and wave. The throng roared. A thrilling jolt of energy coursed through my body. I thought the former Vice-President might win based on the enthusiastic reception he received that afternoon in Cleveland! I wanted him to win. I wanted him to represent those of us who didn't have a voice. I guess you could say we were part of the Rainbow Coalition!

Instead, much of the John Carroll student body rejoiced at a very different outcome. Mondale lost by a landslide, carrying only his home state of Minnesota and Washington, D.C. Reagan cruised to a second term. Both Josie and I felt heartsick, convinced that the better candidate had succumbed to a doddering, old man with backward views. We felt isolated as many of our classmates whooped and hollered with glee.

That same year *Newsweek* Magazine hailed 1984 as "The Year of the Yuppie." I didn't know whether I even aspired to become a young, urban professional, yuppie for short. Yuppies held white-collar jobs, dined out all the time, and consumed an assortment of high-end products and services. All I knew was I wanted to help people and use my creativity in ways that made the world a better place. In yet another way, I felt alienated from the mainstream.

I continued to wrestle with feeling on the outside, different from most students on campus who subscribed to a more socially accepted vision of life: go to school, graduate and get a job, and settle into marriage and raising a family. Something different awaited me and that both thrilled and scared me.

***

IN the spring of 1985, I saw many of my upper classmen fraternity brothers, like Lizard, Brooks Lawson, and Pledge Master Sam Smith graduate from John Carroll and move on with their lives. I knew I'd especially miss my fraternity pledge brother Patrick Francis, the diver and my dorm Resident Assistant. He made the pledge process both fun and memorable. Our streaking through campus and successful panty raid during Hell Week, in addition to the time we spent on our mission to Buffalo, Niagara Falls, and back, were seared in my memory. Like Stephen, Patrick had awakened my heart with his kind, empathic personality. A new pledge class graduated, admitting fifteen more sophomores into the fraternity

My interest in drinking and carousing began to wane. Approaching the final semester of my senior year, with a fifth-year semester remaining until graduation, I chose to focus on my studies and getting the most out of my education. I was done chasing girls at frat parties or trying to impress guys who'd never understand me anyway. Finished with my attempts to fit into the fraternity mold I grew more distant from the Kaps brotherhood. I wanted to forge my own path, "make my own kind of music" like the iconic band The Mamas and Papas sang in the 1960's, like I saw Philippa do when she travelled to Europe, and like Josie when she joined the International Student Association.

I moved off campus, boxed up the preppy clothing, bought my first pair of jeans, and began to explore how I might engage the world after graduation.

One thing I knew: I wasn't ready to launch a career. I had too many questions. Instead of applying to law school, my parents' hope for me, Stephen's decision to commit a year volunteering with the Jesuit Volunteer Corps (JVC) in the Pacific Northwest spurred me to consider the same calling. For the first time, Seattle flashed on my radar. I began dreaming of what it might be like to live in that far corner of the U.S.

"Who's your favorite musician?" I asked Stephen one night while studying in the library.

"Well, you know I like jazz. In fact, I like all kinds of music," he said. "I'm starting to get into new wave. I like Lee Ritenour. He's a great jazz guitarist."

"I haven't listened to much jazz," I said, "but I'd like to." I sheepishly admitted my childhood music preferences leaned toward the vanilla music of The Carpenters and John Denver and then shifted toward disco upon meeting RJ. "Now I like Madonna, Cyndi Lauper, Boy George, and The Eurythmics," I explained as if namedropping would convince him I'd grown more sophisticated in my tastes.

Inspired by my friendship with and attraction to Stephen and a desire to explore the music that intrigued me, I followed him into the radio world and launched my own jazz hour at WUJC, John Carroll's radio station. Every Tuesday afternoon from 3-5 pm I'd kick off Jazz Classics by spinning the latest from artists such as Herbie Hancock and the Yellow Jackets. I loved the feel of thumbing through the old and new album covers in the station's record bin, selecting a few prized artists, and gently handling the shiny vinyl platters. People said I had a smooth voice that sounded like velvet over the airwaves. Their affirmation boosted my confidence.

Stephen taught me how to cue my first record. He demonstrated how to place my finger lightly on the needle and with the opposite hand spin ninety degrees backward on the vinyl while the current song played out to the finish on the second turntable.

I loved hearing the glorious fusion of one song coming to an end as the strains of the next song emerged. I could feel the hum resonating in my body and throughout the studio while I sat alone in the tower, on top of the world, creating a seamless panel of music, an unending cosmos of sound.

One afternoon I played Joe Jackson's "I'm the Man," the song I'd memorized during pledge period for my tobacco-chewing frat brother. I laughed recalling how silly, yet empowered, I had felt bouncing up and down on Jeff's bed, strumming air guitar.

Stephen hosted his own radio show at WUJC on Sunday nights from 10 until midnight. He enjoyed playing new age music and female admirers would often drop by the station to sit and talk during his shift. They would often spend late nights in the Grasselli Tower studio while he spun records by Kate Bush and George Winston.

We'd often sub for each other when we needed to study for an exam or ran into a scheduling conflict. Grasselli Tower and the deejay station offered us an escape into a hideaway universe.

Our exploration of music led to more discussions about meaning in the world. Stephen shared stories about the seminary, his disillusionment with studying for the priesthood, his desire to meet someone special, and yet still nurture a spiritual life.

"I just want to meet a girl and fall in love, ya know?"

I nodded, my heart once again hurtling down a silo. I couldn't admit the truth to myself, so how could I tell him?

CHAPTER 28

Revelations

THE FINAL weekend of December of my senior year my parents and I drove to nearby Lakewood to visit my 85-year-old great aunt Lola and her daughter, my beloved Re-Re. The two had lived together for as long I could remember.

I loved Lakewood with its big old family homes dotting Lake Erie, its charming duplexes, and old-world brick apartments. Lola and Re-Re occupied the top-unit of a duplex on Parkwood Avenue; Mom had lived with my maternal grandparents in the lower unit until she married Dad.

From the age of seven onward my most cherished memories involved the Saturday evenings my parents went on date nights and dropped me off on Parkwood for a sleepover. Aunt Lola and I cozied up on the white, leather swivel chair watching *All in the Family*, *Mary Tyler Moore*, and *Carol Burnett*, back-to-back on television. When Re-Re wasn't on a date, we made it a cozy trio. We'd concoct root beer floats and have a party.

Mom and Re-Re, born three months apart and raised like sisters by Lola and my grandmother, grew up with a close but often contentious relationship. They attended the same grade school and high school, and sometimes even wore the same matching clothes sewn by Lola and my grandmother.

Mom often criticized Re-Re when she'd hang out at our house espe-cially when she came for dinner. "Can't you see how she just puts her feet up on the couch and reads the newspaper while I'm getting dinner ready? She could at least bring something to contribute to the meal," Mom would harp, expecting me to chime in, which I never did.

I refused to take sides when Mom complained about Re-Re's shortcom-ings because I loved her and chose to see her wonderful qualities rather than the faults Mom pointed out.

The day after Christmas we arrived at Re-Re's and Lola's early for dinner. My father and I turned on *The CBS Evening News* in the living room while my mother sat in the kitchen with Re-Re and Lola while they chopped onions and carrots for a beef stew. Making herself at home Mom rum-maged around for a snack and discovered a box of candy underneath the Christmas tree in the dining room. She cracked open the lid and slipped a piece of chocolate in her mouth. Like a mad hornet, Re-Re flew out of the kitchen, "Ruthie, I told you to wait until after dinner."

"Oh, for crying out loud, Renata. It's just a piece of candy. Can't you share?"

I hurried into the dining room in time to see Re-Re grab the box from my mother's hand. Pieces of chocolate flew every which way and landed on the aqua and green-speckled rug. Before I could say anything, Mom took hold of Re-Re's blond wig and yanked it off her head. There Re-Re stood, her mouth agape, holding an empty box. For a split second, we all froze, silent as stone.

I lunged toward them. "Stop it, stop it, you two." I fell to my knees scrambling to collect all the chocolates. "Don't you know how upset this makes me, seeing you squabble for no reason? It's Christmas. Can't you get along?" My voice broke. I'd seen these two people I loved escalate into tense confrontations time and again. I hated it. Why couldn't we just be together and get along, happy in each other's company?

My mother pointed with an accusatory finger, "Jack, it's her fault. She's not the sharing type. All I wanted was something to nibble. There's no snacks, crackers and cheese, or anything in this house."

"But Jack, couldn't she wait?" An exasperated Re-Re whined retrieving her wig off the rug. "After all, I'm making dinner for goodness sakes. She didn't even ask. These chocolates were a Christmas present to me."

Suddenly, the tears came, my voice cracking, then exploding. "Can't you see what you're doing to me? I love you, both of you. I don't want to get dragged into the middle of your feuds. But it happens all the time."

My father came into the dining room. "Jack, will you calm down? It's not such a big deal. Just cool it. Let them be."

"No, I'm tired of ignoring it, it's been happening for years, their fights. I don't want to sit back and be hostage any longer. It's not fair."

Great Aunt Lola petted my hand trying to reassure me, but I headed to the front closet and ripped my coat off the hanger.

"I can't be here right now." I stormed down the creaky wooden stairs and disappeared into the night.

All I want is to love them both without having to pick sides when the shit hits the fan, I repeated to myself.

The biting cold December wind blew through my jacket as more tears flowed. Rage coursed through my veins, rage for striving to be the perfect son. I bristled thinking of all the times I found myself in-between warring parts of my family. Whether it was Mom's strained conversations with Dad about taking the initiative to spend more time with me, or Re-Re and Mom fighting over some silly disagreement, or Mom directing judgement towards relatives who didn't meet her moral high ground. I felt like a pinball in a machine, flicking back and forth between one goal post to the next. I was sick and tired of her spats. I decided this was the end of it. No longer would I play the referee. I knew where I could go.

When I arrived at the house on Belle Avenue I peered in the window and saw inviting Christmas tree lights: warm, sparkling, red, green, blue, and yellow. Boxes of presents lay unwrapped underneath the tree. I rang the bell. RJ's mom answered the door.

"Hi, honey, what a nice surprise."

She called up to RJ from the stairwell and then returned to me, looking into my eyes, placing her hand on my shoulder. "Are you okay?"

I exploded in tears recounting the story of the family fight. "I don't want to be around them right now," I sniffed. "I'm sick of getting drawn in and having to take sides."

RJ bounded down the steps wearing slippers, jeans, and a sweatshirt. I wiped my wet face with my shirt cuff.

"Hi, I wasn't expecting to see you." He smiled but then grew serious when he noticed my red face. "How about a soda?"

Mrs. Fallon fixed me some dinner, a small steak, some leftover potatoes and gravy and broccoli. RJ just sat and watched while I slowly chewed and finished the meal. "Do you want to sleep over tonight?" he asked.

I swallowed. "Sure, it'll be like old times."

Minutes later the phone rang. Mrs. Fallon answered then handed it to me.

"Jack, you should never have left here," my father said. "You embarrassed your mother and me. We'll be there soon."

I tried to tell them not to bother, that I wanted to stay the night at RJ's, but the phone went dead. They arrived fifteen minutes later.

Mrs. Fallon answered the door. "Frank, I think it would be better if Jack stayed here and returned in the morning. He's very upset and more than welcome to spend the night."

I peeked around the corner to see my father standing on the porch, my mother behind him. "Jack, buddy, don't you think you should come home with us tonight. C'mon, we'll go for some ice cream at Malley's."

I stepped towards the front door. "Dad, I'm wrecked. I'm staying here tonight."

"We can drive him back after church," said Mrs. Fallon.

My mother's face looked sour, but she nodded and turned to walk down the icy porch steps, clinging rigidly to my father's arm and the rail. I heard the Monte Carlo's engine ignite, and the tires crept out of the snowy driveway.

Away. Gone. Relief poured over me, despite my miserable mood. I could wait another day before facing them.

That night, I unleashed more tears in RJ's attic room. I felt comforted by the smell of the fresh timber in the ceiling above our bed and the warmth of the fireplace several floors below that floated up the stairs. "Jack, I don't think I've ever seen you cry like tonight. It's kind of amazing." His brown eyes were like reflecting pools of my own.

"I don't know," I sniffed. "I feel like, like you know me. We're brothers. I'm a part of your family. Even though you're in college in New York, we're still here for each other. That hasn't changed. I don't think it ever will."

He passed me some Kleenex and quietly nodded. Then RJ slung his arm around me, and I rested my head on his chest, my nose running and all snotty until I blew it again. My entire body felt so heavy, so tired. RJ turned off the light. Quickly, soundly, I fell asleep in his arms. My problems disappeared – for the moment.

***

THE next morning RJ took me home. The temperature hovered above freezing. Light rain hardening into ice pellets bounced off the hood of the station wagon. "How do you think your parents are going to be?" he asked.

"I don't know. They didn't look very happy last night when your mom suggested I stay over."

"I guess most parents wouldn't appreciate someone butting into their business."

"Yeah, but I didn't want to go home with them. I think they knew better than to make a scene."

RJ drove along the winding bend that paralleled the Rocky River Metroparks. The trees, naked and grim, stretched towards the ice gray sky. Crusty, old snow mottled the ground. As we rounded the corner, I could see our empty driveway.

I sighed. The house looked dark inside. "I don't think they're back from church yet. They'll be home soon."

After I got out of the car, RJ rolled down the window. "Call me, if you need me."

I plopped down on the front porch steps and waited. My underarms felt wet and uncomfortable, and I couldn't sit still. I prepared for a confrontation. Ten minutes later the Monte Carlo pulled into the driveway. My parents emerged from the car, funereal looks on their faces. I followed them into the house.

In stone silence they sat down at opposite ends of the kitchen table surrounded by the cheerful daisy wallpaper.

My mother with a downward glance nodded at my father, who began. "We'd like you to join us at the table. We have some important matters to discuss with you."

Standing at a distance buffeted by the refrigerator and kitchen pantry I remained on my feet refusing to budge.

My parents glanced at each other, and my father rose to his feet. "Son, I think you should sit down right now." He pointed to the empty lime green chair between them at the table.

"No, Dad."

My mother's voice cracked. "If you don't sit down, we're going to immediately withdraw you from John Carroll. We'll not contribute a cent to your tuition. You'll be on your own when it comes to your schooling."

An unbearable silence overwhelmed the room. I felt fury coursing through my bones, racing up my spine. Countless years of trying to dance, faster and faster, to please them and follow their lead. All these years of trying to play the part of the best son, the reliable young man, the good student, the obedient one. I was done.

Suddenly, a new, defiant person took charge. My posture stiffened. "Go ahead," I snapped. "I'm twenty-one and can support myself. I don't need your money."

"How dare you take Renata's side and embarrass me," my mother roared. "You know how flinty she's been all these years. When she comes here for dinner she expects to be waited on hand and foot. We shuttle her back and forth to the airport for her skiing trips. Our door is always open to her. And yet she can't even share one piece of chocolate?"

"The issue has nothing to do with chocolate, Mom. You want me to take sides, and I won't do it anymore. I love you both, I won't choose."

"And you humiliated us in front of Mrs. Fallon," she continued pointing an accusing finger at me. "I'm sure they're already saying, 'Oh, Mrs. Hilovsky, she doesn't even have the respect of her only son.'"

"I'm not going to stand here and listen to this. I've had enough."

"Well, if you don't want to listen, you can get out." Rising from the kitchen chair, the sea of daisies a stinging backdrop, her face grew dark crimson and her eyes simmered like boiling cauldrons. "Because I'm finished keeping house when I'm not appreciated."

She pushed past me and headed for my bedroom. My father and I followed close behind her.

"You can get o-u-t, OUT," she screamed. Throwing the closet door open she began tearing my clothes off the rack and hurling them on the cherry carpeting. "You don't need me; you don't need a mother anymore so you can find a better place to stay."

"All right, it's a deal," I thundered back. I yanked my suitcase from underneath the bed and began shoving clothes into it. Sweaters and shirts and pants and shoes began piling onto the floor from the closet as she tossed one thing after another into a heap.

"You don't appreciate us," she bellowed. "You'd rather live with your little friend in Lakewood. Well, they don't know anything. They're ignorant when it comes to raising a family." My mother's wild-eyed face looked like it would explode.

"Stop it, stop it," my father shouted in the middle of the clothes fight. "Do you know how long I've watched you two from the outside, looking in? I've felt separate. You're tearing me apart. Ruth, will you stop this tantrum? Jack, you don't need to go. We can talk about this."

My father, streams of tears pouring down his face, wiped his eyes. He looked so hopeless and abandoned. Staring at him I felt pain and empathy and guilt flood my heart. Never had he allowed us to see him so broken up, broken down.

My mother stomped from the clothes-strewn bedroom and headed toward the living room. From the mantle above the fireplace, she grabbed a Currier and Ives keepsake dish I'd given her several Decembers ago. The inscription read *All Roads Lead Home at Christmas*. Tucked in an elegant display case, the dish featured a sentimental scene of a sleigh gliding over a snow-covered bridge. In high school I picked it out from the Higbee's

Department Store especially for her. She threw open the front door and hurled the curio toward the front lawn.

Then she locked herself in my parent's bedroom and wouldn't let us in, no matter how many times we knocked. Silent, my father and I stood in the kitchen while he prepared a ham sandwich. It sat on a plate uneaten. At a loss for what else to do, we retrieved the Currier and Ives dish wedged in its cracked powder blue container lying in the dirt under a snow-covered bush.

Everything changed following that Sunday afternoon uproar. Despite my mother's tirade and insistence I remain subservient, I'd finally stood my ground. I'd made my voice heard, I refused to be intimidated or forced to bend to my mother's will. I saw myself in a different light, no longer a boy but a man in the making, and it felt liberating.

I'd taken another step toward becoming separate, toward establishing my independence. Toward no longer needing my mother's approval. And toward understanding my father's sorrow about feeling excluded from the special relationship, the closeness, he instinctively knew my mother and I shared. For 21 years he'd kept it buried, a secret from us.

She and I maintained our distance the rest of that Sunday and into the following week while I bided my time at home before the new semester started. Once I returned to school our relationship began to thaw with the spring-like weather. But I remained cautious and guarded as the snows melted. The episode allowed me to start thinking of myself as different from my parents and prepared me for an eventual break. I needed air. I wanted to make my life my own.

***

In January I made the decision to go on an eight-day silent retreat. Stephen had suggested we give it a try, and I knew others in the Christian Life Community who'd gone and reported that they'd gained more clarity about their life goals. On a cold, grey day 25 of us boarded a chartered bus for Columbiere, Michigan, to participate in the age-old Catholic retreat program known as The Ignatian Spiritual Exercises. Foot-high snowdrifts blanketed upstate Michigan by the time we arrived for our adventure.

We called it an adventure because silent meant no talking, except with a spiritual director, for eight days straight, a major challenge for a talkative person like me and other students, who thrived on the noise and clatter around us. We were assigned to read passages from Scripture, met with our spiritual director to discuss how the readings informed our lives, and took time in the afternoon for journaling and silent reflection. It surprised me how easily I fell into the rhythm of quiet and contemplation, and I grew to love this time of calm introspection.

The Columbiere Retreat Center sat on several hundred acres of forest-land. In the afternoons I'd cross-country ski into the snowy wilderness. There in the streaming sunshine I would kick and glide, kick and glide, and listen. My ear grew attuned to the quiet of the country. Away from automobiles, telephones, television, and newspapers, my heart softened, and my interior world opened wide. The quiet helped shift me from a world of doing, movement, and accomplishment toward one of being, reflection, and acceptance.

One afternoon I skied to a peaceful overlook on a hill. I adjusted my sunglasses to avert the glare, wiped my runny nose and planted my ski poles in the ground. I found a stump and bathed in the sun's warmth and intensity. I relished being alone. I imagined I could hear the snow melting, and the universe spoke to me. My eyes opened wide. My heart broke open and something precious took hold of me.

The blue sky, the white snow, the purity of the place, breathtaking and limitless, all joined to create a whole. Like a gorgeous tableau--the French term I'd learned in theatre class beautifully expressed what I was seeing. I held my breath, afraid that if I moved, the beauty of the moment might vanish.

A deepening bond with a creator, a power beyond me, a force like a lover and protector, overcame me. The sky, the earth, the sun, and the moon all became one. Nothing could separate me from my abiding love of this moment for nature, humanity, and myself. I felt unified, complete, and content and one with God.

A voice called out and kept repeating *you are okay, you are perfect. follow your path, listen.*

Humbled and in awe, I rested for a long time, allowing this sacred presence to sink into my mind and body.

Colombiere granted me many gifts: I discovered how to find meaning in silence and reflection; I learned to trust – without question – my deepening desire to contribute in a way that reflected my values and beliefs, and I realized that I had something that only I could give to the world.

On the trip home I turned to Stephen who nodded off in the seat next to me, his blond hair framing his brow. He confided that he too had experienced an epiphany on this trip—like I, he realized he had a strong desire to serve, to better the condition of society through helping others. A warm feeling washed over me as I imagined how our post-graduate paths might intersect as we pursued our separate callings. I felt closer to him and sensed the bond we shared would endure – even without my physical attraction to him.

CHAPTER 29

Move On

FOLLOWING MY EXPERIENCE at the retreat in the snowy wilderness I
sought out a priest at John Carroll in whom I felt I could confide. Father
Paul Hennesy, a tall, elegant Jesuit in his late 40's, hailed from Boston and
taught religion. He always spoke in honest, direct terms during his homi-
lies at Sunday night services for students within and outside of the Christian Life Community. Professorial and authoritative, Paul was thought by
some students to be aloof; I respected his quiet, thoughtful demeanor. I
appreciated how he approached moral quandaries society faced like the
U.S. nuclear arms buildup in Europe, apartheid in South Africa, or racism
in our own country.

Of all the priests at the college, I sought out Paul's counsel because I believed he would be the most open to discussing my newfound insights and
revelations. I didn't need or want a formal confession to receive expiation
for my sins. I already knew my desires were in no way sinful. I wanted to
share my experience with someone wise whom I respected. I wanted to
talk, plain and simple.

When I stepped into Paul's private quarters filled with rich, mahogany

furniture and wall-to-wall paneling I fell into awe. The surroundings appeared formal, almost judicial, as I entered his office and sat down in front
of his large desk. Tall picture windows overlooked the campus quad. My
fluttering stomach refused to settle down as I searched for the words to tell
him.

"Father, I came here today to discuss my life . . . a very personal . . .
private part of my life." I gulped, as my throat grew scratchy, and my heart
raced. I looked him straight in the eye. "I've been carrying this secret, but
I'm tired of holding it so tight and concealing it from everyone."

Paul shifted in his chair. He swept his fingers through his Scottish red
beard tinged with flecks of gray. His face looked quizzical, as if he were trying to anticipate the nature of my confession. His eyes narrowed, he leaned
in closer toward me. I could see the lines settling into his jaw, the white
around his temples. I sat silent across from him, almost paralyzed about
how to proceed, yet convinced I needed to confide in someone.

He cleared his throat. "Well, Jack, I know you were on a retreat and had
some time to reflect. What would you like to share with me – your secret
– your insights?

I smiled nervously and fidgeted with my folded hands. The room felt
drafty as I peered out the large windows capturing the fading light on the
snowy quad. I looked into Paul's cool, blue eyes. "I learned two important things about myself at the retreat. I want to volunteer after college in
a service organization, whether it's the Peace Corps, or Jesuit Volunteer
Corps." Paul's eyes looked approving as he nodded his encouragement. The
knot tightened in my stomach because this insight was the easy one. Now
I had the final whammy to impart. My chest hurt, like all my organs were
compressing into one final statement of my be-all and end-all. So, I leaned
forward and said it, half expecting I would explode as I released the words.
"And my second realization is I have feelings for men. I have feelings for

my best friend at school. And I've concluded this is part of who I am, how God made me, a blessing, and I need to accept it." I swallowed hard and sank into my chair, a sense of relief sweeping over me.

Paul sat back and stared at me in silence. At times I'd seen him smoking a pipe, and he looked like he had the urge to light one, something, anything, right now as his eyes darted between me and the molded ceiling above us. Instead, he crossed his hands on top of the desk. The long pause, his vacancy of words, felt interminable. I wanted him to say it would be all right, to trust my instincts, to trust that voice I heard in the snowy wilderness. He sat up straight and took a long, deep breath.

"I congratulate you for having the courage to come and discuss these matters with me." He sounded so formal. I sat there, studying him, only the large desk separating us. For a moment I felt like I'd disrobed and was awaiting a physical examination. Except rather than examine my body I feared he was preparing to examine my moral state, my soul. I sat on the edge of my chair, anxious for what he would say next.

"You are right to seek out spiritual guidance. I can't condone or encourage your thoughts about homosexuality since the Church has spoken out against it." When I heard his words my heart plummeted, my ears started to ring. "It's unwise to act on your feelings," he continued. "They'll only lead to a further reinforcement of a behavior the Church disapproves."

I nodded in shock feeling the ice creeping over my entire body. I gritted my teeth. I refused to lose the warmth I'd experienced several weeks before standing in that snowy expanse overlooking limitless possibilities with the sun in my eyes, igniting my soul, and reassuring me everything would be all right if I simply abided by the quiet voice within. I felt very alone. Now this man of God told me the Church could not condone what I'd found in my very heart and soul, my being: *You are all right. You are perfect.* I wasn't about to give up on what I knew and held dear.

The bells of the grandfather clock in Paul's office began to chime, six times. Dusk descended darkening the campus, chasing out the remaining light. "I can give you absolution, Jack. And I encourage you to seek out your desire to be of service. But these other desires are destructive. They are unnatural." A sourness, a bile, climbed up my throat, like when I'd battled my ulcer. My body experienced an overwhelming urge to spit in disgust.

He leaned over me with his big hands and intoned the prescribed words of the confessional absolution "The Father, the Son, and the Holy Spirit..." but I'd already dismissed him, and his remaining mumbo-jumbo tumbled into the oblivion.

I had reached out to Paul hoping for compassion, but I'd received a judgement, a harsh sentencing, that my deepest heart's desire was sinful and destructive. I knew I deserved better. I knew he was toeing the Vatican line. He certainly hadn't made the connection that my feelings were a gift from God, a given I couldn't change. I would forgive his glaring oversight, I could see he felt uncomfortable, almost disturbed in my presence, did I touch a nerve? Was Father Hennesy struggling with his own sexual doubts and feelings? That I didn't know. What I did know is I didn't want – or need – his absolution. He was insensitive and unaware of his damning words. He didn't understand how intolerance for same-sex love rivaled the sins of apartheid and racism.

"Thank you for meeting," I said as I rose from my chair. "I'm hard pressed to agree with you, Father. How could a God who created me in love, to love, make me unacceptable?" He remained silent and gripped the arm of his desk chair.

I left his ecclesiastic stronghold and made my way across the freezing cold campus. I felt crushed by the encounter and decided I would follow my conscience, a compass the Jesuits taught should guide all Catholics on their moral journey.

I would not confide in any other priest what I shared with Paul. I didn't feel safe. I had thought he would see things in a more empathic way. I was wrong.

***

"JACK, what's your plan after graduation?" Stephen asked. I watched him finger comb his light blond hair away from his eyes, revealing a handsome forehead and dark eyebrows that reminded me of exuberant punctuation marks. His smile, always contagious. My heart danced observing him.

I shrugged. "Still considering the Jesuit Volunteer Corps. All I know is I want to work with people who are voiceless. I've been thinking it would be fun to explore a placement in the Northwest, maybe Seattle or Portland. The Peace Corps is a two-year commitment," I explained, "a long time to be away from my parents. I know they would miss me, probably freak out if I disappeared for two years."

Stephen laughed and rolled his eyes. He understood my predicament. With a younger sister and brother, he wasn't tied down to his parents in the same way.

"Hey, I'm considering JVC too. Not sure yet, but I want to check out Alaska. Go somewhere in bush country."

I smiled, a warmth overcoming me, recognizing we both shared a do-gooder gene and a thirst for adventure. He inspired my idealism with his passion for helping others less fortunate. He was earnest and forthcoming; unlike any other college guy I'd met. In his quiet, simple way, Stephen challenged me to be a better person just by being his friend. My heart softened, made gentler and more thoughtful whenever we spent time together. And I was frightfully attracted to him.

The conversation shifted to girls. "I don't know, Jack. They expect too much," Stephen said. "They want to get more serious, but I'm not interested."

The more I listened to his romantic woes, the more I wanted to reach out and make him forget all about any woman that brought him pain or confusion. I was falling harder, and deeper. I wished we could go off on our own to a desert island, away from everything and everybody. But that was not in the cards.

***

AFTER allowing several casual relationships to fade away Stephen began spending time with a new girl by the name of Karen.

Karen Karmichael, a junior marketing major, lived on the third floor of our co-ed dorm, Miller Hall. I couldn't help noticing her fashion flair. She wore denim miniskirts and jean jackets with pastel-colored moccasins. Bright-colored bracelets jangled on her wrists. Her sunny personality and playful, bohemian style starkly contrasted with the more buttoned-down, kilt skirt-wearing girls that attended JCU. Slim, personable, and plainspoken, Karen exuded a softness despite her matter-of-fact personality. Once you got to know her, her warmth became evident. I wanted to touch her soft, long, honey blonde hair, very different from the more rigid bobs of many John Carroll women.

Stephen met Karen in a psychology class. They were teamed up on a project studying multiple personality disorders. At one point, Stephen joked that it gave him insights into Marvin, which I thought was a bit mean, but understood the comparison. Little by little I watched their relationship flower. Karen's independence and sense of humor brought out the best in him, as he was free to not feel responsible and take himself so seriously.

I watched Marvin, who still wanted one-on-one time with Stephen, growing more jealous by the day. He'd elbow into their conversations while Stephen and Karen were strolling on the campus quad. He'd purposely not acknowledge Karen by name when he encountered her. And he tried to monopolize Stephen's time when they did meet up. Marvin and I were no longer sidekicks to Stephen at meals or class.

Though I found it hard to admit to myself, I too felt envious that Karen got to spend so much time with him. I reminded myself that's what happens in early stages of relationships, when you are getting to know someone. When I saw Stephen and Karen walking to dinner on the quad, I'd wave, really wanting to be supportive. But I felt excluded, crushed, disappointed. I realized they were growing closer and more intimate.

At least he was getting to know a woman I found worthy of him, unlike some of the other girls. I was happy to see them out of the picture, but I mourned the loss of Stephen's easy availability and the possibility that maybe, just maybe, he'd be my boyfriend.

***

Despite my encounter with Father Paul, I enrolled in an elective class, unrelated to my major, called Christian Spirituality. Sean O'Brien, the soft-spoken Jesuit scholastic and head of John Carroll's Campus Ministry, taught the course. Stephen and I both met Sean through our involvement with Christian Life Community at Sunday night services.

Sean began the first class by saying, "Remember, my friends, true love involves respect and cherishing. Regardless of whom we choose to love, these attributes are most important." He went on to describe different types of love: *eros, agape,* and *philia.* Eros involved the physical and romantic kind of love, agape was unconditional love and caring regardless of the circumstances, and philia was shared between friends.

"And remember this," he said, "same-sex love is not sinful but one of many ways people love." Several voices stirred in the back of the classroom. Sean projected his voice to reach them and strode toward the back. "The important thing to remember is that each person is an embodiment of spirit, of soul, in fact is the embodiment of God and must be treated with reverence and dignity. We cannot change or alter whom we choose to fall in love with," he repeated. "Follow your conscience and you'll never go wrong. It is our moral arbiter and wiser than pronouncements in a book."

My head exploded. This earth-shattering revelation like an arrow pierced the center of my heart, my very being—I couldn't believe my ears! I reflected on my encounter with Father Paul. He had disputed the validity, the reality, of my feelings tossing me on the junk heap of sinners if I acted on them. Now with Sean's revelation, I knew I could follow my innate desire, and it would never mislead me. While my encounter with Father Paul unnerved me, I was grateful that another man of the cloth expressed a more compassionate point of view.

Shame, doubt, anxiety, fear--all the emotional forces imprisoning me— began melting away. All I wanted was to love with a big heart and be loved with a big heart.

Sean gave me a lasting gift. If any course prepared me for graduation, and the world I aspired to live in, his teachings based on the Christian ethos of the nature of love pointed the way.

I had arrived at a truth: God made me exactly the way he intended me to be, whole and complete. I didn't need to change; I was perfect simply the way I was. My perceived imperfections—the acne on my face, my sexuality, whether I fit in somewhere--could not take away the radiance of God's love for me. My relationship with RJ served as a sign, gave me a taste of what could be when I was ready to share my body and spirit with another man.

Sean O'Brien's course validated my own understanding of the meaning of love. Every time I entered his classroom, I could feel my heart opening to new possibilities, my soul soaring to unrealized heights.

***

IN the summer of '85, with one final fall semester awaiting me before I could graduate, my entry into the real world loomed. I retired my lifeguard suit for an internship with the Cleveland *Plain Dealer* newspaper, an experience that taught me more about my relationship with women then how I'd move forward in a career.

My first day, I arrived in an air-conditioned lobby full of natural light and leather furniture. A young platinum blonde woman with a pageboy haircut sat down across from me and crossed her legs. "Your first day too?" she asked looking up from a printout with a pert smile on her lips. I nodded. "The new suit gave it away and the tie," she said. "Me too."

She looked me straight in the eye like a cat eying a canary and extended her hand. I gulped, a little intimidated by her confident demeanor but at the same time intrigued by this fashionable blonde dressed in a red suit. "By the way, I'm Laura. I imagine we'll be working together, unless the sharp duds get you a job at *The New York Times*.

Not since Mary Kathleen, Hope, and Melissa, had I met a girl who was both smart and funny not to mention a total flirt. We'd see each other come and go in the office en route to sales assignments but never had the chance to chat.

Toward the end of summer, I got up my nerve to ask Laura out on a date. I wanted to see if maybe this time, going out with "the girl with something extra," my nickname for her, I would feel different. "Sure, I'd love to," she responded when I suggested.

Several evenings later we drove down to the Flats, the nightclub and entertainment district in downtown Cleveland. We boarded the Good Time Two tugboat that sailed the Cuyahoga River, now home to a variety of rowing clubs after the notorious incident 16 years earlier when it caught fire leading to Johnny Carson's famous Mistake on the Lake comment.

As the boat sailed away from the dock, I wrapped my arm around her shoulders as we leaned together against the ship's railing. She relaxed sideways into me, and we watched the prow of the vessel cut into the waves. The floral scent of her perfumed hair tickled my nostrils, as did the fresh jasmine fragrance on her neck. "Hmmm, this feels good," she whispered.

She burrowed under my arm as we stood on the deck of the boat with a gentle breeze teasing our hair and the sun setting on the horizon. While the waves ebbed and flowed, my upset stomach continued forcing me to face the truth. What was I getting myself into? I was laying the groundwork for romance but had no inkling about whether I really could deliver. I couldn't even go there in my mind.

And then I turned toward her, and our lips touched, Laura's and mine. A tender bite, a caressing tongue, an invitation to something else--but it felt all wrong, and I stepped back. Laura looked a bit confused. I tried to cover by not removing my arm from around her shoulder.

Truthfully, I wanted something rougher, with the pull of a whisker, not the soft and tender smoothness Laura offered. I realized once again that I hungered not for Laura, but for Stephen. Images of him with a wet, sweat-drenched t-shirt after a game of racquetball floated into my mind. I felt pangs of hurt, rejection, even anger that I couldn't have him because he was straight. Laura wasn't the answer. I needed to go outside my comfort zone and explore another world. Yet I was terrified to take the first step and felt like dashing, running, screeching away. I wanted to wretch, empty my overactive gut overboard, but I held myself in check. Laura took a step back and asked, "Are you okay?"

"Just an upset stomach. Probably the rough water." I couldn't tell her. I didn't know how.

My experience with Laura demonstrated once and for all that I couldn't make myself fall in love with a girl. It would never feel natural. There would always be tension and doubt. I wanted more than that. I wanted it to feel good, and right, and crystal clear.

***

In July, Rock Hudson made international headlines when, with his cinematic sweetheart Doris Day by his side, he announced at a Paris news conference he'd contracted AIDS. He didn't say how.

A whirl of questions spiraled through my mind. In grade school I'd watched the famed actor in the television series *McMillan and Wife*. I'd never even questioned that he might be gay, and yet he didn't say he was a hemophiliac or IV drug user, two other ways of getting HIV-infected. I read the story in *The Plain Dealer* and rifled through the pages of *People* magazine to try to learn more but there was nothing more about how he became infected. Until a week later when *The Enquirer, Star* and other tabloids had a field day, interviewing his previous lover who spoke out publicly about their relationship.

Once again, I sensed that especially among the famous there was no incentive to come out as gay without becoming a pariah, or worse, a person with AIDS. Hudson's silence about his personal life reinforced the shame and isolation I felt. There was no one who stood out as an example of how to live a happy, healthy, and open gay life.

My loneliness grew into an ever-present companion. I felt as if a shadow lurked around me, waiting to descend. My secret stayed locked away, hidden by defenses that I erected. I really wanted to date women, but my body said no. I wasn't comfortable going to public places where gay people spent time. Bars and nightclubs seemed to be the only options – both unappealing to me due to the greatest paradox of all. They were anonymous and off the beaten track and yet I feared running into someone I knew who would blow my cover. I would lose control of my reputation and forever be labeled an out-in-the-open homosexual.

I longed for safety and security, but my insecurities about my identity, who I was, haunted me like silent ghosts and merciless goblins. And the people I felt least safe confiding in were my parents. I was frightened all roads would only lead to heartbreak.

CHAPTER 30

The Final Inning

Marvin couldn't contain his growing resentment of Stephen spending most of his time with Karen and soon began undermining his reputation. Seated with his posse of giggling gossip girls in the cafeteria, he'd whisper, "Y-y-you'll never guess—Stephen's been spending a lot of time with that seminarian friend of his. His friend's a queer so he must be one too. Can you believe it?"

It angered me to see Marvin, whom I'd suspected was gay, accusing others of the sins he was guilty of—daring to love, to desire someone of the same sex. Just as the high school divers Luke and Dylan had suffered from Marvin's wagging tongue, now Stephen was the one to take the gay-bashing heat. And I was too afraid to defend Stephen for fear Marvin would turn his guns on me.

I realized I didn't want any part of the gossip mongering, the hiding behind a false persona, the bullying, the in-your-face mockery: Marvin and his determination to sully people's reputations. Rock Hudson and his secretive life. Victor and his gang's thuggish, cruel behavior. Weren't there any healthy gay role models, guys who didn't gossip, hide, or undermine other people?

Because I wrestled with my own feelings toward Stephen, ones that grew more confused and tortured by the day, I tried my best to ignore Marvin's trash talk. Stephen and I engaged in countless conversations about love and God, his dreams and ambitions, his girl crushes and romances. He confided in me that he had a high sex drive, which worsened my sexual frustration, and I couldn't get him out of my mind. I wanted him, but I didn't want to admit it.

"Sometimes I just wanna' fuck the whole world," he confided in me on one night walk. He had recounted to me his first time with his first summer love. He described her soft skin, her luscious kisses, the way she laughed at his silly jokes.

After listening to my friend, I felt sick to my stomach. So much of what I felt revolved around fear: I was scared of being found out and exposed; fretful of Marvin and his vicious gossip, and the Church and its judgment; afraid of disappointing my parents if they were ever to discover their only son loved men; petrified of the burgeoning AIDS crisis and the resulting stigma; and fearful I'd never meet a guy like me: family-oriented, responsible, wanting to make a difference in the world, and more than a showboat or a big personality.

More than anything I wanted my life to mean something, but all I could see were the demeaning and demoralizing jokes, so popular in the 1970's of my youth, about Jews, the Polish, or other ethnic minorities. At St. Angela Merici grade school I'd experienced people making fun of me because my name ended in "sky." *Pollack!* kids would scream. "I'm not Polish," I'd yell back. "I'm Slovak." It didn't matter. And the same insults were hurled at gay people without a thought—*faggot, sissy, girly-boy, fudge packer.* People liked to pigeonhole and ridicule groups that didn't fit. Gay people didn't fit, and I didn't fit.

I knew I had a beautiful body that I yearned to celebrate and share with another person– a man. But I remained imprisoned by the moral judgments that I watched playing out all around me. I couldn't see beyond what people thought.

That fall Stephen began getting more serious with the free-wheeling, fashion loving Karen Karmichael, who'd begun to remind me of my own high-school muse, Hope.

As time passed, I grew more and more aggravated with my inability to construct a romantic life, compared with Stephen who found it so easy. In a moment of frustration, I yelled at him, "God, they just flock to you, like groupies to some rock star." Right there in the middle of the dance floor at Turkey Ridge as a blonde flirted with him. He looked stunned but I was tired of watching him lap up girls without lifting a finger. I slammed my beer on the bar counter, ready to storm out the door. The Beatles' "Let It Be" echoed in the background.

"Don't try so damn hard," Stephen said following me outside of the bar. "You're making girls uncomfortable, they aren't able to see the real you, if you're making such a strong pitch. You're too intense."

My sexual frustration grew. I looked for opportunities when my roommates were not home to relieve my tension. I wrote in my journal-- "I'm tired of whacking off alone, I want more than a relationship with my own hand." My heart and my head engaged in a pitched battle about why, why it was so difficult for me to have a relationship, to find a special someone.

After my epiphany at Columbiere and my post-retreat encounter with Father Paul, I still found myself in a tug of war about my desires. It was a fruitless question, which only led to more self-denial. I found it difficult to reconcile my yearning with the person I tried to force myself to become—mainstream, acceptable, and straight. But I still tried.

In October I met a new girl in my Spanish Culture class, who asked me to introduce her to Stephen. Julia stood six feet tall, with saucer brown eyes, a pixie haircut, and a cherubic face. She often used Spanish slang, words I didn't know, but she taught me their meaning.

"Who's that cute blonde *muchacho* you're always meeting for lunch?" she'd ask. "What's his name?"

I shrugged, "Oh, yeah, everyone wants to know Stephen."

Julia invited Stephen and me to a Halloween costume party she threw at her parent's home in tony Chagrin Falls. Dressed in a skipper's cap and a boat neck sweater, I masqueraded as one of the castaways from *Gilligan's Island*. A la Bonnie and Clyde, Stephen donned a gangster hat and carried a toy machine gun, while Karen slipped into a grey, pencil thin skirt and beret. An avid movie buff, Karen was the Faye Dunaway to Stephen's Warren Beatty.

When we arrived at Julia's house we were awestruck. The property included an indoor swimming pool, a home theatre, and a stable for horses. "I'm so excited to have you guys here," She ushered us into the atrium with a crystal chandelier and bannister staircase. "*Mi casa es tu casa*," she giggled.

Her father had hired a caterer to serve beer and appetizers. We tried to keep our drinking to a minimum; however, the beer flowed and by the end of the evening we were so giddy we dove fully clothed into the swimming pool.

"C'mon everyone," I called out while bouncing on the diving board. "Let's play Simon Says. Simon Says let's get wet."

I charged off the board with a cannonball splash into the deep end. My skipper's hat sunk to the bottom of the pool. I felt like a character in *The*

Great Gatsby and couldn't stop laughing. I loved the free spiritedness I discovered in such luxurious surroundings, but also realized the alienation, separation from what Stephen inherited without effort –being part of the acceptable, male-female, heterosexual center of life. I would never experience that. The separateness fueled my desire to at least create an attention-grabbing memory that would cement us all together.

After the dive in the deep end, Julia, Stephen, Karen, and I stood shivering in the laundry room with nothing but towels wrapped around us waiting for our wet clothes to come out of the dryer. I felt aroused catching glimpses of Stephen's hairy chest and the treasure trail traveling below his belly button. I began to shiver and gyrate.

"What are you doing?" Karen giggled, as I mimicked a striptease, revealing the tan line I had acquired last summer. She soon got into the act, and the two of us performed a mini burlesque. I flashed a leering smile at both Karen and Stephen while Julia fell into uncontrollable laughter. Yeah, it was obvious I was flirting. But I felt bonded to them on this evening of silly, carefree abandon. I decided to let go of trying too hard and just allowed my words and actions to flow unedited.

Within a week of the party, Julia had begun burrowing her way into Stephen's heart. By Thanksgiving he'd broke off his relationship with Karen and started to date Julia.

***

On December 26, 1985, I watched my life flash before my eyes. Heavy snow fell on the expressway as I drove toward I-480 West. I turned the windshield wipers on full speed and zoomed onto the entrance ramp. I'd given Stephen the gift-wrapped record I knew he'd love. Now the gift giving was done, and time was wasting to return from the East side back home and beat this storm.

Only a few cars were on the highway as I glanced in my rearview mirror and prepared to merge. Smooth and steady, cavalier in my confidence, I accelerated to 55 and entered the middle lane. I thought about Stephen and his surprise at my gift. I'd taken care of business and now would escape back into my fantasy world, my protective bubble on the West Side of Cleveland. I looked again in the rear-view mirror and saw headlights rapidly approaching.

As the windshield wipers flew back and forth across my line of vision, images flashed through my mind. I thought of Stephen and his too-cute-for-words grin, his delighted reaction to the *Seascapes* LP, the fact he hadn't purchased a gift for me. I didn't take it personally. I knew he didn't share the same special feelings for me as I did for him. He wasn't gay.

With snow falling thicker and thicker and making the sky whiter and whiter, more recollections accumulated like drifts piling in my mind: first meeting Stephen at Miller Hall, spring break on Clearwater Beach, our talks about God and life, our hopes and dreams. Lost in my desire for him, I could feel my groin coming alive, an unrepentant hard on bulging in my pants.

Suddenly, the approaching headlights…a black SRX sports car… zoomed from behind, passed on the right, pulled in front of me, and flashed its brake lights. Alarmed I pumped my brakes, but it was too late, I was going too fast, and I careened into his bumper. As the SRX sped forward, my car spun out of control. I gripped the steering wheel trying to right the automobile, but it continued to whirl, like an ice skater performing a 360-degree pirouette. The car finally stopped at a ninety-degree angle to oncoming traffic.

Frozen in silent time and space I sat breathless in the middle of I-480 while the snow blew across the highway. The SRX was long gone in the distance. A miracle, I thought, that there were no cars or trucks anywhere near me nor were any approaching.

Stunned, I sat there, paralyzed, buckled in my seat. I tried to start the car, but the ignition had locked. I pumped the brake, tried the ignition again. Then, thank God, the engine came to life, and I righted the car and aimed for home.

Mom and Dad knew when I entered the house something had happened. "I have good news and not so good news," I announced. "The not-so-good news is coming home from the East Side I got in an accident." Their faces turned serious, my mother's eyes wide and fretful. "The good news is that I survived without getting hurt. It was only a fender bender, the front grille's a little dented."

I wondered how pissed they'd be at me for messing up my brand-new car. Dad inspected the grille and shrugged "It could have been worse."

Mom just wagged her head. "Remember, we told you to adjust your driving to the weather conditions." For a moment I wondered whether Mom cared more about the damaged car than me.

Dad interrupted, "The important thing, Ruth, is that he's okay." I knew they were relieved I was in one piece, but I could feel their disapproval that I hadn't shown more caution on the road.

That night I couldn't sleep. I felt more and more haunted by the incident. The car spinning out of control on the slick highway morphed into a symbol for my double-edged life. I thought about my rush to give Stephen the special *Seascapes* album I'd handpicked at Record Revolution. How he smiled at the door saying, "Gee, you didn't have to do that," and gave me an even bigger bear hug.

The moment preceding the collision my mind, my dick had been obsessing about a man, not a woman, in my life. My recklessness on the highway, ignoring driving conditions and failing to slow down, could have ended in tragedy. I didn't believe in death wishes, but I could have perished. I broke out in a cold sweat, shivering between the now damp sheets. When would I begin to face the truth? Stop trying to please people, to convince Stephen to love me the way I wanted him to? I was chasing a mirage.

I shuddered at the thought of losing my life. I had so much to offer the world. And yet I'd nearly thrown it away on an icy highway. I wanted to live. I wanted to love. But it didn't seem like life was cooperating because I wanted to love a man. Why couldn't I just be honest and start living my life out in the open? Who would I hurt? Who would I shame? Mom? Dad? Myself? Who would I offend? Stephen? Did it matter if I experienced more rejection? From classmates who already suspected I was gay? From frat brothers who didn't think I was cool, or might feel guilt by association if I came out?

What if my parents threw me out? What if they disowned me? I knew the Catholic Church influenced my parents, my classmates, and society with their anti-gay teachings. *An unhealthy lifestyle, AIDS is God's punishment to gays for their aberrant behavior.* I wanted to spit in disgust at how loving thy neighbor, a Christian tenet, had turned into judging and condemning thy neighbor. Well, whether my parents, frat brothers, or society accepted me, or not, didn't matter. Soon I'd be free.

I opened a book about the Pacific Northwest, recently given to me by Josie in my poly sci class, who knew I had greater ambitions. I closed my eyes and imagined myself in this distant, rugged land with rocky shores, seascapes, and jagged mountains – a land where nature ruled. The Northwest looked like a place where I could just be me, allow my natural wind-blown personality to prosper, get lost in the beauty of the elements and start over again, fresh and open to possibility, something different. Could this place be calling me, could it be my escape? An exile from all I was obligated to satisfy…maybe there I could finally satisfy the most important person of all—my own self.

***

"ARE you okay?" RJ asked. "You don't have whiplash, do you?" It was the morning after the accident. I sat in my parent's kitchen fiddling with the phone cord and getting lost in the sun flickering across the daisy-patterned wallpaper.

"No, I was lucky nobody came from behind, swerved, and t-boned me."

"Do you want me to come over?"

I didn't know what to say. I didn't know what I needed.

Our physical relationship transitioned into a deeper, abiding friendship, a bond that had continued for a decade, surviving ups and downs, brotherly-like one-upmanship, and my conflicted inner turmoil around our on again-off again sexual relationship. While we'd seen much less of each other since he started school in New York we remained constants in each other's lives.

After a long silence he said, "Well, I'm glad you didn't get hurt."

Then he changed the subject. "Now that half the 1980's are over, is the decade what you thought it would be?"

This is what I loved about RJ, and how he was similar and yet different from Stephen. While Stephen engaged me in philosophical discussions about God, the universe and the meaning of life, RJ plumbed different, almost familial, aspects of my life. RJ knew me on a much deeper, more intimate level since he'd observed and understood my struggles with sexuality, my relationship with my parents and other members of my family, my history, my dreams and hopes for the future, and everything in between.

"It's been tough," I admitted. "I had no clue who I was when I graduated from high school and started college. I thought I did, but not really. And while we're like brothers, and I did feel competitive with you, I was determined to not make myself a carbon copy of you. That's why I had to break away for a while, to figure out where I stood in the grand scheme of it all."

"What do you mean competitive? You beat me out for the Prince Charming role in *Snow White* while I got stuck playing the Mirrored Prince holed up in a cardboard box. Remember? Talk about sorry seconds." He laughed. I smiled.

"No, it went beyond theatre," I continued. "I wanted to differentiate myself, find my own talents and do my own thing. That's why I picked the outdoors and athletics. If I couldn't beat you at your own game, I wanted to find my own. You'll always be the better dancer, and the better sketch artist, that's just the way it is."

"But look how much you know now. You can couple's dance with Mary Kathleen or Shelley or any other girl. Transport them across the dance floor, hoist them up like a bird over your shoulder, and return them to ground zero, just like I can."

Now I laughed picturing his earnest grin on the other side of the phone line. His confidence and artistry, his pure love on the dance floor had inspired my own dancing.

"But I wanted to be different from you. I wanted my own signature activity. So, I started swimming and lifting weights to build myself up. I liked how it made me look, how it made me feel. And I became a lifeguard. And when I got to John Carroll, for once I wanted to be part of the "cool" group. So, I pledged the fraternity, and adopted wholesale the preppy look, remaking my image like I was auditioning for a Hollywood screen test." RJ interjected an affirming sigh. I continued. "Now all of it feels fake. I'm sick of trying to fit in. I'm ready to graduate."

"You can always come to New York. There are plenty of misfits here," he laughed. "I mean, people who aren't interested in conforming, you know what I mean."

I shifted on the kitchen stool and fidgeted with the phone cord. "I have this book about the Pacific Northwest. You should see it. The cover is beautiful—it shows this craggy rock-strewn coastline with waves crashing along the shore and green, snow-capped mountains rising in the background. I've never been there but I'm curious to try something new. New York doesn't really feel like me with all the grit, crime, and graffiti all over the place. But I can come visit."

"Good, because I plan to stay here and look for work after graduation. After my summer experience with Alfred Sung, I've got interviews lined up with Ralph Lauren, and some other designers. I'm gonna put that fashion illustration degree to work no holds barred. You promise you'll come visit?"

"I'm there, you can count on me. We aren't going to lose touch this time."

When I hung up, I walked into my room and dove on my bed. I could feel it coming--waves of frustration and emotion building then crashing over me. Tears began cascading down my cheeks, and I wiped them away with my shirtsleeve. I felt so connected to him yet didn't want to pursue anything more serious. For all we had in common why didn't RJ make me feel the same way Stephen did? We shared a common history, a physical and emotional bond that I prized. Laughter was a constant whenever we were together. We shared similar values--honesty, loyalty, friendship, and directness.

Yet with Stephen some sort of magnetic attraction ruled; it verged on indescribable. I wanted him, all of him, his body, mind, and soul. He confided in me, made himself vulnerable, in a way that RJ, being the grand provocateur, couldn't or chose not to. RJ opened but there was a moment when he paused and couldn't, or wouldn't, go further. It's like he laid down a self-imposed boundary. Had he ever told me he loved me? I couldn't re-member; I hadn't said I loved him. Stephen and I never exchanged the L-word but then we weren't romantic, at least not in the physical sense. Yet I found in him a spiritual companion, someone who didn't pretend to know it all, even though RJ didn't act that way. I tried to remember if RJ and I had ever talked about God. Maybe we had but not in the way Stephen and I shared. There were so many contradictions, paradoxes. Maybe I was fooling myself, imagining somehow Stephen would come my way, after all, RJ and I already had our turn.

Was I in search of a soul mate? Is that why Stephen appealed to me in a way RJ didn't or couldn't? And what was I to do with that feeling? Stephen was never going to switch-hit. He liked girls.

Confused and alone, I was unsure where to turn. I rolled over on my stomach and plopped my head on the pillow, allowing my tear-strewn face to sink into the cool white cotton cover. Myriad voices crept into my head and then one overtook the others. I looked out my bedroom window into the snow-laden backyard with drifts submerging the birdbath and tracing the branches of the cherry tree. I remembered hearing this quiet voice be-fore--on the snowy trails of upstate Michigan while cross-country skiing one year ago. It was beckoning me to leave Cleveland and search for the answer somewhere else: away from the watchful eyes of my parents, family and friends who had known me my entire life. My heart began beating more rapidly and then calmed as I relaxed into a realization. I needed to make a break.

A few weeks later I contacted the Jesuit Volunteer Corps Northwest and asked them to send me placement materials for Seattle and the Pacific Northwest region.

***

I was at loose ends. Stephen's new relationship with Julia flourished. The happier he became in their romance, the more jealous and angrier I grew. A sort of passive-aggressiveness crept into our relationship: I needled him about getting laid all the time, and the poor little rich girl he'd rescued from the lap of luxury. They spent weekends at her house.

"Do you make time for your friends anymore?" I asked. I knew I should be pleased for him, but I felt stung by the loss of companionship we once shared together.

I came to realize I would never win this competition. In February, March, and April I slowly let go, accepted that our relationship would change, and it would be better to treat Julia nicely than wage a battle I was sure to lose. By accepting Stephen as an unwavering straight man, I now needed to face my own reality: Jack Hilovsky loved men. Jack Hilovsky likely was gay. Laura, or Melissa, or Hope, or Mary Kathleen, could no longer be my cover. Stephen wasn't going to come over to my side. Not the way I wanted him. I needed to walk this journey on my own and accept who I was.

Sitting in my apartment one lonely Saturday night, very aware I'd lost the battle to win over Stephen, I stretched out on the couch and got lost in the lyrics to Starship's "Sara" on the Hot 100. I felt haunted by the lyrics as fragments about moving on, letting go, fire and ice, floated through my psyche.

Nobody other than RJ knew about my ten-year struggle. We'd managed to keep our own sexual relationship a secret; nobody ever approached us or insinuated that we were gay. We were two boys, who loved to disco dance, and attend matinee movies, and who seized the opportunity to run buck naked through backyards, gardens, and alfalfa fields, and who were obsessed with Farrah Fawcett-Majors.

What would I be now that I couldn't hide out in college anymore?

I thought back to the summer of 1984 after I returned from Mexico, how I told my grade school friend Philippa about my confused yet exciting feelings. I thought about meeting the young actor from Madison. His warm smile and Midwestern good looks, blond and tan and toned. Another male version of Farrah, he too exuded a glow, an all over goodness. But I hadn't pursued him because I didn't know what I wanted and even thinking about what it meant to pursue him became too scary to contemplate.

Compassionate and loving, Philippa had turned to me that moonlit night in the playground and said, "I've felt attraction to women before. I think it's common for females to admire and appreciate aspects of other women they like."

She had paused and caressed my cheek that August eve and said, "Jack, all I want for you is to be happy. That's all."

***

IN May I received a letter from the Jesuit Volunteer Corps (JVC) confirming my placement at the Northwest AIDS Foundation in Seattle, my first choice. As a client advocate starting in August, I'd help people unable to work and living with HIV/AIDS apply for disability assistance, affordable housing, and other social service benefits.

My parents knew about my plans to take a year off and ponder my future but were unaware of the population I'd be assisting.

"Jean O'Flaherty would sooner tie her daughter Susan to the kitchen table before she'd let her go to Seattle and work with AIDS patients." My mother's voice quavered. "Are you sure you're doing the right thing?"

I swallowed hard. I didn't want a fight. I just wanted their support. I took a deep breath and reached for the words. "I'll be okay, Mom."

I looked into her deep blue eyes and saw her depth of love and concern, but also her nervous uncertainty. In 1986 many people still questioned how AIDS was transmitted, and there was an underlying hysteria in the air.

"You can't get it through casual contact," I told her. Dad bit his lower lip. "Do what you need to do, son," he said. "We'll be here if you need us. Just be careful, you're the only one we've got."

Mom added, "And you can always come home."

***

THAT summer I waited tables in Rocky River at a fancy lunch spot in a renovated 1920's movie house. Two of the waiters there, Jeff and Tony, were openly gay, and the hostess was rumored to be a lesbian mom with a little boy at home.

During my off-hours I drove to my beloved lifeguarding turf Foster Pool and swam laps. One afternoon a slim guy sunning on the pool deck kept looking over at me. I stared back meeting his eyes with a smile. God, he was sexy. He wore a light blue Speedo swimsuit. I summoned up my courage and walked over to say hello.

"I've watched you swim the last couple days. You set a good pace," he said. "I'm Ross."

"Jack," I responded crouching down to shake his hand. "I've noticed you over here. You've got a great tan." I felt shy suddenly making direct contact in such a public place, but I couldn't help myself. I alternated between looking in his eyes and shifting my vision to the distant lake. My feet felt tingly on the hard, scratchy cement surface of the pool deck. We sat for a while and talked. The suntan lotion on his skin smelled like cinnamon. His blue eyes sparkled. I wanted to run my fingers through his curly, sun-streaked blonde hair.

"I work at Glow, a tanning salon and gym on Detroit Avenue. Not far from here," he continued. He gave me his business card and encouraged me to visit sometime.

One afternoon after work I dropped by to say hello. "Hi. You found me," he said. I stood there for a minute looking around at a loss for words. "Want a tour?" he asked. He showed me the weight room and sun tanning booths. "If you ever want a complimentary membership for a month, let me know." I looked straight into his blue eyes and saw my own reflection. He made me feel comfortable, welcome, like we'd known each other for longer than the 30 minutes we spent on the deck of the pool. And he was soft-spoken and thoughtful, the sort of guy I'd want to get to know better.

I began to drop by every few days to visit him. Sometimes we would lift weights together; other times we'd meet at Foster Pool to sunbathe and swim. He was my ideal--lithe and fit, like a dancer, with smooth skin, except for his legs and arms, which we're covered with golden trails of hair, bleached blonde by the sun. His lips were slim and the small gap between his two front teeth reminded me of some famous model in a Maybelline commercial

Shy and very gentle, one day Ross asked me in a voice so quiet I could barely hear him, "You don't mind that I'm gay, do you?"

"No, I don't mind. For God sakes I attended Lakewood Little Theatre, and I'm going to work with people at an AIDS Foundation. And . . . and . . . I might be . . ." I looked up into his blue eyes, fiddling with my hands unable to finish the sentence.

I was thrilled he said it out loud. I couldn't. I didn't have the guts to go down that road, still wrestling with how I'd arrive at the other side because once I said it there was no going back.

I wagged my head in answer to his question and repeated, "No, I don't mind one bit. I have other people in my life who are gay, and they're nice people."

Ross and I never ventured beyond the salon or the pool. I never saw him naked while changing in the pool locker room, although I would have loved to. His body was so statuesque, his cocoa brown skin so beautiful. I felt like I had an overwhelming, puppy-dog crush different from the grounded friendship with Stephen that grew over time, and where feelings had developed over shared experiences in college and our Catholic upbringing.

My attraction to Ross came from a more visceral place and happened quickly. I felt lonely and yearned for company, for someone who'd understand me and with whom I could share my feelings. He just wanted to live in a safe place and not be mocked or abused. That's why he left his small-town Marion, Ohio, for the big city of Cleveland.

But I felt more and more that even Cleveland wasn't big enough, or safe enough, for me.

***

I leaned over and touched his slim, soft lips before planting my own on them. I could taste his cherry lip balm. I inhaled, and air rushed into my nostrils. I opened my eyes and saw a streetlight flicker above us. The sunset over Lakewood Park colored the sky purple, orange and red. Fireflies danced in the warm summer air.

"Beautiful sky," I said, waving my hand towards the deepening colors of evening over Foster Pool.

Ross nodded. "Beautiful man."

We both smiled. "Yum," I said caressing the small of his back.

He nodded and patted my cheek. "I guess it's obvious I like you. But I know you're getting ready to move away. Maybe I'll come visit you in Seattle."

My eyes lit up. "That would be nice."

The kiss felt so innocent without any expectation that it would go further. I was living at home and didn't feel comfortable inviting him back to my house. Ross had a roommate who rarely left their apartment. I gave him my new Seattle address. It felt so abrupt, we'd just met, but I had a new life, a new beginning, awaiting me in Seattle. I was excited to look to the future. And I hoped we'd see each other again.

My time with Ross allowed me to start reflecting on my intentions going forward. I'd take what I learned from him about communication, attraction, and desire and build on it in my new city. I would never forget his gentle spirit and quiet demeanor.

That summer little by little I continued letting go of Stephen. My encounters with Ross and some of the wait staff at Heck's were my first real exposure to engaging gay people in my world, at least ones that had jobs and lives and didn't resemble drag queens or club kids. I learned not all gay people were untrustworthy and gossipmongers like Marvin, whom someday would have to face his own gay reality in the mirror. They had jobs and families of their own. And then there was Ross: generous, kind, and hoping to live in a less hostile place and make his way in the world.

***

"How's your friend Stephen?" my mother asked out of the blue. I had just helped her finish mowing the lawn, and we were sitting in lawn chairs and basking in the late afternoon sun, a shared activity we both enjoyed.

"Okay, I guess. He's seeing a girl I introduced him to last fall."

A long silence punctuated the conversation. I cleared my throat. "I wish we had the chance to spend more time together. I feel like during college we were so close, but now he's not available. It makes me feel sad. . . and a bit jealous." Without intending it, in my pure honesty, I'd allowed my disappointment to see the light of day.

I felt jittery and began to perspire as the silence stretched between us, and then she pounced, "Well, be careful, that kind of attachment isn't healthy. You need to accept he's found a girlfriend."

My heart sank. I shook my head. "I can't help it."

She gave me a withering look and then said, "You're not in love with him, are you?"

I didn't know what to say. I fumbled with my shirttail and felt my spine begin to freeze, as I sat glued to the lawn chair with a fixed stare on my face. I avoided looking into her eyes.

She shifted in her seat and continued. "You know you're treading in dangerous water, Jack. Remember your body is the temple of the Holy Spirit." Her eyes glanced downward as if she couldn't bear to look at me when delivering her message of moral rectitude. After all, I wasn't a distant relative or a neighbor boy down the street she could easily dismiss for lowdown behavior. I was her only begotten son.

Crippled, I swallowed hard the tiny voice in my throat, taunting me to scream out loud "How dare you?" at the top of my lungs.

And then my mother drove home her point with a dagger that penetrated my heart: "Don't you have feelings for girls? Remember we raised you with good values, Jack."

I felt incriminated, and my face froze into an indecipherable mask. Her unsympathetic stare, so unusual for a woman I'd watched show empathy for those in need, failed to crumple my spirit though; I vowed to protect myself and never again share my feelings with my mother when it came to my desires and need for intimacy and closeness with men. I pictured myself with a giant scalpel, and I did what I long wanted to do: sever the umbilical cord that had bound me to her for 23 years.

This was the first time my mother--often the first to point an incriminating finger at the loose behavior of my cousins when it came to sex and dating--ever questioned my moral core. Parroting the stance of the Catholic Church, she was consistent in vocalizing her strong feelings against couples living together "in sin," engaging in pre-marital sex, using contraception, and of course the greatest sin of all, abortion.

I knew of no family members who had ever sought an abortion, but several close relatives, including my mother's goddaughter, earned her scorn by living with their significant other or showing excessive displays of affection in public.

"It's in poor taste," Mom would pronounce after we left the scene. "They're déclassé. Vulgar," she'd say. "It's like they're in the bedroom for all of us to see."

She was a devout Catholic, and yet had her own personal quirks when it came to propriety: while criticizing open displays of affection that went beyond a simple kiss or handholding, she loved to sunbathe in the backyard wearing only her brassiere and panties.

Now here I sat with my mother in the front yard on a sunny July evening feeling muddied in shame. What did she know? How could she ever understand what I'd wrestled with in my heart? Memories of her reaction to the queer men in wigs and heels strolling the streets of Provincetown in 1974 flooded my mind. I recalled how Mom pulled me aside and pointed at them—hissing *look at those queers*—and how the objects of her derision just laughed and sashayed on their merry way. All for the sake of attention, demanding the attention of a society that ignored and castigated them. Now I imagined them pointing and laughing at me as I suffered the fate they encountered daily. "Poor sucker," they'd probably scream.

But I didn't want to flaunt my sexuality and shock people for attention. I just wanted to live and love in a way that felt natural and good, like Ross.

I looked at my mother in the intense summer light and realized I could never change her opinion, even if I tried. Her righteous morality was emblazoned on her breast, the equivalent of a Good Housekeeping Seal of Approval from the Catholic League. I saw her face as hard, unaccepting, and unchanging. Indoctrination, from religion and the mores of her time, prevented her from seeing gay people as normal and human, the offspring of a God who made us in His image, deserving of compassion and acceptance, like the immigrant children she tutored and the African American women she happily engaged when we took public transportation. She mustered compassion for people on the outside—the poor and vulnerable, the immigrant and the stranger—all God's children. But homosexuals were different—in her mind they made a choice to follow a lifestyle condemned by the Church and society.

I couldn't address the gay issue—not then.

"I guess I'll put away the lawnmower," I mumbled as I stood up and folded the lawn chair. The freshly cut grass reminded me of all the times I'd mowed our lawn over the summers of my youth. Those structured, obedient days had come to an end. Something new, unpredictable, and free was to replace them, but I wasn't quite ready to divulge all that I knew and suspected about myself. I couldn't yet face a full-on confrontation.

My mother was frightened by the possibility of my homosexuality. And I wanted to protect her and my father. I didn't think they needed to know about Ross, or my gay struggles—not yet. Had RJ not come into my life, my path would have been solitary and fraught with isolation. In that moment it became clear that Mom couldn't reconcile the good son she raised with my same-sex desires.

***

On a warm August day, my parents drove me to Cleveland Hopkins Airport. I was to begin my yearlong placement in the Jesuit Volunteer Corps. They hugged me at the departure gate before I boarded the Continental Airlines jet. I looked in their aging eyes and saw our history.

In my mother I saw her innate love for me, her never-ending encouragement, her desire that I be happy, that I do the right thing, that I hold fast to the faith they nurtured in me, and that I spread my beautiful light into the world. I also saw her contrasting shadow—her fear that I was leaving her behind, upending the nest, and relinquishing her as an arbiter of my moral values.

In my father I saw his pride that I was venturing out on my own, leaving the nest and spreading my wings, that I'd completed my college education—a feat neither one of my parents had accomplished. I knew Dad understood they had to free me and allow me to make my own life. He gave me his unqualified permission while I sensed Mom would struggle with letting go.

I thought about how important it was for Mom, in her own words, to "be a good mother." But whether she believed it or not, she had prepared me for the big wide world I was soon to discover 3,000 miles from home. Thanks to her example I learned how to interact and develop relationships with people. My experience in lifeguarding and on baseball leagues, along with my theatre background, exposed me to a variety of personalities. I'd studied hard in college, learned to think on my own, understood the value of self-discipline, and how to delay gratification today for a better life tomorrow. All those Midwestern truisms and lessons she taught, some of which I'd modify to suit my own life, I'd carry with me.

Dad had provided for me, exerted a stricter style of parenting, a healthy perspective, and counterbalanced the lenient playfulness of my mother while reminding me to keep a sense of humor. I yearned to grow closer to him but viewed him more as an authority figure. One day maybe I'd get to know him, understand more of what made him tick.

Being gay, or addressing the fears they had surrounding it, no longer crossed my mind; no longer felt compelling to discuss with them as we said our goodbyes.

Tears flooded Mom's eyes. "Darling, I feel like there's so many life lessons I wanted to impart but haven't told you. Promise you'll always be the sweet boy we raised, that you'll never change."

I threw my arms around her and blessed her in my heart, remembering that most of what she gave me was real and good. The moral inflexibility and tendency to judge other's motives I would confront, in her and myself, another day.

"Hey, kiddo," my father added, planting his hand on my shoulder with the other arm poised to give me a full-on bear hug. "Be careful and have a great time. Don't forget about us here at home."

My father had learned the one-arm hug from my godfather Hugh, and it was the most affectionate show of love he dared impart. My throat caught, and for a moment, I felt like I might not be able to choke back my own tears.

"We'll miss you, sweetheart," my mother said wiping the wet from her eyes. "Don't forget to call. And remember everything I taught you."

I waved goodbye to both and sauntered down the long sky bridge to board the plane. I could feel my breath grow deeper and shallower, like I was entering an airless chamber. My steps felt measured as if I were counting down to blastoff and a new life. I felt nervous and excited all at once. I turned around to see my mother waving at the far end of the bridge. Then I turned, ducked into the plane entrance, and located my seat.

As the warm August heat radiated through my window, I plugged my headset into my Walkman. RJ had mailed me a mixed tape of our favorite songs from the disco years: "I Love the Night Life," "Boogie Oogie Oogie", and Donna Summer's "Last Dance." The plane began to taxi down the runway. As we accelerated, I pushed the play button to discover he'd included Dionne Warwick's call to friendship during the time of AIDS, "That's What Friends Are For."

Soon we were gliding into the blue and pink and orange of dusk and an infinite night sky. The bright light grew dimmer in my window portal, and I watched the fiery sun make its descent into Lake Erie and the horizon beyond. Salty tears streamed down my cheeks, endless and profound, mixed, and confused and full of happiness and regret and excitement and apprehension.

I looked down at the city lights, twinkling along the coast of Lake Erie. I thought of past events—*The Rocky Horror Picture Show* with Mary Kathleen, bloodying Cousin Jimmy's nose and the cantankerous nuns, St. Ignatius High School with all its joys and disappointments, Lola and Re-Re, my godparents Hugh and Fran, meeting RJ at Lakewood Little Theatre, the fraternity with Brooks, Patrick, and Lizard, my heartbreaking college crush on Stephen, and singing "I'm a Man, I'm a Man, I'm a Man" from that Joe Jackson LP. And then there was Philippa loving me unconditionally, and Ross' kiss and goodbye with a hint he might visit me someday.

I thought of everything I loved and struggled to accept and understand. And what was yet to come. As I flew westward, I realized Cleveland was in my past. And the future was a plane ride away. Strangely, even though I was leaving behind everything and everyone I'd known and loved, I was saying hello to me for the very first time.

AFTERWARD

Coming Out

AFTER I ARRIVED in Seattle and had met a beautiful man named Carl, I began to give my mother small clues. I told her in my letters how I rode with him on the back of his motorcycle and spent a weekend at his quaint farmhouse on Bainbridge Island, but Mom didn't confront me or even ask questions about Carl – at a distance.

Nine months later in 1987, when my parents came to visit, Mom confronted me. "How would a mother know if her son were gay?"

I tried to deflect her inquiry and stammered, "Mom, you have nothing to worry about." She had taken me by surprise, and I wasn't prepared to come out at that moment. My mother refused to relent. She marched upstairs and dragged my father into the interrogation. While the three of us descended the front steps of my rental house, Dad blurted out, "You aren't being submissive, son, are you?"

I cringed at his blunt questioning, never having dreamed that my parents would ask such specifics about my sex life. I didn't answer him, but said, "Dad, I'm attracted to men and women." It was partly true: I did find women attractive; I just didn't want to sleep with them. Then I said to him,

"I'm focused on men right now." It was a tense, uncomfortable moment that lingered.

I had no idea that my father, who had served in WWII deciphering messages in Morse code from the German enemy, had been exposed to homosexuality in the Army. I was dumfounded, awed, taken aback. My father with obvious pain in his eyes later told me, "All the guys in the Army came home and married women. That's what you do. You get married."

The next day on a windy morning my parents and I boarded the Victoria Clipper to British Columbia. I struck up a conversation with a young woman on the deck, laughing with her at how her long chestnut hair kept flying in her face. "Do you like that girl?" Mom asked.

I'd had enough! I couldn't straddle the fence any longer. I shouted into the wind, "Mom, I like men. I'm not interested in women."

My mother stepped back as if I'd flung acid on her. She staggered and struggled to find words. "All I know is that I'm afraid we won't be together in heaven. And I don't know what will happen to your soul." Her face sagged, her hair blew wildly in the wind, and my dad who rushed over to her, couldn't conceal his gloom. It was as if I had tossed all their dreams overboard and the vestiges of our past happy life were slowly sinking into the cold waters of the Strait of Juan de Fuca.

Another year would pass until I could look my mother and father straight in the eye and say, "Yes, I am gay, and I'm still your son."

They continued to struggle, despite having close friends who also had a gay son. During a summer visit in 1990, these friends accompanied Mom, Dad, and me to a PFLAG (Parents and Friends of Lesbians and Gays) support group in Cleveland but the open, affirmative environment there was no salve to their wound.

Despite my own feelings of guilt and shame, I stood strong, and I accepted that both my parents had grown up in an era when being gay was considered deviant, a mental illness, and illegal. Until the 1970's the medical and psychiatric community, and society-at-large, had reinforced these biases, and it was the norm. They continued to love me, but for my mom, more devout in her Catholicism than my father, it was a crushing blow.

Now that both are deceased, I choose to believe that their larger, more evolved spirits have found understanding, peace, and acceptance. And that all they wish for me is a happy life.

POSTSCRIPT

FARRAH died in the summer of 2009 at the age of 62. How weird it feels to say she's dead. I guess I thought her youthful radiance would last forever, even though she faced many personal challenges the last decade of her life. I avoided *Farrah's Story*, the documentary she filmed of her valiant fight to beat cancer. I wanted to remember her the way she'd always been in my memory. I guess even glamour can't overcome what we all must face--that life sooner or later must end.

The friendships from my formative years continue. Philippa, the sister I never had, remained in the Cleveland area, and raised 4 children. She recently began working with an animal rescue non-profit and the joy in her voice when she tells me about the dogs and cats she cares for, well, it warms my spirit. Whenever we hear Elton John's "Don't Go Breaking My Heart," we call or text each other. I'm still the Elton to her Kiki Dee.

Mary Kathleen married another thespian after graduating from John Carroll with her English degree. She and her husband reside in Chicago, a stage actor's town, where she occasionally performs and plans to pursue voiceover work. Whenever we speak on the phone, I tell her how much I love her voice.

And Stephen, after spending a year in Alaska with the Jesuit Volunteer

Corps returned to Cleveland and married Julia. I take credit for their 30 years of wedded bliss. When he passed through Seattle on the way home from Alaska, I found the courage to let him know I'd fallen in love with him while we were in college, but that now I was over him. He greeted the news with a graciousness that renewed my faith in the friendship we'd built during a confusing time in our lives.

For RJ and me, our friendship endures as one year passes into the next. He continued to work in the fashion industry, before pivoting to merchandising, branding, and design. There were years he struggled during the fiscal crisis, finding it difficult to land work so he put out a shingle and began freelancing for greeting card and toy companies. That's RJ: resilient and always finding ways to reinvent himself.

We talk on the phone once a month, sometimes more. When he gets frustrated with the freelance industry, I listen and play cheerleader.

Often, I ask myself, could we be a couple? Our friendship stretches four decades, and we are united by a storied past and a complex present. I care for him deeply, but we now occupy different universes. He loves the four seasons, especially the sweater weather of autumn, while I love the West Coast. He's a homebody while I'm an active outdoorsman and athlete. We are a study in contrasts: suburban/urban, designer décor/eclectic tastes, silk and leaves, hairy and smooth. And the differences continue.

We shared our bodies during a time of adolescent yearning and exploration. We held space for each other in our hearts and in our families. And then time took hold, and we stepped into new experiences and separate lives. He into a 17-year relationship and me into multiple relationships each one teaching me a little bit more about myself and the nature of love. After all these years, we continue to laugh with and at each other, yet the values we cherish--honesty, loyalty, friendship, and truth--are still the cornerstones of our relationship.

RJ and I will continue living our lives, harboring our eternal flame for a woman whom we never had the pleasure to meet and yet united us in sustained, forever-after ardor.

For my part I chose to make Seattle my new home, though I still identify, and always will, as a native Clevelander. Reclining in my backyard hammock on a breezy summer day, the bluest skies you've ever seen take me back. I activate Pandora on my Smartphone and my ear pods come alive with the gleeful harmonies of the Bee Gees and "You Should Be Dancing." My body moves on the canvas of the hammock as if I were still that 14-year-old-boy at the YMCA disco night. I think back to those days with wonder and joy, acknowledging the twin agony and blessing of coming to terms with my adolescence and my sexuality.

And then the phone rings, and it's RJ. I smile and swipe to accept the call. "What's new, buckaroo?" I breathe into the phone. And the story continues.

No regrets. No regrets.

Acknowledgements

Without the support of Anne Biklé and Elizabeth Fowler, the core of my writing circle, I would have never made it this far. From 2010 when I first completed my manuscript through all the countless re-writes, both these incredible women stood by my side egging me on, giving me constructive feedback and making editing suggestions ad infinitum. To them I am eternally grateful.

They say it takes a village and so there are others who helped along the way. The late Professor Hubert Locke, my mentor, teacher, and friend, read my initial draft and told me "Jack, you must get more naked." My young, trusted cousin Jacob Barkley, during a family vacation asked to see my pages and by his sheer interest and unconditional love gave me the juice to keep going.

Thank you to fellow author Christopher Drajem, who shared his experience negotiating the world of publishing and introduced me to Mark Pogodzinski. Thank you Mark for taking me on and guiding me through the publishing process. And thanks to Ellie Rummell, Mark's associate and reader, who reviewed my book, saw its value and recommended Mark publish it.

There are countless other friends and family members who kept me going just by asking about my progress over the past dozen years. Thank you for your care and your encouragement.

Finally, before I even owned a personal computer, I would take myself to Hugo House, a literary arts center, 5 blocks down the hill from where I live. I'd sit down in front of a screen in their quiet library and write columns and essays for a community newspaper and a local LGBTQ magazine. Thank you for providing me with a writer's refuge, a place where I felt safe and embraced.

Made in the USA
Middletown, DE
12 June 2023

32152993R00195